# Trekking in Turkey

Ma...
Env...

**Trekking in Turkey**
  **1st edition**

**Published by**
  Lonely Planet Publications
  Head Office: PO Box 88, South Yarra, Victoria 3141, Australia
  US Office: PO Box 2001A, Berkeley, CA 94702, USA

**Printed by**
  Colorcraft, Hong Kong

**Photographs by**
  Marc Dubin (MD)
  Enver Lucas (EL)

  Front cover: Head of Düpedüz Deresi, below Mezovit (MD)
  Back cover: Makri (Kayaköyü) ghost town, Turquoise coast (EL)
   Gerbekse church, Turquoise coast (EL)

**Published**
  February 1989

National Library of Australia Cataloguing in Publication Data

Dubin, Marc S.
  Trekking in Turkey.

  Includes index.
  ISBN 0 86442 037 4.

  1. Hiking – Turkey – Guide-books. 2. Turkey –
  Description and travel – 1960– - Guide-books. I. Lucas, Enver. II. Title.

  915.61'0438

### Marc S Dubin

Marc was born and educated in California and interrupted university in 1976 to teach English in South America. While he did eventually finish his formal schooling, this started a habit which continues to the present day. His career as a travel journalist and author began in 1979. In addition to this book he is author of *Greece on Foot: Mountain Treks, Island Treks* (The Mountaineers/Cordee) and the upcoming *Spain & Portugal on Foot*. He is also an editor and consultant for the Rough Guides series, being the co-author of the Greek volume and major contributor to the Spanish, Kenyan and Portuguese titles. Marc is also an accomplished photographer with numerous publication credits.

### Enver G Lucas

Enver Lucas was born in California to a Turkish mother and an American father. Having spent half his life in each country, he is a dual national and fluent in both languages. After secondary school in Turkey and university in the US, he became an avid kayaker and nature lover during an eight year stay at Yosemite National Park. He completed the OARS whitewater guiding school and became a guide for Wild River Tours and SOBEK Expeditions, then returned to Turkey to lead trips on the Coruh River. More recently he has conducted treks and yacht tours in Turkey for Inner Asia and Wilderness Travel. Enver is currently director of Turkish Operations for Wilderness Travel in Berkeley, California. When not living in Turkey he can be found skiing and guiding raft trips in California.

### Dedication

For our many Turkish friends

### Lonely Planet Credits

| | |
|---|---|
| **Editor** | Peter Turner |
| **Maps & Cover Design** | Vicki Beale |
| **Design, Illustrations & Typesetting** | Ann Jeffree |

Thanks also to Debbie Rossdale for proof reading and Vicki Beale for paste up assistance.

## A Warning & a Request

Things change – prices go up, schedules change, good places go bad and bad places go bankrupt – nothing stays the same. So if you find things better or worse, recently opened or long since closed, please write and tell us and help make the next edition better! All information is greatly appreciated and the best letters will receive a free copy of the next edition, or any other Lonely Planet book of your choice.

Extracts from the best letters are also included in the *Lonely Planet Update*. The *Update* helps us make useful information available to you as soon as possible – it's like reading an up-to-date notice board or postcards from a friend. Each edition contains hundreds of useful tips, and advice from the best possible source of information – other travellers. The *Lonely Planet Update* is published quarterly in paperback and is available from bookshops and by subscription. Turn to the back pages of this book for more details.

## Acknowledgements

In retrospect, the writing of this book would have been well-nigh impossible without the assistance of most of the individuals singled out below.

Before we left the United States, we had committed ourselves to a portable computer/word processor which, while powerful and adequate to get the job done, had been decreed obsolete by the marketplace. Bruce Birkman, Adam Heilbrun, Kenji Nagedegawa and the friendly staff of SnyderScope took repeated phone calls in good stride and did their best to track down arcane spare parts and components and to furnish us with public domain software.

C Kamil Müren, formerly of the Ministry of Tourism & Culture, New York branch, did the initial processing of our request for complimentary transportation within Turkey, while Ayten Tunakan of the İstanbul office and Zehra Sulupınar at Ankara headquarters actually nailed down the specific arrangements. We are also obligated to Mehmet Başen and Hasan Turhanoğlu of the Forest Service for granting us permission to use their ministry's guest lodges and providing us with transportation to these remote spots. Marc is indebted to Fetih Parça, *bekçi* (guard) of the Pinara archaeological site, for an unforgettable private twilight tour.

We knew that there would be something of an information 'blackout' on Turkey's mountains, and that we would experience feelings of being outcasts, crazies or worse for attempting to shed light on the subject, but were initially taken aback by the extent and thoroughness of such phenomena. Before we were tempted to give up entirely, though, Enver renewed his acquaintance with Batur Kürüz and Kaşif Aladağlı of the Anatolian Mountaineers' Union and we were off and running again. Lucky 'chance' meetings made all the difference as well; a particularly good day on Tahtalı Dağı gained us the friendship of Tosun and Josette Sezen, and Izzet and Rozzette Keribar. Tosun and Jo were kind enough to put their summer house at our disposal for the final stages of the book writing, and Izzet became our informal photographic consultant.

John and Ayşe Carden, whom Marc found among the ruins of Assos at sunset, told us about hiking on Marmara Adası (although we were never able to get there) and gave us an introduction to Professor Hadi Özbal at Boğazici University. After priming us with information on the Bolkar Toros, Hadi in turn passed us on to Haldun Aydingün, a gentleman and a scholar if there ever was one, who kept us supplied with a steady stream of maps and intelligence. Where Haldun left off Yücel Üzmen and Josephine Powell filled the gap,

Acknowledgements continued on page 145 ...

# Contents

# Introduction

Turkey is currently experiencing a boom in tourism of the sort which occurred in Spain in the 1960s and Greece in the 1970s. It is definitely the 'in' destination for the 1980s, and seems to have recovered from the combined effects of *Midnight Express*, sundry hijackings and assorted fallout from the coup of 1980.

Not surprisingly the last few years have also witnessed a virtual explosion in the number of English-language guidebooks to the country. But with all the plethora of information, there was nothing addressed to the walker or trekker who planned to visit a land with some of the most beautiful scenery, and certainly the highest mountains, anywhere around the Mediterranean.

While dayhiking, let alone trekking for extended periods, may not be the first thing that comes to mind when potential visitors consider a trip to Turkey, it is one of the best ways to get acquainted with this sizeable and fascinating country. The variety of terrain and climate on the Anatolian peninsula is such that there will be something for every taste.

If you're keen on simple peak-bagging and snowfields, there are a handful of conical volcanos on the central plateau to challenge you. Lovers of the classical pine-covered landscape of balmy Aegean Turkey can follow old trails between ancient ruins and modern Turkish settlements, and do so almost year-round owing to the low altitude.

For the best taste of rural Turkish life, head for the limestone contours of Aladağlar or Bolkar zones of the Toros Mountains, or better yet, to the Black Sea

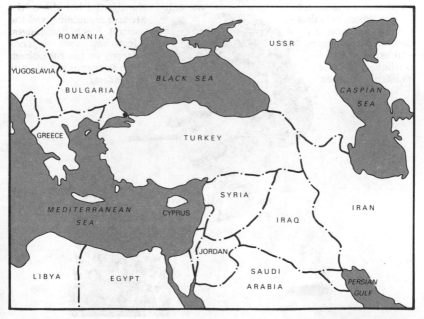

ranges, which have been home to a variety of colourful peoples (at least for the summer) since time immemorial. Security conditions permitting, we can recommend the gorge-slashed Munzur mountains in central Anatolia or the jagged, wild Cilo/Sat massifs on the Iraqi border for those who wish to immerse themselves in Kurdish culture for a time.

A walk through the Turkish backcountry is not a wilderness experience as in a North American or Australian national park. Rather it is an opportunity to come into close contact with the substantial part of Turkish culture which is still rural; trekking in India might be a better approximation of the experience available in Turkey. For however brief a period, you will be participating in the daily life of villagers, herb-gatherers, loggers and (yes) officials who treat the mountains as their back yard, and perhaps also with a familiarity that may make it difficult for them to understand what you find special about their environment.

Even among outsiders – and urban Turks are included in this category – trekking in Turkey is still very much in its infancy. Therein

lies its appeal. If you are looking for a landscape that is impressive but still relatively unravaged and litter-free, inhabitants who are not yet jaded in the presence of visitors, and an opportunity to explore various historical remains at the pace (walking) and from the perspective (eye level) which their builders intended, then Turkey is the right place.

In terms of our own personal preferences, we were most taken with the Kaçkar range on the Black Sea, where the trekking compares favourably to that in Nepal, and accordingly a large part of the book is devoted to it. We were disappointed in not being able to visit the Cilo/Sat mountains, which are said to be even more spectacular, owing to the ongoing Kurdish troubles. Ağrı Dağ (Mt Ararat) gets the debunking we feel it deserves and frankly neither of us is keen on scaling it or any other Anatolian volcano again, not when so much that is more worthwhile awaits for a new edition. We hope to return shortly, not only to the Cilo/Sat but also to the Munzur mountains, and the central Black Sea ranges. Just how soon depends largely on the enthusiasm and response of our readers.

## MAP LEGEND

| | |
|---|---|
| —— | Major Road |
| - - - - | Minor Road |
| •••••• | Walking Track |
| ·········· | Cross Country Route |
| +++++ | Railway Line |
| ⪰ | River, Stream |
| ▲ | Mountain, Peak |
| ⚑ | Campsite |
| —750— | Contour, Contour Interval |
| ▬▬ | Major Ridge System |
| ⪥ | Mountain Pass |
| ⊣⊦ | Bridge |
| ⬟ | Hut |
| ⛉ | Church |
| ⦂⦂⦂ | Glacier |
| ◎ | Spring |

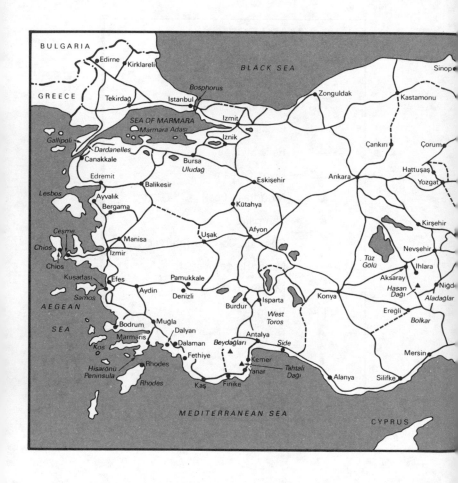

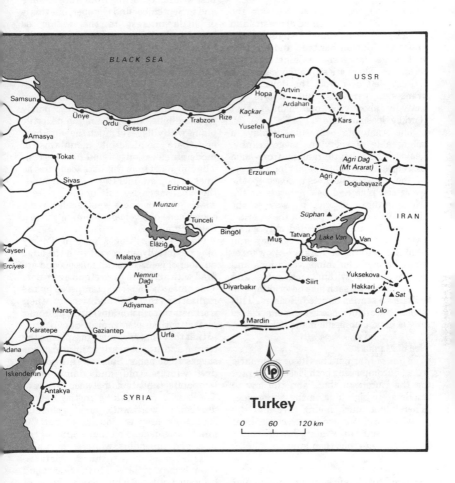

Turkey

# Facts about the Country

## GEOGRAPHY & CLIMATE: WHEN TO GO WHERE

Many foreigners seem to harbour the notion that Turkey is a land of deserts and camels, a misconception fostered by the country's Muslim heritage and perhaps by the legendary scene on Camel cigarette wrappers. There are still a few camels in Turkey, left over from the days of the trans-Asia caravans, but deserts are actually about the one habitat that Turkey does not have.

The Anatolian peninsula displays a remarkable diversity in its geography, geology and climate, ranging from such extremes as the subtropical cloud forests of the eastern Black Sea coast to the evergreen pine and oak habitats of the Mediterranean littoral, by way of the deceptively barren steppes of the interior.

The following is intended only as an overview of the regional geography and climatic patterns of Turkey. Allowances must be made for minor variations and micro-climates within each zone, and accordingly with each hike description you will find a section entitled 'Season'. This should be carefully heeded and supersedes any general comments made below.

### Sea of Marmara

The Sea of Marmara has its own climatic zone, encompassing both Eastern Thrace on the European shore and the low to moderately high hills on the Asian side. There's not much hiking here and the season is relatively short, with continental summers and dank winters that are better for abundant crops than humans.

### The Aegean

Between the Asian Marmara ranges and the Gulf of Gökova, Aegean Turkey extends inland from the Aegean Sea to the tops of several parallel river valleys which furrow the region. The climate is more salubrious than further north, with the best weather occurring from April to June and in September and October, but this is of little interest to the walker as surprisingly there are very few noteworthy hikes in the area.

### Central Anatolia

The Central Anatolian heartland begins beyond the sources of the rivers in Aegean Turkey, and consists of rolling, partly forested hills, dull-coloured but fertile plains with villages of much the same hue, and bare nondescript mountains of moderate elevation (around 2500 metres). The only relief from this bare scene are the lines of poplars marking a watercourse, the expanse of a dry, salt, or (rarely) fresh water lake, or more spectacularly the snowy cone of a volcano looming above a field of grain.

Novices consulting a map of Turkey may be initially impressed with the large number of peaks or small massifs and are fired with ambition to go climb every one. This enthusiasm is soon tempered by the realisation that in addition to their starkness these mountains spring up from a plateau with an average altitude of 1000 m, so that they appear as mere pimples on the terrain and are not nearly so impressive as suggested on paper. Summers are hot and dry, winters cold and damp, with temperate transitions between the two. The season for trekking in the limited number of worthwhile areas generally lasts from May to September but the exact dates depend on the severity of the past, and impending, winters.

This landscape, with minor variations, extends most of the way to the Soviet and Iranian borders. The major rivers of Anatolia – the Kızılırmak, the Sakarya, the Fırat (Euphrates), the Dicle (Tigris), the Murat, and the Aras – all rise here and flow, not just to the Black Sea and the

Mediterranean, but to such far-flung points as the Caspian Sea and the Persian Gulf.

The upper reaches of the Fırat and the Dicle enclose the beginning of their joint flood plain, which spreads south into Syria from an arc roughly connecting Siirt, Elazığ, Malatya and Kahraman Maraş. There is little in this flat, surprisingly dry (soon to be massively irrigated), agricultural expanse that would interest the trekker, but the Lake Van basin is another story. This is the beginning of Central Asia and the basin is ringed by several dormant volcanoes and the rugged Cilo/Sat peaks along the Iraqi border. Minimum elevation rises to 1500 metres and the barrenness, occasionally off-putting further west, here acquires an aesthetic perfection. The climate, too, goes to further extremes, with cool summers and Siberian winters, resulting in the shortest trekking season (June to early September) of any region in Turkey.

Central Anatolia is sandwiched between the two most rewarding hiking areas in the country, namely the Black Sea coastal mountains and the Mediterranean barrier ranges.

## Black Sea Coast

The Black Sea coast mountains begin just north of Ankara as pleasantly wooded hills, and extend east beyond Kars and Artvin to the Soviet frontier, gaining in altitude and majesty along the way. The north slopes, which face the Black Sea with its surprisingly mild climate, are lushly vegetated with hardwood and coniferous forests at the higher altitudes, and chestnut, hazelnut and cherry groves lower down.

The coast is rainy but warm throughout much of the year (though of course winter higher up is severe as in any mountain range), and this pattern becomes more pronounced as you travel east, culminating in the perennial mists and tea plantations of Artvin, Rize and Trabzon provinces.

To the south these mountains fall away less sharply to the great central plateau, but since the opposite side catches most of the precipitation from the moist Black Sea, the inland flank has the craggy appearance and dry weather of a rain-shadow zone. Although the Black Sea swimming season is brief – June through August – the climate for walking at the higher elevations is generally satisfactory from mid-June to early October.

## Mediterranean

The geography of the Mediterranean shore, from the Gulf of Gökova to that of İskenderun, is dominated by the Toros (Taurus) mountains and its various offshoots such as the peaks of the Lycian peninsula. Collectively they are the terminus of a great geological unit, consisting mostly of karstic limestone, which begins in the Carso region of Italy and Yugoslavia, forms the spine of Albania and mainland Greece, and continues through Crete and part of the Dodecanese before ending above Malatya.

As this formation generally runs from west to east, it is furrowed by short, swift rivers running from north to south. Vegetation close to the sea is the typical Mediterranean mixture of maquis, Aleppo pine and scrub oak, though higher up true alpine forests of other conifers and hardwoods occur.

For the hiker, this region has the greatest concentration of tourist facilities and the longest walking season in Turkey. In the mountains the climate is influenced both by altitude and by the high steppe behind, so jaunts between October and April are not advisable. In mid to late summer, because of the southern latitude, heat is a factor and water is scarce owing to the properties of the area's limestone core.

Temperature and dryness also rule out coastal walks in July or August, but otherwise hiking can be comfortably undertaken at just about any time. It is wet from December to March, but even then walking is apt to be pleasant between the storms, which rarely last more than a few days.

## PEOPLE & CULTURE OF RURAL TURKEY

Settlement in Turkey dates back as far as 7500 BC and in the following millennia the region was peopled by invaders from around the Mediterranean, such as the Hittites, Greeks and Romans, and from Persia in the east. It was not until the beginning of the 9th Century AD that Turkey was settled by the central Asian tribal people generally known as the Turks.

They came in successive waves from the territory between the Ural and Altay mountains, though the reason for this migration has not been firmly established. The two main theories are that the migrants were either fleeing a prolonged drought or had multiplied so successfully that they required new and larger pastures.

Before leaving their original homeland in central Asia the various Turkic tribes had been shamanistic, deifying natural phenomena and conferring the title of shaman on those individuals whose duty it was to mediate with these natural forces on behalf of the larger community. After initial contacts with the Islamic Persian and Arabic cultures, the Turkic peoples adopted Islam, and it was a Muslim Seljuk Turkish army that defeated the Byzantines at Manzikert (today Malazgirt) in 1071, thus establishing Anatolia as the new Turkish homeland.

The Seljuk kingdom was succeeded by the more durable Ottoman empire in the late 13th century. This expanded around the eastern Mediterranean for the next three centuries, and as a result new and heterogeneous elements were introduced to Anatolia. Numbers of Balkan Greeks, Slavs, Albanians, Bosnians, Pomaks (Islamicised Bogomils), Circassians, Laz, Georgians and Kurds joined, through voluntary movement or conquest, the existing Greek, Armenian, Assyrian, Persian and Arab populations which the Ottomans had 'inherited'.

Most of these ethnic groups are concentrated in the cities and form the largely homogeneous population of the modern Turkish Republic. Yet traces of the tribal or clan divisions within the original Turkic peoples can still be discerned in contemporary Turkey, though they are diminishing through the process of assimilation. These are the people you are most likely to meet in the rural areas of Turkey.

### Yörük

Perhaps the most romantic of these groups are the *Yörük*. The name is derived from either the adjective *yürük* (active, swift) or the verb *yürümek* (to walk, march), which obviously both refer to the original nomadic habits of these people. Today they are no longer nomadic but rather transhumant, ie they oscillate between established summer and winter quarters, having been compelled in late Ottoman times to maintain a fixed address for taxation and conscription purposes.

Yörüks are found principally in the coastal foothills of Muğla and Antalya provinces, with smaller populations to the east in Mersin and Adana provinces. Their traditional occupation of livestock-raising and the yearly circuit between summer and winter pastures is assuming less importance as a settled farming life becomes ever more lucrative.

It is difficult to tell by sight if someone is of Yörük background. They may have a darker complexion but the most reliable indicator is the still-splendid and colourful headdresses of the women.

### Türkmen

The Türkmen (Turcoman), if they are of pure descent, have the distinctively round faces and slanted eyes that affirm their kinship with the Uigurs of western China, the most eastern Turkic group known. Otherwise the home territory and lifestyle of the Türkmen is almost identical with those of the Yörük, and this has led to a lot of confusion on the part of both observers and the people themselves. It is probably safe to say, though, that there are individuals who are both Türkmen and Yörük, persons who are merely Yörük (ie given to seasonal movement), and genuine Türkmen who gave up wandering habits generations ago. One thing at least is certain – there is no confusing a Türkmen rug with a Yörük one!

Kurdish man
from Lake Van area

## Kurds

The Kurds speak an Indo-European language and make up a large part of the population of south-eastern Turkey. Within a rough rectangle connecting Doğubayazit, Erzincan, Adıyaman and Hakkarı there are some seven million Kurds and many live outside this territory. They are principally engaged in livestock-raising and are reputed to be excellent horsemen. You are most likely to meet Kurds on any of the mountains discussed in the Around Lake Van chapter and in the Munzur range as well. Most of the men will understand and speak Turkish, having learnt it in school and/or the army, but women and children are usually monolingual.

## Tahtacılar

The Tahtacılar are often mistaken for the Yörük, and the two groups are concentrated mostly in the same areas. The Tahtacılar are discussed in depth in the section on the Beydağları in the Turquoise Coast chapter.

## Laz

The Laz are a people of Caucasian origin who inhabit the north slopes of the Kaçkar and speak their own language as well as Turkish. When not in their summer pastures they are formidable fishermen and sailors. For many outsiders the Laz country has come to mean (incorrectly) the whole Black Sea coast east of Trabzon, although the Laz homeland is in fact much more compact. More reasonably, the Black Sea is identified with one of the hallmarks of Laz culture, the *horon* or lively circle dance performed to the strains of a bagpipe (*tulum*) and lap fiddle (*kemençe*).

## Hemşin

The Hemşin are believed to be a very ancient Turkic tribe – perhaps stragglers from the original migrations – who speak their own dialect of Turkish and who are restricted to the area around Çamlıhemşin, Ayder, and Çat in the Kaçkar mountains.

## Other Groups

There are few, if any, people of purely Georgian descent remaining in the Kaçkar; those that may exist live mostly on the Georgian side of the range. We have heard a few reports on tiny communities of Armenians and Pontic Greeks living in the hills above the Black Sea, though according to the 1923 Treaty of Lausanne the latter are not really supposed to be there. The generation of 60 years ago probably adopted Islam outwardly to avoid deportation, and so were able to retain their ancestral villages and pastures and bequeath them to those living today.

### Life in a *Yayla*

All of the preceding groups, and in fact any village Turk, have one thing in common – an abiding attachment to the land which is the heritage of life on the steppes of Central Asia. The most visible manifestation of this for the trekker is the institution of the *yayla*.

'Mountain plateau' and 'summer pasture' are the dictionary definitions of the word but they tell only part of the story. Yayla is derived from the verb *yayılmak* (to spread out or disperse), as in the action of a grazing herd of goats or sheep, but the *yayla* is much more than a meadow to the locals. It is home for the summer, almost always successive summers, and *yaylalar* (plural) belong to particular villages whose individual livestock owners pay a tax to the provincial administration for the use of the pasture.

Yaylalar can consist of anything from a single *yurt* – a dark goat-hair tent suspended on a number of wooden poles – to a cluster, virtually a village, of substantial wood-and-stone chalets. The latter are found almost exclusively in the Kaçkar, where the need for protection from the weather and the availability of building materials have made it necessary and feasible to build semi-permanent structures. Pure wood-and-fibre *yurtlar* are heavy and expensive to maintain, and accordingly have become collector's items.

What you will mostly see

are hybrids, with a metre of stone wall and above that a shanty-style patchwork of plastic sheeting or flour-sacks. The frame is often made of hastily cut branches instead of the carved tent poles that were once used.

A Kurdish *oba* (another word for yurt, also a group of them) tends to be billowy, and irregularly shaped, with protruding poles. Türkmen tents can be either round like an igloo or tunnel-like with extensive lattice work, but they are now rare. Other Yörük tents are box-like, almost rectangular, and it is this type that you will see the most of, particularly in the Toros range.

The *yaylalar* are inhabited in the early summer as soon as the snow melts and the grass regenerates. They remain occupied until forage is exhausted and increasing cold and rain signal the beginning of winter, a date which varies from place to place. A typical *yayla* in the Toros might consist of two or three tents inhabited by one extended family or two related ones. It is rare for every member of a family to be present at any given moment; there is a great deal of coming and going and someone is always down in the winter village looking after the house.

The women cook, milk the cattle, sheep or goats, and prepare butter, cheese and yogurt from the milk. They also spin wool, weave carpets and knit socks and gloves in

preparation for the coming winter. Men hunt, cut wood (if any is nearby), and of course graze and shear the animals. Shepherds are often armed, as they must stand all-night vigils to protect the flocks from predators (four-footed and otherwise). The men also gather fodder for the winter, though the actual transport of the cut grass is considered women's work. Both sexes make and stockpile cow-pats for use as fuel.

When the work is done the *yayla* is a centre for socialising and, occasionally, celebration. With good company, a battery-powered radio, a fire and a boiling teapot, a yurt can seem more like a *çayhane* (teahouse) than an outpost in the wilderness.

The *yayla* is simple, labour intensive and in harmony with the environment, but its future is jeopardised by the allure of contemporary life. More than half of Turkey lives in a city or town and the urban population is up 15 million from what it was 15 years ago. Wealth brought back by Turks working abroad has spawned such anomalies as a VCR in the corner of a mud-and-straw hut, or the lyrics of Madonna competing with the *ezan* (call to prayer) being chanted over the loudspeaker of a nearby mosque. Urban Turkey is increasingly a drab affair of monstrous concrete apartment complexes; perhaps their inhabitants will only realise what they have lost when it is too late.

## STAYING IN THE BACKCOUNTRY

Hospitality, *misafirperverlik* in Turkish, is deeply rooted in Turkish culture, and probably predates the conversion to Islam. A Turk is secure in a network of the immediate family, relatives and friends and therefore feels able, even obligated, to take under his or her protection a traveller who is far from home.

Accordingly you will receive many offers of food and possibly shelter as you travel through rural Turkey. These offers are almost always sincere and nothing is expected in return except your company

and possible entertainment value. Potential hosts may even become offended if you refuse an invitation, and doing so gracefully takes some skill. If you really are in a hurry, you can mime 'thanks' by placing one hand on your chest and pointing with the other to your watch and then in the direction you're headed. Even a cup of tea will take some time because you should stop for at least two, or none at all; drinking only one glass might be interpreted as a slight on their tea.

Upon accepting an invitation to enter a dwelling, whether in a *yayla* or a village, remove your shoes at the threshold (unless nobody else does) and wait to be shown to the *misafir odası* (front room for guests) if there is one. By this time news of your arrival will have circulated like wildfire and you will soon be the centre of attention for relatives and curious passers-by alike.

After tea, food will appear, brought in unobtrusively by the women of the household and set down on a large tin-plated copper tray. In both *yaylalar* and villages everyone sits on the carpeted floor around the tray, which is usually surrounded by a dropcloth. This cloth serves both to catch stray crumbs and for you to hide your feet under; stockinged feet near food are considered little better than dirty boots. All those present dip into the common dishes with a spoon and/or pieces of bread until they are satisfied.

A village menu generally features *yufka* (unleavened bread) or *bazlama* (leavened bread), an onion and tomato salad, olives, yogurt or cheese, a cooked vegetable dish, occasionally soup, and sometimes a light sweet. Meat is a luxury and is rarely prepared; count it a special honour if you get any. If you are carrying any food that complements the meal, you might offer to share it, though in most cases this is not necessary and your offer may even be strongly resisted.

In a *yayla* the fare will be slanted even more toward dairy products and various kinds of bread - a happy coincidence, since these are precisely the types of food that are difficult to carry for long distances. It's usually okay to ask for small portions of such items to fill these holes in your diet but you can't really count on doing massive restocking of your larder; there are many mouths to feed in the average *yayla*.

It is polite to refuse spontaneous offers of take-away food at least once, since your hosts may try and load you down with more than you can possibly carry. Rather than offering money for such goods – although on one occasion this was expected of us – it might be better to take a family portrait with your camera and send them a print later. (Addresses may appear to be utterly rudimentary, but your mail will probably get through.) Basic over-the-counter medications such as aspirin, cold medicines, zinc oxide paste and sun cream are greatly appreciated by the mountain folk, who seem universally afflicted with mysterious pains, sniffles and chapped or cracked hands. More curiously, we were asked several times if we had any binoculars (*dürbün*) for sale, and if you were to stay anywhere for some length of time it might be appropriate to part with a pair for little or no money.

If you need to spend the night at a *yayla*, you should initially offer to pitch your tent close by and drop in for tea and food when it's appropriate; space in the *oba* is generally limited. In a remote village you should first ask for the *köy odası* (a room or lodge set aside for travellers), though in most cases you will end up in the house of the *muhtar* (headman). In a village house and in any of the more elaborately constructed *yaylalar* of the Kaçkar you sleep as well as eat in the *misafir odası*.

After the meal and socialising are finished, *yorganlar* (quilts) and *yastıklar* (pillows) are taken from corners or cupboards and your bed is prepared on the floor. There is rarely any running water in the typical village house, but your hosts will be happy to *su dökmek yıkanmak için* – pour some water out of a jug for you to wash outside. Variations of the same term are used for urinating (*küçük su dökmek*) and defecating (*büyük su dökmek*), and for those operations you will be shown the outhouse or pointed in the direction of a likely tree or rock.

By this point you will have noticed that, unless their menfolk are absent, women are seldom seen and never heard, and do not eat with the men when they are entertaining in the *misafir odası*. If you are trekking as a couple the lady will be accorded the status of 'honorary man' for the duration of the visit, since you are foreigners, and you can expect to eat and sleep in the same room. The women of the house by convention remain in the *mutfak* (kitchen) and take their meals there when company is around. (When there are no guests everyone eats there, near the cooking and heating fireplace).

In the morning you are more likely to meet the women when they get up early to rekindle the fire and prepare a breakfast of hot milk, tea and fresh bread. You can't expect to sleep in, as the villagers are up and about at dawn. In the *yaylalar* the animals have to be milked and then dispersed on the slopes before the growing heat makes the beasts disinclined to move.

## LANGUAGE
### Turkish Alphabet
Since Turkish terms and place names appear in their vernacular spellings in the text, the following table is presented so that the reader may use and utter them, and stand a good chance of being understood.

A modified Roman alphabet was devised for modern Turkish in 1928 and is much better suited to the language than the Arabic script previously used. Pronunciation is phonetic, with all letters having the same values in every situation; furthermore the only dipthongs are those produced by the combination of a vowel and the letter 'y', and these also are constant in their pronunciation.

The Turkish alphabet contains all the letters of the English alphabet except 'q', 'x', and 'w' (though the latter is often seen on the 'WC' signs posted over toilets). Moreover all these letters are pronounced approximately the same as in English, save for the exceptions covered below. In addition there are a handful of special letters which need to be learned.

## Vowels

*Letter   Pronunciation*

| a | Somewhere between the 'u' in *but* and the 'a' in *far* |
| e | 'e' as in *bed* |
| ı | the dotless 'i' is pronounced like the short unstressed 'a' in *probable* |
| i | 'i' as in *hit* |
| o | 'o' as *no*, never as in *nothing* |
| ö | like the same letter in German, or 'eu' in French *deux* |
| u | somewhere between the 'u' in *push* and that in *blue* |
| ü | like the same letter in German, or 'u' in French *tu* |
| ˆ | This accent occurs exclusively over the vowels *a* and *u*, usually in words of Arabic origin. It serves to introduce a very slight 'y' sound between the affected vowel and the preceding consonant, but this convention is on the wane. |

## Dipthongs

| ay | like 'uy' in *buy* |
| ey | like 'a' in *make* |
| oy | like 'oi' in *oil* |
| uy | like first syllable of French word *puissance* |

## Consonants

| c | 'j' as in *jam* |
| ç | 'ch' as in *church* |
| g | hard 'g' as in *goal*, never as in *gentle* |
| ğ | never initial; when final after a vowel, or between a vowel and a consonant, or two vowels, serves to slightly lengthen the preceding vowel. This letter is virtually silent, although when found between two vowels a very faint 'y' sound can be detected. |
| h | 'h' as in *him*; never silent, even when final |
| j | soft 'j' as in French *journal* |
| s | 's' as in *snake*, never as in *phase* |
| ş | 'sh' as in *shall* |
| v | weak 'v', almost like 'w' in *wash*, especially after a vowel |

**Stress** A good topic to start arguments with. Some grammars claim that it is usually on the first syllable, others that it is on the last, which should indicate that it is not that critical of an issue. The one thing that everyone seems to agree on is that place names are the big exception to whatever rule is established, and each one must be learned as encountered. Thus: *Mar*maris, *Fet*hiye, Istan*bul, Diy*ar*bakır, Iz*mir, and so forth.

### Turkish for Trekkers

A desire to travel in the manner advocated by this book also implies a willingness to learn at least some *grammatical* Turkish. Memorised phrases of the 'Waiter, there's a fly in my soup' variety will not get you by in the hills. If you must learn something by rote, it should rather be the list of greetings in this section. Even if you never learn to hold extended conversations you need, for your own safety at the very least, to understand directions, and to answer or pose simple questions.

For a systematic grammar course, *Teach Yourself Turkish* by Geoffrey L Lewis (David McKay) is recommended. It is compact, lively and, though almost 30 years old, is still remarkably current.

The best dictionaries are those published by Langenscheidt, which come in both miniature and coat-pocket size, and

Redhouse, which has a full line of products for every taste and wallet, ranging from the miniature bilingual to the definitive, four kg set of two volumes – just the thing to take trekking! These all are published in Turkey so they can be bought on arrival.

Outside the country you might consider purchasing *The Concise Oxford Turkish Dictionary*, especially if they have finally come out with a bilingual paperback edition.

Without going into a lengthy discussion of the language, it can be said that Turkish is an agglutinative language, ie changes in meaning are brought about by attaching one or more suffixes to a basic word or verb stem. It also exhibits vowel harmony, ie a given vowel can only occur with certain others within the same word, although there are a few exceptions to this rule. For anyone who has studied Latin the syntax will be vaguely familiar; Turkish commonly puts the subject of a sentence first (often set off by a comma in writing), then necessary qualifiers, with the verb usually coming last.

You will notice a couple of abbreviations in the following vocabulary: 'lit' for literally and 'pl' for plural. The latter will not only designate plural objects but the also formal (plural) second person, which Turkish, like many languages, uses.

### Greetings & Partings

| | |
|---|---|
| Hello (informal) | *Merhaba* |
| Peace be on you | *Selâmün aleykum* |
| And peace be on you (reply) | *Aleykum selâm* |
| Good morning | *Günaydin* |
| Good day | *İyi günler* |
| Good evening | *İyi akşamlar* |
| Good night | *İyi geceler* |
| Welcome (pl) | *Hoş geldin(iz)* |
| We (or I) have found you well (in reply to *hoş geldin(iz)*) | *Hoş bulduk* |

| | |
|---|---|
| Permission for me/us to leave (said when resuming travel) | *Bana/bize müsaade* |
| Good-bye (said to those staying) | *Allahaısmarladık* or *Alasmarladık* |
| Remain well (pl) (said to those staying) | *Hoşça kal(in)* or *Esen kal(in)* |
| Bon voyage | *Güle güle* |

### Useful words & phrases

| | |
|---|---|
| Have a good trip | *İyi yolculuklar* |
| How are you (pl) | *Nasılsın(ız)* |
| I am well | *İyiyim* |
| I am pleased (to meet you) | *Memnum oldum* |
| Please | *Lütfen* |
| Thank you (very much) | *(Çok) teşekkür ederim* or *Sağol* (lit 'be well') |
| You're welcome (lit 'It's nothing') | *Şey değil* |
| The same to you | *Bir mukabele* |
| Yes | *Evet* |
| Certainly | *Tabii* |
| Okay | *Peki* |
| No | *Hayır* |
| Nope (colloquial) | *Yo* |
| Extreme negative, not available | *Yok* |
| Okay | *Tamam* |
| Understood (between two people) | *Anlaşıldı* |
| Agreed (lit 'done, occurred') | *Oldu* |

The suffix particle *-mı* appended to any of the above three words turns it into a question.

| | |
|---|---|
| How many, how much | *Kaç* |
| How much is my bill? | *Borçum ne kadar?* |

May it remain with you, eg keep the change   *Kalsin*

## Forms of Address

If you don't know someone's name, and even if you do, you can and should address them by the following terms appropriate to their age and station in life relative to you.

| | |
|---|---|
| *Dede* | 'Grandpa' (to an old man) |
| *Nine* | 'Grandma' (to an old woman) |
| *Amca* | 'Uncle' (to someone of your father's age) |
| *Abla, bacı* | '(Big) sister' (to a woman your age or somewhat older) |
| *Abı* | '(Big) brother' (to a man your age or slightly older; contraction of *ağabey*) |

## Turkish Questions

| | |
|---|---|
| Where are you from? | *Nerelisiniz?* or *neresi?* |
| Your country? | *Memleket?* |
| Are you (pl) married? | *Evlimisin(iz)?* |
| Where are you going? | *Nereye gidiyorsun(uz)?* |

## Nationalities

| | |
|---|---|
| American | *Amerikalı, Amerikan* |
| Australian | *Avustralyalı* |
| Canadian | *Kanadalı* |
| Dutch | *Hollandalı* |
| English | *İngiliz* |
| French | *Fransiz* |
| German | *Alman* |
| Irish | *İrlandalı* |
| New Zealander | *Yeni Zellandalı* |
| Swedish | *İsveçli* |

| | |
|---|---|
| Swiss | *İsviçreli* |

You can make a complete sentence by preceding any of these adjectives with *Ben* – I (am).

## Common Requests

| | |
|---|---|
| Can I camp here? | *Burada kamp kurabilimiyim?* |
| Can I leave this here? | *Bunu burada bırakabilirmiyim?* |
| How many hours to . . .? | *. . . buradan kaç saat?* |
| I'm looking for the path to . . . | *. . . giden patikayı ariyorum* |
| Where is the toilet? | *Tuvalet nerede?* |
| Is there/are there any . . . (tickets, trails, etc)? | *. . . var mı?* |
| There is/are | *Var* |
| There isn't/aren't | *Yok* |

## Other Useful Verbs

Verbs are listed below, and in dictionaries, with their -*mak/mek* infinitive endings. We have provided a few conjugated examples in various tenses and moods.

| | |
|---|---|
| I have/haven't | *bende var/yok* |
| To occur, become, be | *olmak* |
|   It is possible | *olur* |
|   Out of the question | *olmaz* |
| To find | *bulmak* |
|   I found | *buldum* |
|   It is found, available | *bulunur* |
| To stay, remain | *kalmak* |
|   Where are you staying? | *Nerede kalıyorsınız?* |
|   Is there any left? | *Kaldımı?* |
|   None left | *Kalmadı* |
| To come, arrive | *gelmek* |
|   it's arrived | *geldi* |

| | |
|---|---|
| To go, depart | *gitmek* |
| I'm leaving | *gidiyorum* |
| He has left | *gitti* |
| To understand | *anlamak* |
| I didn't understand | *anlamadım* |
| To want | *istemek* |
| I want to go | *gitmek istiyorum* |
| To see | *görmek* |
| I saw | *gördüm* |
| I don't see | *görmüyorum* |
| To watch, look | *bakmak* |
| Look! (imperative) | *bak!* |
| To wait | *beklemek* |
| I'll wait (for someone) | *bekleyeceğim* |
| I'm waiting for a minibus. | *minibüs bekliyorum* |
| To take, buy | *almak* |
| I took, bought | *aldım* |
| To pay | *ödemek* |
| I paid | *ödedim* |

## Eating

| | |
|---|---|
| Are you hungry? | *Acıktınmı?* |
| Are you thirsty? | *Susadınmı?* |
| I am hungry | *Acıktım* |
| I am thirsty | *Susadım* |
| Food (also 'to eat') | *yemek* |
| Water | *su* |
| Bon apetit | *Afiyet olsun* (lit 'may it further your health') |
| Health to your hands (to compliment someone's cooking) | *Elinize sağlık* |
| May there be excess (said when refusing an invitation to eat) | *Ziyade olsun* |
| You shouldn't have (gone to the trouble) said for a particularly elaborate meal | *Zahmet oldu* |

## Accommodation

| | |
|---|---|
| I'll be staying here . . . days | *Burada . . . gün kalacağım* |
| single room | *bir kişilik oda* |
| double room | *iki kişilik oda* |
| triple room | *üç kişilik oda* |
| key | *anahtar* |
| bed | *yatak* |
| sheet(s) | *çarşaf(lar)* |
| pillow | *yastık* |
| blanket | *battaniye* |
| quilt | *yorgan* |
| hot water shower | *sıcak sulu duş* |
| cold water shower | *soğuk sulu duş* |
| lantern or flashlight | *fener, kandil* |
| electric light | *ışık* |
| candle | *mum* |

## Numbers

| | |
|---|---|
| 1 | *bir* |
| 2 | *iki* |
| 3 | *üç* |
| 4 | *dört* |
| 5 | *beş* |
| 6 | *altı* |
| 7 | *yedi* |
| 8 | *sekiz* |
| 9 | *dokuz* |
| 10 | *on* |
| 11 | *onbir* |
| 12 | *oniki* |
| 20 | *yirmi* |
| 21 | *yirmibir* |
| 25 | *yirmibeş* |
| 30 | *otuz* |
| 40 | *kırk* |
| 50 | *elli* |
| 60 | *altmış* |
| 70 | *yetmiş* |
| 80 | *seksen* |
| 90 | *doksan* |
| 100 | *yüz* |
| 200 | *iki yüz* |
| 600 | *altı yüz* |
| 1000 | *bin* |
| 4000 | *dört bin* |
| 7368 | *yedibinüçyüzaltmışsekiz* |

## Time

| | |
|---|---|
| What time is it? | *Saat kaç?* |
| It's . . . o'clock. | *Saat . . .* |
| At what time . . .? | *Saat kaçta . . .?* |
| At . . . o'clock. | *Saat . . . de* |
| When? | *ne zaman?* |
| hour, also clock or watch | *saat* |
| half-hour | *yarım saat* |
| quarter of an hour | *çeyrek* |
| two hours | *iki saat* |
| two-and-a-half hours (unlike yarim, buçuk cannot stand alone but must follow a whole number) | *iki buçuk saat* |
| minute | *dakika* (usually slurred to *dakka*) |
| twenty minutes | *yirmi dakika* |
| sunrise | *şafak, seher* |
| at sunrise | *şafak,da, seherde* |
| sunset | *güneş batımı* |
| dark | *karanlık* |
| it gets dark | *karanlık olunca* |
| morning | *sabah* |
| noon | *öğle* |
| afternoon | *ikindi* |
| evening | *akşam* |
| night | *geçe* |
| now | *şimdi* |
| then | *o zaman* |
| later | *sonra* |
| always | *her zaman, hep* |
| continual(ly) | *devamlı* |
| never | *hiçbirzaman* |
| today | *bugün* |
| yesterday | *dün* |
| day before yesterday | *evvelki gün* |
| tomorrow | *yarın* |
| day after tomorrow | *yarından sonra* |

## Weather (*hava*)

| | |
|---|---|
| good, clear | *açık* |
| bad, ruined | *bozuk* |
| sun(ny) | *güneş(li)* |
| cloud(y) | *bulut(lu)* |
| rain(y) | *yağmur(lu)* |
| snow(y) | *kar(lı)* |

| | |
|---|---|
| storm | *fırtına* |
| lightning | *şimşek, yıldırım* |
| wind | *rüzgâr* |
| fog, mist | *ois* |
| mist, haze (also 'smoke') | *duman* |

## Hiking Equipment

| | |
|---|---|
| backpack | *sırt çantası* |
| boot(s) | *postal(lar)* |
| canteen, water bottle | *matara* |
| cartridge (for butane stoves) | *tüp* |
| compass | *pusula* |
| fuel | *yakıt* |
| fuel (alcohol) | *ispirto* |
| kerosene | *gaz yağı* |
| map | *harita* |
| matches | *kibrit* |
| pocketknife | *çakı* |
| sleeping bag | *uyku tulumu* |
| down | *kuştüyü* |
| fibre | *elyaf* |
| stove | *ocak* |
| tent | *çadır* |
| walking stick | *baston* |

## Directions

| | |
|---|---|
| straight ahead, toward | *doğru* |
| straight | *düz, dümdüz* |
| a bit further | *az daha uzokta* |
| near/far | *yakın/uzak* |
| right/left | *sağ/sol* |
| uphill/downhill | *yokuş/yokuş aşağı* |
| above/below | *yukarı/aşağı* |
| level/steep | *düz/dik* |
| uneven, not level | *arızalı* |
| wide/narrow | *geniş/dar* |
| good/bad | *iyi/kötü, fena* |
| nice, pleasant/ugly, unpleasant | *güzel/çirkin* |
| big/small | *büyük/küçük* |
| here/there | *bur(a)da/or(a)da* |
| from . . . | *. . . dan* |
| until . . . | *. . . kadar* |
| before/after | *evvel/sonra* |
| behind/in front of | *arkasında/önünde* |

| | |
|---|---|
| above/below | üstünde/altında |
| across from | karşısında |
| adjacent | yanında |
| in between | arasında |
| bottom, base | dip |
| along the base | dibinden |
| to follow | takip etmek |

**Trails**

| | |
|---|---|
| road, way (general term) | yol |
| main road, highway | anayol, karayolu |
| auto road | araba yolu, asfalt |
| jeep road | şose (susa in some dialects) |
| tractor track | traktör yolu |
| mule/donkey track | eşekyolu, hayvanyolu |
| trail, footpath | patika |
| cobbled footpath | kaldırım |
| goat trace | keçiyolu |
| fork, junction | çatal, ayırım |
| shortcut | kestirme |
| sign, waymark | işaret |

Fethiye area, old cobbled kaldırım up to Makri

**Places**

| | |
|---|---|
| province | il |
| county or subdivision of an il (also its main town) | ilçe |
| subdistrict of an ilçe; also its main village | bucak, nahiye |
| hamlet, or neighbourhood of a village | mahalle |
| summer residence pasture | yayla, yaylalar (pl) |
| village | köy |

**Landmarks**

| | |
|---|---|
| mountain(s) | dağ(lar) |
| rounded, eroded (lit 'old') | ihtiyar |
| jagged, uneroded (lit 'young') | genç |
| peak, summit | zirve, baş |
| couloir, or scree | çarşak |
| glacier | buzul |
| chasm | yarık |
| pass, saddle, gap | geçit, bel, belen, aşırt, gedik |
| hill, knoll | tepe |
| slope, hillside | yamaç, yüz |
| ridge | sırt |
| rock | taş |
| boulder | kaya |
| gulch, hollow | çukur |
| cave | mağara |
| gorge | kapuz (sometimes kapız) |
| cliff | yar, uçurum |
| valley | vadi |
| stream (or its valley) | dere |
| dry stream | dere yatağı |
| running stream | çay, su |
| river | İrmak, nehir |
| lake | göl |
| sea | deniz |
| shore, bank | kıyı |
| dock | iskele |
| sandy beach | kumsal |

| | |
|---|---|
| swamp | *bataklık* |
| mud | *çamur* |
| forest | *orman* |
| grove | *koru, koruluk* |
| meadow, turf | *çayır* |
| meadow, clearing | *meydan* |
| plain, plateau | *ova* |
| plateau, level spot | *plato, düzlük* |
| field | *tarla* |
| parcel of land, lot | *arazı* |
| corral | *ağıl* |
| shed or livestock pen | *ahır* |
| hut | *kulübe* |
| house | *ev* |
| tent in a *yayla* | *yurt, çadır* |
| yayla tent or the whole collection of tents | *oba* |
| beehive | *kovan* |
| flowing spring | *pınar* |
| irrigation canal, aqueduct | *kanal, su yolu* |
| water tank | *depo* |
| fountain (contructed) | *çeşme* |
| sources (of a river) | *kaynak* |
| well/cistern | *kuyu/sarnıç* |
| quarry | *taşocağı* |
| cemetery | *mezarlık* |
| bridge | *köprü* |
| tower | *kule* |
| castle (or ruins) | *kale* |
| ruins, remains | *harabe, ören, yıkıntı* |
| church | *kilise* |
| monastery | *manastır* |
| sign, placard | *tabela, levha* |
| plaza, central square | *meydan* |
| coffee/teahouse | *kahve(hane)/ çayhane* |
| lodge for travellers | *köy odası* |
| shop, grocery store | *dükkan, bakkal(iye)* |
| restaurant | *lokanta* |
| mosque | *cami* |
| police or *jandarma* post | *karakol* |
| turkish bath | *hamam* |

**People**

| | |
|---|---|
| bath-house attendant | *tellak* |
| foreigner, stranger | *yabancı* |
| forest ranger, field warden | *korucu* |
| friend | *arkadaş* |
| gendarme(rie) | *jandarma* |
| guard, watchman | *bekçi* |
| guest, traveller | *misafir* |
| hunter | *avcı* |
| islamic priest | *imam* |
| pilgrim to Mecca | *hacı* |
| schoolteacher | *öğretmen* |
| shepherd | *çoban* |
| shoe repairman | *ayakkabı tamircisi* |
| tailor | *terzi* |
| village headman | *muhtar* |
| police(man) | *polis* |

Ihlara Valley water-bearer

## Trees (Ağaçlar)

| | |
|---|---|
| arbutus | *koca yemişi* |
| beech | *kayın* |
| cedar | *sedir* |
| cedar of Lebanon | *katran* |
| cypress | *servi, selvi* |
| chestnut | *kestane* |
| fir | *köknar* |
| holm oak | *pırnal* |
| juniper | *ardıç* |
| linden | *ıhlamur* |
| maple | *akçağaç* |
| oak | *meşe* |
| oleander | *zakkum* |
| olive | *zeytin* |
| oriental plane tree | *çınar* |
| palm | *palmiye* |
| pine | *çam* |
| plum | *erik* |
| poplar | *kavak* |
| white poplar | *su kavağı* |
| walnut | *ceviz* |
| willow | *söğüt* |

## Beasts (*hayvanlar*), Birds (*kuşlar*) & Bugs (*böcekler*)

| | |
|---|---|
| bear | *ayı* |
| bee | *arı* |
| butterfly | *kelebek* |
| flea | *pire* |
| chamois | *dağ keçisi* |
| deer | *geyik* |

| | |
|---|---|
| donkey | *eşek* |
| eagle | *kartal* |
| falcon | *şahin* |
| fly | *sinek* |
| fox | *tilki* |
| frog | *kurbağa* |
| goat | *keçi* |
| hawk | *doğan* |
| horse | *at* |
| jackal | *çakal* |
| jellyfish | *denizanası* |
| lizard | *kertenkele* |
| louse | *bit* |
| mosquito | *sivrisinek* |
| mouse | *fare* |
| mule | *katır* |
| owl | *baykuş* |
| partridge | *keklik* |
| rat | *sıçan* |
| scorpion | *akrep* |
| sea urchin | *denizkestanesi* |
| sheep | *koyun* |
| sheep guard-dog | *çobanköpeği* |
| snake | *yılan* |
| stork | *leylek* |
| tick | *kene* |
| tortoise | *kaplumbağa* |
| viper | *engerek* |
| wasp, hornet | *eşekarısı* |
| turtle | *su kaplumbağası* |
| weasel | *sansar* |
| wolf | *kurt, canavar* |

# Facts for the Trekker

### VISAS & IMMIGRATION

Holders of most passports are given 90-day tourist visa stamps upon entry. If you're going to be staying longer, the easiest way to extend such a visit is to leave the country for a few days – Greece is the most convenient solution. However, on his last Greece-to-Turkey re-entry, after having been in the former country for a very appreciable six weeks, Marc was initially denied entry by a border guard at Edirne, who pointed out that he'd already been in Turkey a total of five months that calendar year. It is entirely possible that a law exists governing cumulative, as opposed to consecutive, periods of residence.

### MONEY

The national unit of currency is the Turkish *lira*, which tends to inflate against hard currencies at a rate of about 2.5% per month. Thus any prices given in this book will be in US$, as the dollar value of things changes much more slowly. Coins are common; those of 25, 50 and 100 TL are essential, while smaller ones have strictly nuisance value. Notes come in denominations of 20 (useless), 50, 100, 500, 1000, 5000 and 10,000. Keep lots of 500s and 1000s handy and be sure not to confuse the latter with the look-alike 10,000!

You should always get a few *lira* at airport, land-crossing and maritime-entry change booths if they're open; such service is comparatively efficient and the rates minimally less than banks (which vary microscopically among themselves in this respect, but read on).

Any large post office will accept cash and Eurocheques. Again a slightly discounted rate prevails, but no commission is levied and you usually get quick service at odd

hours. One of us changed two US$20 bills in Kayseri GPO (open around the clock) at 5 am!

Most banks are open 8.30 to noon and 1.30 to 5 pm, Monday to Friday, but on the heavily touristed south coast, particularly at Antalya, Alanya, Finike and Fethiye, there is always at least one *nobetçi* (night/weekend) bank. If a bank is closed a sign on the door will indicate other banks in town that are open. Tutun Bank is often open weekends no matter what.

Banks vary considerably in their performance. İş Bankası charges a hefty commission (US$1.25) per transaction; fortunately other banks are slow to adopt this practice. The Türk Ziraat Bankasi is the most efficient – you're usually in and out within 10 minutes, as opposed to a half hour elsewhere – and they are the only bank that is consistently able to cash American Express travellers' cheques. Their ads to the contrary, American Express cheques are difficult to change in Turkey – hardly anybody aside from the Ziraat Bankası has their specimens! Take Thomas Cook cheques or some other brand Visa or Citibank. All this will probably convince you that *dövis* (foreign paper money) is very handy in Turkey.

There is also a very small black market for cash, generically referred to as 'Tahtakale' after the flea market near Eminönü in İstanbul. The premium is slight – maybe 10% over the official rate – and probably the only reliable place to indulge *is* the Tahtakale area area or the adjacent Covered Bazaar. Needless to say, shopkeepers engaged in this trade don't hang signs out to that effect. If you loiter purposefully in the neighbourhoods cited, one of the many scams that you will be invited to participate in is money-changing.

## GENERAL INFORMATION
### Post

The PTT ('peh-teh-teh', short for Post Telefon ve Telegraf) handles mail and phone services in Turkey; look for their black and yellow logo. If you plan to be sending a lot of material out, you should get hold of a little (13.5 by 9.5 cm) yellow pamphlet, updated yearly, which lists the rates for every conceivable service and surcharge in French, German and English. This is indispensable to avoid unproductive arguments with the many clerks, especially in small towns, who don't know the international rates and will over or undercharge you. Some clerks in eastern Anatolia may claim that the pamphlet rates are valid only for İstanbul province, but they are in a distinct minority.

For packages, the best advice is not to send them, at least not anything over two to three kg. If you have must, do so from some medium-sized town with good air connections, but try to avoid İstanbul. Employees are generally terrified to do anything unusual or on their own initiative so it's best to enlist the services

of a supervisor who knows the rules. In İstanbul go to the new, relatively efficient Beşiktaş branch (open seven days in a new shopping mall across from the ferry dock).

Incoming mail is probably best received at *Türk Ekspres*, the representative for American Express in Turkey (just carry a few of their cheques). Poste Restante at İstanbul's Sirkeci central PTT is a zoo.

## Telephones

All public telephones in towns bigger than a fly-speck are being rapidly converted to automatic direct-dial type, and they work very well for calls within Turkey (slightly more wobbly for international circuits). Tokens (*jeton*) are sold in small, medium and large size (*küçük*, *orta* and *büyük boy*) theoretically for local, long distance and international calls respectively.

For a local call, dial the number (two to seven digits depending on city size). For Turkish trunk calls, dial 9 twice, wait for a change in tone, then the city code (a list is usually posted), then the subscriber number.

For international calls, dial 9 twice, then the country and city codes (omitting zeros in the latter), then the local number. Don't attempt to dial on phones with the square red light illuminated – that means it's out of order. You drop the tokens into the slot when your party answers, and keep doing so whenever you hear the about-to-be-cut-off tone (very soon on long distance calls!) A token whose value is fractionally used is not returned, so start with a big one and feed in smaller ones as you go along. Left-over *jetonlar*, despite notices to the contrary, can usually be exchanged for postage stamps or tokens of different size.

Calling-card phones have arrived in Turkey; the cards cost about US$8 at PTT desks, and permit, for example, more than three minutes of chat to the USA – a substantial savings over token phones.

From the high-tech to the primitive: don't hope to successfully place or receive calls from little mountain villages. Equipment, when present, tends to be of the antique, crank-dynamo-vigorously-and-scream-repeatedly-at-operator variety. The PTT's optimistic slogan is 'A phone in every village (by 1990)', but whether or not they will work is another matter entirely.

## Time

Turkey has one time zone, Eastern European Time, which is two hours ahead of GMT. Daylight savings applies from the beginning of April to the end of September. The Turkish attitude toward time can be described as relaxed without being lax; they're certainly not the Swiss, but nowhere near as careless about appointments and schedules as Latin, African or South Asian cultures. Be punctual in the big cities; in the villages plus-or-minus 20 minutes is good enough.

## Business Hours

Civil servants and white-collar workers keep conventional 9 to 5 schedules. Craftsmen and bazaar shopkeepers keep unbelievably long hours, often working from 8 am to 10 pm, Monday to Saturday and sometimes Sundays, with no visible siesta. This is convenient if you want to have something attended to at some ungodly hour, and demonstrates the blurring of lines between work and socialising in Turkey. You are often expected to have a *çay* and a talk with anyone who has sold you something (other than groceries) or repaired an article.

There is a sadder side to these marathon workdays – they strongly imply that home is not even as nice as the shop for some reason, and that also these people are so on the edge of subsistence that they're willing to sit endless hours on the off-chance that a customer will happen by.

## INFORMATION & OFFICIALDOM

The attitude of government departments toward mountaineers and trekkers seems to be benevolent neglect, except for those individuals whom we have singled out in the Acknowledgments. While we were not hindered outright – with the exception of one office – neither did we find many officials who would go out of their way to assist us with information or travel arrangements. The best strategy would seem to be to let well enough alone and rely on those individuals in the *özel sektor* (private sector, a favourite word of the current regime) mentioned under Helpful People & Guides.

## Ministry of Culture & Tourism (Tourist Information)

Local branches of the tourist information network, even when well-intentioned, were universally uninformed about any hiking opportunities in their zone of responsibility. They usually had no maps on hand with a scale that would be meaningful to a walker, except for the Kayseri office, which stocked good maps of Erciyes Dağı.

This becomes more understandable when you realise that the Ministry exists primarily to promote what might be called industrial tourism – ie planeloads of individuals who are set to spend vast amounts on luxury hotels and yacht charters – and can't really be bothered with the nickel-and-dime impact of lone hikers living in the village economy. Plus the tourism information staff is highly prone to utter amazement and lack of understanding when faced with an individual who wants to walk.

Plans to develop 'mountain tourism' do exist in the archives of the Ministry but these mostly take the form of proposed winter sports centres on virtually every peak and an expanded programme of guide certification and fee standardisation.

## Orman Genel Müdürlüğü (The Forest Service)

In the Black Sea areas and the ranges paralleling the Mediterranean you are likely to encounter installations of the Orman Müdürlüğu or Forest Service. These usually take the form of *bakim evleri* (guard stations), *misafir haneleri* (lodges for VIPs), or research plots, sometimes a combination of all three. We have indicated the few occasions where it is possible for foreign visitors to use these facilities.

On the very few occasions that we imposed on the Forest Service for transportation or accommodation we found them guardedly helpful and polite, when they had every reason not to be. Our publicising of areas under their control could only result in an increase in fire and littering problems, so under the circumstances they were probably as generous as attention to their own best interests would allow. If you do avail yourself of this ministry's services, do so sparingly and appreciatively.

## Köy Hizmetleri (Village Services Division)

The Turkish governmental agency *Köy Hizmetleri* oversees the provision and maintenance of roads, water and power to the outlying communities of each province. If you will be venturing into a very remote area with limited public transport or accommodation, it might be worth contacting the office of Köy Hizmetleri responsible for the area in question.

Their offices are usually found on the outskirts of most medium-sized towns, and are marked with a yellow-and-black sign. In cities they are in the *İl özel idaresi* or Special Provincial Management building. If there is a project currently underway in the area you will be visiting, often a *şantiye* or work yard will have been set up nearby. You may be able to catch a ride out to the work site in an official truck or even obtain permission to stay at such a camp, in a pinch.

## The Army & Jandarma

Unless you approach a sensitive border region, such as Ağrı Dağ or the Cilo/Sat Dağları, you are unlikely to receive any attention from the Turkish Army or the local *jandarma* (gendarme) post. We were never stopped, questioned or otherwise impeded in all our rambles through the rest of the country, and you will probably also find this to be true in other parts of Turkey, if you don't draw undue negative attention to yourself.

## MOUNTAINEERING ORGANISATIONS
In Turkey there are two major mountaineering bodies and a host of smaller, local clubs. Of these latter organisations, only those that are likely to be of most interest to the foreign trekker are listed.

### Turkey Mountaineering Federation (TDF)
The official, government-sponsored organisation is the Türkiye Dağcılık Federasyonu (Turkey Mountaineering Federation) or TDF. Their headquarters are in the Beden Terbiyesi Genel Müdürlüğü, Ulus İş Hanı, A Blok, Ulus, Ankara, (tel (4) 310-8566 ext 356). Beden Terbiyesi Genel Müdürlüğü means 'Physical Education General Directorate', which should give you a clue as to how trekking is officially regarded: as a means to an end, specifically to advance national prestige and influence youth in a wholesome manner.

Accordingly the TDF mostly organises large-group expeditions, with a distinctly military flavour, to Turkish and foreign peaks, usually on state holidays. It is not noted for catering to the needs of solo trekkers, especially foreigners, and they don't overly exert themselves to make trail maps readily available or to mark and maintain trails.

Nonetheless you may find the organisation useful if you are looking for an alpine guide. One of the TDF's duties is to register guides, *mihmandar* in Turkish, and the Ankara headquarters maintains a complete list of qualified people, broken down by region/province.

The TDF itself is subdivided into agencies, *Dağcılık Ajanlıkları*, which are represented in the larger provincial

capitals. These regional offices tend to be more helpful than the Ankara headquarters, where the bureaucratic atmosphere is apt to be stifling. The employee at the Ankara desk may not be an active mountaineer or trekker and will probably have very little information at hand, however, they will do their best to put you in touch with knowledgeable people, who are usually (surprise!) in the regional *ajanlıklar*. Even if you don't intend to hire one of the local guides for the standardised fee of $US40 per day, you may still find very helpful individuals among their ranks. Despite the shortcomings of the TDF organisation, it does have very competent, personable members.

A case in point is the current president of the TDF, Dr Mecit Doğru, a professor of medicine at Ankara University. Though well into his 60s he remains an active mountaineer and is excellent campfire company, always ready with provocative (if unproven) theories on place nomenclature and the origins of Turkic culture.

### Anatolian Mountaineers Union (ADB)
The Anadolu Dağcılar Birliği (Anatolian Mountaineers Union) or ADB, is a non-profit club based in Ankara (P.O. Box 750, Kızılay; tel (4) 136-9476). This group was founded by individuals with a genuine love and appreciation of mountaineering, and its members have interests ranging from simple dayhikes to big-wall and ice climbing. They are amateurs in the best sense of the word – though of course some of them are not averse to guiding for a fee – whose principal motivation is the promotion and encouragement of mountaineering in Turkey without regimentation or hidden agenda.

ADB members meet most weeknights, at around 7 pm, in the outdoor tea/beer garden of the Mülkiyeliler Birliği (the Political Science University clubhouse). This is not on the grounds of that university itself, but off Karanfil Sokak and behind the Gima Gökdelen highrise at Kızılay Square. The current president is Muzaffer Tıraş; other members likely to be most welcoming to guests are Ömer Tüzel, Batur Kürüz, and Kaşif Aladağlı (see Helpful People & Guides).

The club also issues a twice-yearly newsletter which often includes good sketch maps of trekking and climbing routes – good to browse even if you don't read Turkish. If you're looking for first-hand information or even a trekking companion, than you should consider attending an ADB nightly meeting.

## Kayseri Mountaineering Club (KDK)

The Kayseri Dağcılık Külübü (Kayseri Mountaineering Club) might be considered an offshoot of the TDF, since its founder, Dr Bozkurt Ergör, once served as the president of the TDF. Dr Ergör commands the respect of all Turkish climbers and has made his reputation with a recently prepared series of excellent mountaineering maps. The club itself functions as a professional guiding centre specialising in, but not limited to, nearby Erciyes Dağı. One of Dr. Ergör's associates, Tekin Küçüknalbant, is also a competent guide and a good source of information. It is possible, though not a certainty, that retaining either of their services as a guide might net you a set of their maps. (See Helpful People & Guides for contact addresses).

## Other

The Niğde Dağcılık Ajanlığı is one of the branch agencies of the TDF described before, and one that is known to be particularly helpful owing to the qualities of the past local representative, Mr Mümtaz Çankaya. This office specialises in the Aladağlar and Bolkar Toros; also, if you are planning to use the *Dağ Evi* or alpine lodge in Demirkazık village, it would be a good idea to first check in at the Niğde office (tel (483) 16031) at Burhan Mahallesi, Kale Altı Sokak 15/3, Niğde.

The Boğaziçi Üniversitesi Dağcilik Külüb (Bosphorus University Mountaineering Club) should be helpful in locating maps, finding hiking partners or just for general information, but the main advantage for the visitor is that virtually all of its members speak good English. The club has a programme of excursions to different wilderness areas on most official holidays and over long weekends. You can contact them in advance at PO Box 2, Bebek, İstanbul. Mr Haldun Aydingün (see Helpful People) is a Boğaziçi graduate and ex-member who might still know some current club members.

Other important university clubs include those of the İstanbul Üniversitesi, Beyazit, İstanbul, and the Orta Doğu Teknik Üniversitesi (Middle East Technical University), Ankara. Probably the best way to communicate with these groups is to go to the campus in person and hunt around.

## HELPFUL PEOPLE & GUIDES

The following list is mostly restricted to individuals whose expertise applies to more than one region.

| | |
|---|---|
| Haldun Aydingün<br>Ak-Pa Tekstil İhracat Pazarlama<br>Miralay Şefik bey Sokak<br>Ak-Han No. 15/17<br>Gümüşsuyu, İstanbul<br>tel 151 9200<br>   151 9211 | Author of a guide to the Aladağlar; wide range of Turkish trekking experience. Excellent English. |
| Cemil Bezmen<br>tel 350-0507<br>(İstanbul) | Hiking partner of Haldun's from Boğaziçi University days. Some English. |
| Ömer Tüzel<br>Katip Çelebi Sokak 3/1<br>Çankaya, Ankara<br>tel (4) 127-4658 (home)<br>   (4) 136-6293 (work) | Is researching a guide (in Turkish) to hiking throughout Turkey. Some English, German. |

Top: Wildflowers near the summit, Uludağ (MD)
Bottom: Tahtalı Dağ under November snow (MD)

Top: Baba Dağı from Gemile Island, Turquoise Coast (EL)
Bottom: Flock of sheep below Kız Sivrisi, Beydağları (MD)

Batur Kürüz
Gökçen Sokak 21/A
Şeyranbağları
Ankara
tel (4) 167 5244
(home)
　(4) 136 9476 (work)

Co-manager of the
mountain equipment
shop at this address.
ADB member, speaks
some English.

Kaşif Aladağlı
Kuzgun Sokak 31/13
Aşağı Ayranci
Ankara
tel (4) 230 6347
　(4) 136 9476

Co-manager of
mountain equipment
shop at address above.
ADB member; speaks
some English.

Seyhan Çamligüney
Ankara
tel (4) 230 6157 (home)

ADB member; speaks
English.

Erhan Ersoy
Anthropology Dept
Hacettepe University
Ankara
tel (4) 223 6730
ext 1521

ADB member; speaks
English.

Metin Öz
Instructor,
Yenimahalle Meslek
Lisesi
Ankara
tel (4) 311-0971

TDF-certified guide;
speaks German.

Doğan Şafak
Paşakapı Caddesi,
Bal Apt. 10/4
Niğde
tel (483) 12117

TDF-certified guide;
speaks English,
French.

Dr Bozkurt Ergör
27 Mayis (Millet)
Caddesi 17
38 010 Kayseri
tel (351) 33 767 (home)
　(351) 21 513 (work)

KDK president and
TDF member; drafter
of definitive map
series for Turkish
mountains. Speaks
German.

Tekin Küçüknalbant
Mete Caddesi 36/3
38 010 Kayser
tel (351) 13393 (home)

KDK associate; TDF-
certified guide. Speaks
some English.

Ahmet Piçakçı
*Muhtar*, minibus
driver
Barhal village
Yusufeli district,
Artvin province
tel (0589) 1428 (for
village)

Minibus can be hired
for transfers to
trailhead.

Arif Tokatlıyan
Barhal village
Yusufeli district,
Artvin province
tel (0589) 1428 (for
village)

For hire as a guide to
the Kaçkar.

Galip Körükçü
Avanos (Cappadocia)
Nevşehir
tel (4861) 1543 (home)
　(4861) 1577 (work)

Speaks French,
English, some Dutch.
Contact for horseback
tours through
Cappadocia.

Enver Lucas
Tunalı Hilmi Caddesi
62
Kavkalıdere, Ankara
tel (4) 126 9113 (home)
　(4) 128 2812 (mssg)

Guide; leads custom
tours or those offered
through: Wilderness
Travel, 801 Allston
Way, Berkeley, CA
94710, USA; tel (415)
548-0420

## HEALTH & SAFETY

Turkey is a remarkably hygienic and
secure place in which to travel, whatever
you may hear to the contrary. The water
supply is not a problem as it is in some
countries, and in the cities and large
towns the tap water, though heavily
chlorinated and not very palatable, is
quite safe to drink.

In the country, spring water is invariably
delicious and pure, having usually filtered
down through hundreds of metres of rock
strata – precisely the conditions recreated
by waterworks engineers to purify muni-
cipal supplies shunted from reservoirs or
aqueducts. Just use common sense and
don't take water from below a village or a
grazing area (sheep and goats at the latter
harbour giardia, a debilitating amoeba-
like organism). Only once (near Lake
Van) did we use the purification tablets
that we'd brought along.

A more real danger is over-exposure to

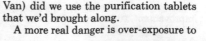

the elements, especially in the eastern half of the country. Necessary protective gear is listed in more detail under Equipment List but suffice it to say that you should never set off without a tent, raingear, headgear for both sun and cold, sunglasses and sunblock cream, and your favourite assortment of clothing capable of handling any weather encountered.

## Altitude Sickness

Altitude sickness is a severe reaction to the low oxygen levels at high altitudes and varies unpredictably from person to person. In theory it can strike at any elevation above 3200 metres, but is unlikely to occur below 4000 metres.

In a mild case, symptoms include headache, listlessness and nausea. If they occur *do not climb any higher* and rest. Aspirin, sweets and hot fluids can provide the necessary relief while normal acclimatisation takes place.

More severe attacks are typified by the inability to urinate, sleeplessness, and heartrate and respiration anomalies. Victims should be transported *immediately* – under their own power or otherwise – to a lower altitude until these symptoms abate. If ignored, acute altitude sickness will result in the death of the affected person from massive pulmonary edema, often within a day. Even after removal to lower elevations oxygen may still have to be administered to critical cases.

The condition is not completely understood as yet but seems to resemble a complex anaphyllactic (allergic) reaction to the absence of oxygen – and of course allergic sensitivity varies enormously from person to person. In Turkey climbers are unlikely to contract altitude sickness except on Ağrı Dağı (5137 metres), where most trekking groups have a client or two who fail to make it to the summit for this reason. If you're in the mountains, and begin to develop the symptoms, without improvement, turn back before you have to be carried back.

## Malaria

There is malarial risk from June through August in the Fırat and Dicle River basins between Gaziantep and Siirt. This guide does not cover that area and we did not use our chloroquine pills.

In the coastal areas mosquitos can be an annoyance. Incense coils (*spiral tütsü*) are sold in affected places and *pansiyon* proprietors often provide you with an *ESEM Mat*, a small electrified tray that slowly vaporises a pyrethrin plaque during the night. These are safe for mammals, effective, and don't reek like the coils.

## Safety on the Trail

There are snakes and scorpions in the backcountry but both are reclusive; we rarely saw either, though the Turquoise Coast seems to have more of both. As for scorpions, it's wise never to stick your hands or feet into places that you cannot see.

Shepherds muttered constantly about bears and wolves but again we never met any or ever saw traces of a nocturnal visit around our camps. The giant Sivas Kangal sheep dogs (*çobanköpekleri*) that we had been warned about turned out to be universally tame and friendly. We should hasten to emphasise, however, that this was strictly our own experience, and should a Sivas Kangal decide that you are a threat to his sheep, it would probably attack without hesitation. Don't walk through or near a flock of sheep when the dog is present and the shepherd isn't.

Nor does the two-legged species pose much threat. This was repeatedly demonstrated to us even when we were prepared for the worst. Several times we went day-hiking, leaving a tent full of gear unattended, and once as we were coming back to camp we witnessed a van drive up to the site. Two individuals got out, unzipped the tent door and went inside. (We were too far away still to do anything about it but could see everything that went on). After a moment the driver honked, the two dashed out of the tent, and they all drove away. We clambered down the mountain, expecting wholesale pillage, but opened the tent to find nothing missing or even touched. Most probably they were curious, came to visit, and disappointed with our absence, left.

Another time I was hitchhiking, wearing baggy pants with an expensive Swiss Army knife in the pocket. As I was getting out the driver pointed out that the knife had fallen out and was lodged between the seat cushions.

On yet another occasion I was hiking along minding my own business when suddenly the hillsides all around resounded with wild yells and repeated gunfire. At first I thought a big-game hunt was on, then that I was the game and was about to be robbed by bandits. As it turned out I was aiming to unwittingly walk down one of the nastiest, most impassable gorges in Turkey, and the mountaineers, all four of them, were strenuously trying to warn me. In the end they came down off the crags and, pointing out the lateness of the hour, invited me up to their *yayla* for the night.

We think these anecdotes speak volumes. The only exception to the general rule might be among certain members of the population around Lake Van (see the appropriate chapter for warnings).

## Medical Facilities

It's a good idea not to hike alone; in case of an accident someone has to go for help. For broken bones, major lacerations, burns and the like, the victim should be transported by any means available to the nearest *sağlık ocağı* (rural health centre), found in most sizable villages. Even if the problem is beyond their capacity to treat completely they will assume responsibility from there on, and arrange for transfer to the nearest *devlet hastanesi* or government hospital. The fee for setting a broken bone, for instance, at one of these establishments is quite nominal – about $US20 – and foreign insurance will probably be accepted.

Attention to injuries in state care facilities is generally quite competent. If you insist on going to a private clinic or hospital for more chronic conditions, you'll find that fees start at around $US20 – even for writing a prescription – with the likelihood that you'll be referred to another specialist who will charge yet another fee.

## FILM & PHOTOGRAPHY

If you shoot Kodachrome or Ektachrome 35 mm slide film, you'll find Turkish prices for it very high – about $US14 for the former (with processing), $US10 for the latter (without). However, Fujichrome 100 can be a very good deal and we used it exclusively. Another advantage of using an E-6 film such as Fuji is that you can get it readily and professionally developed in the big cities. Conditions on the trail often disagree with cameras and it's much better to know sooner, than later, if your camera is malfunctioning, rather than return home and discover dozens of ruined rolls!

### Bargain Outlets for Fujichrome

İstanbul *Can Ticaret*, Büyük PTT Caddesi 2, Sirkeci. About $5.50 per roll, VAT included, if you buy five or more rolls.
Ankara *Telefot*, in Kalabalık Çarşı,

Sakarya Caddesi, Kızılay; about $6 a roll.

**İzmir** Ayhan Ercanlı, Kestelli Caddesi, Kemeraltı District (very close to Konak Square). About $6.20 a roll, tax included.

**Fethiye** Akin Tezel, Turan Sokak 5/A. $7.40 a roll – cheapest anywhere on the Turquoise Coast.

## Quality E-6 Slide Processing
The premier lab in Turkey for processing is *Refo*, with branches in the largest cities. Cost per roll is $US3.50, about a dollar more if you want them framed. Processing time is a day or less.

**İstanbul** Nispetiye Caddesi 18, Etiler
**İzmir – 1.** Kordon, Atatürk Bulvari 252-A, Alsancak
**Ankara** Şehit Adem Yavuz Sokak 8, Kızılay

## Camera Repairs
**İstanbul** *Flaş Optik*, Büyük PTT Caddesi 3, Zafer Hani, 4th Floor, Suite 27. Reasonably priced work done in 24 hours. Ahmet Akdağ, Nuruosmaniye Caddesi, Atasaray İşhanı 37/8-107, Cağaloğlu (near the Covered Bazaar).

**İzmir** *FORS*, Cumhuriyet Bulvari 36/302, Kapanı İşhanı, 3rd Floor, on Emirçaka Bey Meydanı (near Konak). Expensive but good work done in 24 hours.

**Ankara** *Telefoto* (address given above); Aziz Içgüdel or his son Servet are the technicians.

## BOOKS
The following is a selection of the most useful books in English on Turkey, most of which are still in print. Unfortunately relatively little has been written in English about Turkey, especially compared to the literature about other Mediterranean countries, and that which has been written is dominated by three men, Lord Kinross, George Bean and Bernard Lewis.

## Anthropology & Religion
*The Whirling Dervishes* by Ira Friedlander (Colliers, New York, 1975; Wildwood House, London, 1975) is a stunning photo-essay, with reverential text, on the remnants of the Mevlana dervish order of Konya.

*A Village in Anatolia* by Mahmut Makal (Vallentine, Mitchell & Co, London, 1954). Memoirs of a young schoolteacher, stationed in a backwater that remained unaffected by Ataturk's reforms. A sometimes shocking, but often funny, ethnographic classic, and the first written by one of the 'natives'.

*Life in a Turkish Village* by Joe E Pierce (Holt, Rinehart & Winston, New York, 1964). This study of Demirciler is part of the excellent 'Case Studies in Cultural Anthropology' series. It is out of print.

*Turkish Village* by Paul Stirling (John Wiley, New York, 1966; Weidenfeld & Nicholson, London, 1965). Meticulous study of two villages near Mt. Erciyes; unfortunately out of print but listed because there is little else.

## History
*Ataturk: A Biography of Mustafa Kemal* by Lord Kinross (John Patrick Douglass Balfour) (Morrow, New York, 1965). The definitive study, in case you are curious about the man and his legacy, which both still exercise a considerable hold on the Turkish imagination.

*The Ottoman Centuries* by Lord Kinross (Morrow Quill, New York, 1977). A readable chronicle for non-specialists of the fortunes of the Ottoman dynasty and nation, from the 1300s to the 1900s.

*The Emergence of Modern Turkey* by Bernard Lewis (Oxford University Press, New York & Oxford, 1968, 2nd ed). Ideal sequel to the previous listing, as it spans the period between the too-little-too-late reform era of the late 19th century, and the 1950s.

## Belles Lettres, Travelogues, Memoirs
*Through Paphlagonia with a Donkey* by

David Beasley (Davus Publications, New York, 1983). Inspired by Robert Louis Stevensons's *Travels with a Donkey*, the author set out on a donkey through the Black Sea coastal hills in the summer of 1958. Though the landscapes described have considerably altered, the book still accurately conveys the quality of personal interactions when trekking in remote corners of Turkey.

*The Turkish Time Machine* by Monica Jackson (Hodder & Stoughton, London, 1966). This record of an expedition to the Cilo/Sat mountains is not exactly high scholarship, but one of the few accounts of mountaineering in Turkey.

*Within the Taurus; a Journey in Asiatic Turkey* by Lord Kinross (John Murray, London, 1954). An engaging narrative, spanning various eras, on the monuments and peoples to be found beyond the great Mediterranean barrier range. A complementary volume by Lord Kinross is *Europa Minor; Journeys in Coastal Turkey* (Morrow, New York, 1956). Kinross' point is that Asia Minor was in fact one of the wellsprings of early Greek, and hence European, culture.

*East of Trebizond* by Michael Pereira (Geoffrey Bles, London, 1971). This is not so much about trekking as road-walking and bus visits to villages in the Kaçkar, interspersed with generous portions of local history.

*Bolkar* by Dux Schneider (Brockhaus, Wiesbaden, 1982). The author of what was long the definitive guide to Turkey (Jonathan Cape, out of print) spent a summer in this range of the Toros. This German edition is claimed to be translated from an English one, unavailable as yet, but judging from his other work it should be a goodie.

*The Lycian Shore* by Freya Stark (Harcourt, Brace, Jovanovich, New York, 1956). This book focuses on the territory of the Lycians, one of the early civilisations noted above; good background for the Turquoise Coast walks.

*Scotch & Holy Water* by John D Tumpane (St Giles Press, Lafayette, CA, 1981). Although based on the author's experiences as a supplies contractor to the US military in the 1960s and 1970s, his impressions of Turkey are still current – and hilariously told.

## Archeological & General Travel Guides

Four books by George Bean, though slightly dated by more recent scholarship, remain the most readable and authoritative introduction to Turkey's classical and Roman heritage along the Aegean and Mediterranean coasts. *Aegean Turkey* (Norton, New York; Benn, London, 1979) covers antiquities from Bergama to Lake Bafa; *Turkey Beyond the Meander* (1980) from Bodrum to Dalyan; *Lycian Turkey* (1978) covers the coast and inland areas from Fethiye to Antalya; and *Turkey's Southern Shore* (1979) covers the ruins from Gelidonya Burnu to Silifke.

*Turkey – a travel survival kit* by Tom Brosnahan (Lonely Planet, 1987, 2nd edition) is the ideal companion volume to this hiking guide. It has comprehensive city listings of reasonably-priced accommodation, eateries, transport and sights.

*Guide to Aegean & Mediterranean Turkey* (Michael Haag, London, 1987, 2nd edition; Hippocrene, New York) and *Guide to Northeastern Turkey & the Black Sea* (Michael Haag, 1988), both by Diana Darke, together cover the entire country. They are somewhat more expository and upmarket, and have fewer accommodation and restaurant listings.

*The Companion Guide to Turkey* by John Freely (Collins, London, 1979) has no establishment listings but is the best single source on Byzantine, Seljuk, Ottoman, Hittite, and Armenian monuments, which Bean does not cover, plus creditable sections on getting around modern Turkey.

## Hiking Guides

*Aladağlar: Some Routes & Information* by Haldun Aydingün (Redhouse Kitabevi, İstanbul, 1988) is the only other mountaineering guide in English that we know of; it includes some easy rock scrambles as well as straight treks.

## Turkish Literature in Translation

Relatively few Turkish novels or poems are available in other languages. Of the novels which have been translated, most are by Yashar Kemal, a jack-of-all trades from Southern Anatolia who began to write in 1951 at the age of 30. Since then he has made up for lost time, penning more than a dozen novels. Many are set in the foothills of the Taurus where Kemal grew up, and deal with the struggles of the peasant farmers. As such they offer invaluable insights into the lives of the people you will meet in the backcountry.

Kemal's most famous novel is *Mehmed, my Hawk* (Pantheon, New York, 1982). Set in the late 1920s, this tale of a village youth who takes to banditry in response to personal and social oppression, has been widely acclaimed since it first appeared in 1956.

In *They Burn the Thistles (Mehmed my Hawk Part II)* (1982), Mehmed returns in his role as the Turkish Robin Hood.

*The Sea-Crossed Fisherman* (George Braziller, New York; Methuen, London, 1986) is set partly in the İstanbul backstreets of 20 years ago and partly on the timeless Sea of Marmara. This tale of frustrated love and illusions in a community of low-lifes and fishermen is one of Kemal's best.

Other books by Yashar Kemal available in English include: *Anatolian Tales, Seagull, The Undying Grass, The Wind from the Plain* and *Iron Earth, Copper Sky*, which was recently filmed near Erzurum by a multi-national team.

## MAPS, PLACE NOMENCLATURE & TRAIL SCIENCE

The lack of widely available, detailed maps to the Turkish back country is the major sticky wicket for those wishing to plan a trek in Turkey. You'll get no aid or comfort from the Harita Genel Müdürlüğü (General Mapping Directorate) of the Ministry of Defense, as they, like most Turks, are unable to comprehend the notion of hiking as an enjoyable or recreational activity. Furthermore, they are likely to view a request for detailed maps to rural Turkey as intent to commit espionage.

They have prepared a series of some 80-odd quadrangles, covering the entire country at 1:200,000, but it is currently classified – even Turkish citizens cannot obtain it – and dates back to 1944. Most of the place names have changed and it is useful only for its topographical contour lines. However, the security ban was haphazardly applied until the military intervention of 1980 and there are a number of sets in collections abroad. Major university libraries at home may have a set from which you can photocopy portions of interest.

There is also a set of 17 quads covering the entire country at 1:500,000, but these are virtually useless except for showing the general locations of villages and land formations. If you wish you can obtain these for about US$2 apiece at the Harita Genel Müdürlüğü, Dikimevi, Ankara, but you will find these to be 20 or 30 years out of date and riddled with inaccuracies.

The prognosis is not entirely gloomy, however, since usable, high-quality maps of scales 1:100,000 and better do circulate among the dedicated core of Turkish trekkers and mountaineers, who must be incredibly resourceful and persistent to squeeze what they do out of the government. Distribution beyond the original is strictly on a *samizdat* basis and the maps we have are third or fourth generation photocopies. Contact the individuals listed under Helpful People & Guides and see what you can come up with.

Good maps may soon be readily available, though, since Dr. Bozkurt

Ergör of Kayseri has recently completed a series of 1:25,000 sheets for all of the major alpine trekking regions in Turkey. As this book went to press he was open to offers for the rights to publication for the set and such a deal may have been concluded. We suggest you write to him and ask whether the maps are generally available yet.

For dayhikes along the Turquoise Coast, the nautical charts published by the *Seyir, Hidrografi & Oşinografi Dairesi* (Navigation, Hydrography & Oceanography Department) are useful. These are all at a scale of 1:100,000 and usually extend inland from 10 to 20 km; purchase them for about $US7 at yachting and chandlery shops in major coastal towns.

The Municipality of Marmaris has a conveniently sized pamphlet entitled *Mavi Yolculuk ve Marmaris*, which includes eight pages of sections from navigation charts, covering the coast from Bodrum to Fethiye. These are for sale on the first floor of the *Belediye* building for US$1.50, but stocks are limited. If the supply is exhausted you might contact the actual publishers at Kummeydanı Sokak Han 20/3, Sirkeci, İstanbul, tel (1) 512 4330. On neither the full-sized charts nor the smaller pamphlet are trails indicated, and often roads and villages are slightly misplaced; they are mostly useful for their contour markings.

With each hike write-up any detailed maps are listed under Maps. 'None' means that to our knowledge there is nothing other than the 1:500,000 sheet for that area.

The magnetic declination for Turkey varies between 1° and 3° east, so for all intents and purposes you can treat magnetic north as true north; we have done so. Some maps give different altitudes for identical peaks, with a variation of around 10 to 100 metres, but these can be disregarded. Where differences in cited elevation have been found we have indicated the alternative figure in parentheses.

## Nomenclature

Of more cause for concern, however, is a pervasive system of dual place nomenclature in Turkey. Many, though by no means all, villages and mountains have an older name of Greek, Armenian, Georgian or Laz origin, and an official Turkish name which has seldom been in use for more than 60 years and in many cases for considerably less time. Frequently, many villagers have never learned the official name for their community; if you get blank looks when using one it may be time to learn the older, durable title. In cases where more than one name exists we list the most understood name first and give alternates in parentheses.

Finally, the list of 'approved' place names seems to be fairly short and unimaginative, resulting in an abundance of non-unique names, even to the extent of having two identically named places within the same province or even district. We have distinguished instances of identical or nearly identical toponyms in the index with a following qualifier in parentheses, eg Karagöl (Bolkar); Karagöl (Kaçkar).

## Trail Science

The quantity and quality of trails in Turkey, as everywhere in the developing world, have been diminishing of late owing to the effects of 'progress' and its handmaiden, the bulldozer. The only trails waymarked with red paint dots or blazes are along the Turquoise Coast. Elsewhere in the country the convention of piling stones to make a cairn is used and understood, but just barely – there is not even a distinct word for it in Turkish.

As a general rule the only *bona fide* paths you will find in the alpine areas are those connecting villages and their *yaylalar*, ie vital components of the local economy. Beyond the highest pasture, it is strictly cross-country for those interested in peak-bagging. Where villages are on opposite sides of a ridge or mountain that has a convenient pass, there *should* be an old trail connecting the two. This may only be true, though, if it hasn't disappeared from disuse after the construction of a road around the mountain or worse, been buried under the road bulldozed directly over it.

Even assuming that you have successfully obtained adequate maps, worked out place-name aliases, and confirmed rumours about the presence of a trail, there remains one further hurdle – enlisting the cooperation of the people along the way.

First and foremost you must make it clear that you wish to walk along a *patika* (trail), if there is one, and not a road. Villagers may be reluctant to admit that a trail from A to B exists, or may assure you that a route is a trail when it is really a road. This becomes more understandable when you realise that for up-and-coming rural dwellers, walking is associated with the drudgery of day-long forced marches before the advent of the tractor and the taxi. Why walk when you can ride, they reason; car-riding is a prerogative of wealth, all foreigners are wealthy, therefore why aren't you on wheels? A repeatedly expressed desire to walk for its own sake may only confirm villagers' suspicions that you are not quite in your right mind. However, in the end their natural inclination to be helpful will probably overcome their disapproval of your intentions, and thorough directions will be forthcoming.

Rural Turks not only have different ideas of leisure, but also an interesting sense of the time and exertion needed for a particular route. Perhaps not wishing to impart discouraging news, they routinely underestimate the time that will be necessary for you to reach your destination. They may in fact feel they are being quite accurate – it only takes *them* three hours to get to Point X. However, they have been doing it since they were knee-high and won't get lost, they aren't carrying 15-kg backpacks, and in all likelihood they are amazingly fit, probably more so than you.

So add anywhere from 25 to 50% to any time estimations that you are given.

Lastly, if you ask an acquaintance about the terrain ahead and the reply is 'normal', you had better go to the nearest store and fortify yourself with some *raki* (firewater) first, because what's ahead is probably anything but!

## EQUIPMENT LIST

If you were to undertake all of the treks written up in this guide you would find it advisable to have along all of the following items. Most of these accessories will come in handy even for dayhikes along the Turquoise Coast. If you need to acquire, or replace, certain camping-related articles while in Turkey, you'll find a glossary of their names in the Language section.

### Clothing

2 pairs lightweight loose cotton pants
1 pair heavier-duty pants for high-altitude use (corduroy, synthetic, etc)
1 pair shorts or cutoffs
1 long-sleeved cotton turtleneck top, sweatshirt, or similar
1 long-sleeved acrylic or other synthetic ski-type pullover (ie something providing ample warmth for the weight)
1 button-down, high-quality wool shirt
1 shell windbreaker, warm-up jacket, or Gore Tex or similar jacket

The last four items, used in layers as you choose, should protect you in most conditions encountered from May to August below 3000 metres. However, outside these months and at higher elevation, add the next five articles:

1 down or fibre fill parka
1 pair gloves, lined and water-proof
1 pair long underwear
1 pair gaiters
1 hat/cap, wool or otherwise, to extend down over ears
1 other warm-weather hat/cap, brimmed all around, reflective colour

socks – assortment of cotton/synthetic (80%/20% – obtainable in sporting goods stores), polypropylene/natural fibre (various formulas), and wool (90 to 100%) pairs to handle all conditions

hiking boots – 1 pair medium duty or better, leather upper, over-the-ankle, Vibram or equivalent sole; 1 pair lightweight, synthetic upper, normal height, minimally treaded sole, for evenings at camp and hikes on easy trails

leather conditioner for boots if appropriate – natural oil-or wax-based preferable to silicone formulas

## Camping Gear

**Backpack** Your backpack should have a minimum capacity of 60 litres (3750 cubic inches), and be designed to efficiently carry up to 16 kg on long treks.

We will not enter the arena of the frame pack versus soft pack debate except to say that, while we use a convertible, internal-frame and a ski-touring soft pack, respectively, we both recognise that we could have carried heavy weights more efficiently with a frame pack and that we sometimes miss the convenience of rigid struts on which to hang unused day pack, water container, etc. Any pack purchased should have some sort of slit-sockets from which to suspend foam pad, tent, sleeping bag, etc.

**Tent** A tent is mandatory for treks anywhere in Central or Eastern Anatolia, and elsewhere outside of the June-September period. This is one piece of equipment you should not scrimp on; we suggest as a minimum a free-standing product (ie dome design) of rip-stop nylon with a securely mounting rainfly. Cheapo models from army surplus or similar outlets, which must be tied to trees (rare in Turkey), are not going to cut it. Bear in mind that the tent will have to protect you from the often considerable wind and cold in the Turkish mountains as much as from the occasional rainstorm.

Other recommended camping gear includes:

daypack – sufficient to carry snacks, map, extra clothes, water container, toilet paper, etc

camera belt pack – several companies make serviceable carriers for up to two bodies and most lenses. Will pay for itself within a month in terms of falls cushioned and repairs thus avoided.

long-handled ice axe or walking stick – the former is most useful for spring ascents and elevations with permanent or semi-permanent snow cover. Real walking sticks are more versatile and will prevent many a fall on trailless scree slopes. Some folks use ski poles, some fancy items from specialty stores, but you can improvise in the Black Sea mountains and the Aladağlar ranges where there are extensive stands of beech (*kayın* and white poplar (*su kavağı*) respectively. Both are phenomenally strong and supple but slender branches can be cut with the saw attachment on a Swiss Army knife.

groundcloth – not critical but handy as extra rain protection

ground pad – medium-density, blue foam, or ThermaRest types seem to work best

sleeping bag – three-season, down or fibre fill according to taste

poncho/cagoule – large enough (eg 250 cm x 150 cm) to fit over you *and* your pack, plus perhaps double as a groundcloth

campstove – see the discussion about performance and fuel availability in the Trekking Services & Stores section

mess kit – steel sets are less toxic than aluminium ones but food, especially eggs, sticks badly; you should in either case carry cooking oil with you in a small (around 50 ml) plastic bottle

cutlery – in addition to the obvious, note that wide wooden tongue depressors make excellent impromptu spatulas egg case – for six eggs; only 12-paks available in Turkey

water container – Spanish-style *bota* flasks keep water cool but invariably spring leaks after a few months. Metal containers should be interior-coated; plastic bottles should be kept out of direct sun for maximum water purity.

## Odds & Ends

nylon stuffsacks – assorted sizes with drawstrings

plastic bags – especially flat ones large enough to protect maps

swimsuit – nude bathing is usually taboo in Turkey

diving mask or goggles – for avoiding jellyfish and sea urchins as well as for sightseeing and eye protection. Get a good fit!

sunglasses

binoculars or monocular – even if you don't use them the hill people will be more than happy to buy them

compass – essential to follow our directions, especially where good maps are unavailable

altimeter – when maps are obtainable, helps to pinpoint your location

compact flashlight – batteries are universally obtainable in Turkey and we found bulbs for a Tekna-Lite 2 as well. A miner's headlamp-type model might be even better.

candle lantern – great morale booster after dark, saves flashlight batteries. Buy a model that takes standard candles, and pay attention to the quality of candles bought in Turkey; many are too small or melt at room temperature in summer

camp mirror – for shaving, and possibly signalling

portable clothesline – these can be bought or parachute chord and pins can be used

Nalgene or polyurethane bottles – assorted sizes: large for storing laundry powder; medium for mixing powdered milk

tape – strong, lightweight, translucent product such as Micropore, in addition to securing gauze pads, is unsurpassed for mending maps, book bindings, and torn paper money

first-aid kit – as a minimum, should contain an elastic bandage to wrap sprains; band-aids and gauze for minor abrasions; topical antibiotic/antiseptic; itch-suppressant ointment/lotion to keep you from scratching bug bites

insect repellent – a preventative for the last mentioned problem

lip balm – a must for low-humidity areas (ie most everywhere)

sunblock – sunscreen, zinc oxide or similar; absolute necessity; factor 15 at a minimum

moleskin – old boots, not to mention new ones, will find new spots to irritate on each walk

cuticle scissors – used in tandem with the blunt end of a sewing needle, deals with ingrown big toenails

dental floss – for Turkish meat stuck between molars, if you're not already a regular user

sewing kit – assorted needle sizes, thread gauges and patching materials, for any necessary emergency repair to luggage or clothes

Swiss Army or similar pocketknife – invaluable; I have used every attachment on mine, more than once

timepiece with alarm (loud) – if not a wrist watch, then a little quartz clock running on an AA battery

pocket calendar – very easy to lose track of days in the hills

paperback books – at least two to trade with other travellers; foreign-language reading material is very costly in Turkey

moneybelt – in Turkey, where most rural people are scrupulously honest, more for convenience than safety

waterproof broad-tipped marker – both for addressing big envelopes at the post office and for labelling rolls of film photo film – bring lots with you, and see the Film & Photography section

Last, but not least, bring spares and replacements for everything that could conceivably be impossible or tedious to find overseas and doesn't take up much pack space. Examples which come to mind: eyeglasses, contact lenses, bootlaces, backpack parts, photocopy of the front page of your passport, *bota* flasks, special medications or cosmetics, spring for scissors on a pocketknife, oddball watch batteries, flashlight bulbs, etc

## FOOD FOR THE TRAIL

You can find just about any type of backpacking food you need in a *bakkaliye* (grocery store) in a medium-sized town, though certain speciality items are best bought in İstanbul or Ankara, or brought from overseas. Food shops in Turkey tend to keep very long hours; you can usually pick up supplies even on a Sunday or a Saturday evening, and the shops are open most days from about 7 am until 10 pm.

In the following list, a brand name recommendation is usually a suggestion and is not exclusive; remarks on preparation or keeping properties are based on our experience.

### Dehydrated/powdered items

tea – *çay* Brands: ÇAy Kur Altin Süzme Çay. This is the only brand of bagged tea we could find; there are dozens of loose-pack ones

sage tea – *ada çqy* Brand: Island. A wonderful calming evening drink

camomile – *papatya* Found growing wild in early summer

sugar – *şeker* Hard to buy in small amounts; we would just just pocket a few extra cubes when offered tea

cocoa powder – *kakao tozu* Brands: Kent, Golden, Nestle.

milk powder – *süt tozu* Brands: Pınar, SEK. Sold in ½-kg box only in large towns

salep – *salep* Brands: Çapamarka. Ground extract of *Orchis mascula* root; a winter drink but as it is mostly sugar and milk powder, you can substitute it for the latter

oatmeal – *yulaf ezmesi* Brands: Çapamarka. Apparently available only in İstanbul, at Migros supermarkets, and in Ankara

baby pablum – *mama* Brands: Arı. Poor second choice when you can't get real oats

potato flakes – *patates puresi* Brands: Pat. Instant mash; just add hot water

soups – *çorbalar* Brands: Tamek, Piyale, Çapamarka, Knorr. Follow package directions; *yayla* and *tarhana* are mint/rice/yogurt and yogurt/flour/red pepper respectively, and are two of the best flavours.

lentil – *mercimek*
yayla – *yayla*
tarhana – *tarhana*
tomato – *domates*
cream of vegetable – *kremalı sebze*
cream of mushroom – *kremalı mantar*
cream of chicken – *kremalı tavuk*

pudding – *puding* Brands: Piyale, Çapamarka (vanilla – *vanilyalı*, chocolate – *kakaolu*). All brands must be made with milk; beware of sticking to pot. Piyale can be made without egg despite what label says

### Staples, herbs & spices

rice – *pirinç* Ask if it's *çabuk pişen* or 'quick cooking' – saves stove fuel

cracked wheat – *bulgur* Best fast-cooking carbohydrate; packaged brands in cities, in villages get from locals

macaroni – *makarna* Found in all stores: one kg and ½ kg packs, and in bulk

allspice – *yenibahar* In cylindrical plastic wrapper; seasons bulgur

lentils – *mercimek* Packaged or in bulk

thyme – *kekik* Dried; seasons lentils

salt – *tuz*

black pepper – *kara biber*

## Semi-Perishable Items

eggs – *yumurta*

butter – *tereyağı* Brands: Mis, Pınar. Small (100 g) packets

cured meat – *pastırma* Ancestor of western pastrami; eat raw or cooked in entrees, keeps indefinitely

sausage – *sucuk* Brands: Apikoğlu, Pınar. *Sucuk* is either the cured, dry kind with a shelf life similar to *pastırma*, or the moist, plastic-wrapped stuff which will keep only 4 or 5 days

soft salami – *macar salami* Brands: Pınar. Keeps only 2 or 3 days

thick flat bread – *bazlama* Semi-risen village speciality, similar to Indian paratha

whole-grain bread – *kepekli ekmek* Difficult to find but stays edible longer than the usual white stuff

## Trail Snacks

fruit juice – *meyva suyu* Brands: Pınar, Meysu. *Vişne* (cherry) and *karadut* (black mulberry) flavours in 180-ml cardboard cartons

powdered fruit drink – *Lezzo* Apple, orange, lemon flavours

grape molasses – *pekmez* Village product; will last a week before fermenting. Mixed with snow, makes a fantastic sherbert.

cookies – *bisküvi* Brands: Ülker, Eti Fantasia. These are the only two firms making chocolate chip or nut cookies, ie something other than the ubiquitous cream sandwich or 'petit beurre' biscuit.

pressed fruit – *peştil* Made from apricots, mulberries, peaches, and (rarely) grapes. Production season is August-March; hard to get June-September.

chocolate bar – *çikolata* Brands: Nestle. *Damak* is with pistachios; *sütlü* is with milk

cheese – *peynir* The following English equivalents are only approximate, giving an idea of taste. Make sure your *kaşar* is *eski* (aged) or it will smell after a few days! Other kinds will last at least a week.

    parmesan – *tulum*
    gruyere – *gravier*
    kasseri – *kaşar*
    mozzarella – *çerkez*
    string – *dil*
    cheddar – *cheddar*

onions – *soğan*

skinny peppers – *sivri biber* Burning (*acı*) or mild; hard to tell difference, except lumpy, green ones tend to be hotter than pale, smooth ones

olives – *zeytin*

peanut butter – *fistik ezmesi* Brands: Planters.

hazelnut butter – *fındık ezmesi* Brands: Fiskobirlik

honey – *bal* Brands: Evin. This brand comes in a plastic squeeze tube

sesame paste – *tahin* Oil can be skimmed for cooking; mix with *pekmez* for a spread

## Bread

sheer flat bread – *yufka ekmeği* Whole-grain village product, in vast sheets like Indian chapatis; moulds after three days dry fruit & nuts – *kuru yemiş* You get all the items listed at a *kuru yemiş ve kuru kahvecisi* (dry snack and coffee vendor); there's at least one in every sizable town

figs – *incir*
apricots – *kayısı*
raisins – *kuru üzüm*
almonds – *badem*
hazelnuts – *fındık*
peanuts – *yer fıstığı*
roasted chickpeas – *leblebi*

You can also find the following at a *pastane* (sweet shop) as well as at *kuru yemiş* stalls, such as:

*susam helvası* – sesame crunch
*cezeriye* – carrot juice, honey, nut and coconut bar
*sucuk* – fruit, molasses, and nut torpedo; not to be confused with meat *sucuk*

## TREKKING SERVICES & STORES
This section covers items that are not easily categorised but all the same are essential for an enjoyable and safe trek.

### Stoves & Fuel
We came to Turkey with a French-made Bleuet 206 butane stove and a lot of cartridges for it, because we knew from previous experience that this type of fuel was impossible to obtain inside the country. We found that this was still 95% true, though there is now one verified outlet for Bleuet stoves and cartridges in İstanbul.

The dealer's name is Nezih Çarşibaşi, and he's just outside the Mısır Çarşısı (Spice Bazaar) at Sabuncu Han Caddesi 75; tel 522 77 46. The stoves are rather expensive but the cartridges are quite reasonable at about US$1.30 each. Moving the cartridges around Turkey by aeroplane, however, is another matter (see Air in the Getting Around chapter).

If you don't have spare cartridges and find yourself out in the boondocks with an empty one, you have one other recourse.

Go to a *çakmakcı*, the craftsman who refills reusable cigarette lighters – there's at least one in every town. Have him install a *supap* (valve, *subop* in some dialects) in the bottom of the spent cartridge. Then reattach it to the stove and have it refilled with lighter gas through the new accessory. This will work fine, but of course you need to keep your newly modified cartridge for future refills.

Performance-wise, the only drawbacks to butane stoves are that they tend to sulk in cold conditions, and above elevations of about 3000 metres they burn inefficiently and suck up fuel at an astonishing rate. With a combination of the two factors, a cartridge might be good for as little as three meals!

The only locally available portable stoves in Turkey are fairly unwieldy ones which run on either *ispirto* (purple-tinted methyl alcohol, similar to liquified Sterno) or *gazyağı* (kerosene). These models are fairly messy and require a lot of priming and pumping to get them going, but at least you can get the fuel in almost any *bakal* (grocery store), where it's known as *tuvalet ispirtosu*.

We have not been able to locate an outlet for white gas in Turkey, so if you're attached to your Coleman, Optimus or Svea you'll have to bring enough fuel with you.

### Pack & Boot Repairs
First off, make sure you bring a few spare accessories for your pack, ie clovis pin sets, strap buckles (especially plastic ones) and belt clasps. THY and bus companies are very talented at losing or smashing these, and trying to get them replaced with something that works, let alone an exact duplicate, is almost hopeless. As a last resort you can visit a *nalbur*, the man who deals in horse tackle (bridles, reins, clasps, horseshoes, blue beads to ward off the evil eye, etc); often he will have a buckle or clasp that will work temporarily.

If a backpack zipper bursts, there's an excellent zipper store (selling nothing but) in the Tahtakale (Flea Market) district of İstanbul. *Emek Fermuar*, Marpuscular Caddesi 19, Eminönü, has a vast selection of metal and nylon zippers in every conceivable weight and length. They don't install them though; you take your choice to the nearest *çantacı* or handbag-repairer for that. This is also the place to go to have opened seams attended to and any of the above-noted spare parts installed.

For simple rips in boot uppers you can take the item to almost any *ayakkabi tamircisi* and he'll stitch it for you at a nominal price. Anything having to do with with the sole, however, is a problem because there are very few machines in Turkey capable of penetrating sole and upper simultaneously, let alone fashioning a fancy welt.

If you're coming off the Kaçkar range, which seems to specialise in destroying boots, one very good craftsman with a capable machine is Bahri Demirci, Sarrafoğlu Sokak 4/C, Cumhuriyet Mahalle, Trabzon. There is another nameless workshop in İzmir, just north of Anafartalar Caddesi and 150 metres east of Eşref Paşa Caddesi; this is really a factory that will fix split soles as a favour to you. If you find any others, ie in İstanbul, please let us know.

### Backpacking Stores

The outdoor goods industry is just getting off the ground in Turkey, but we imagine that within a few years the problems with stove fuels and equipment repairs will become less important, as retailers will be servicing a large enough market to turn their attention towards parts and service as well as primary production. Most of the mountaineering (as opposed to simple sporting goods) stores that we know of are in Ankara.

**Ankara** *Toros Acikhava Malzemeler* (tel (4) 136 9476) Bağlar Caddesi, Gökçen

Sokak 21/A, Şeyranbağları. This is actually a small factory for the first home-grown Turkish packs, sleeping bags, parkas, vests, gaiters, ponchos, gloves and most other soft goods. They are also retailers and will undertake general repairs. The owners, Kaşif and Batur, are avid mountaineers and members of the Anatolian Mountaineers Union.

*Güven Spor*, Tunali Hilmi Caddesi, Tunalı Pasajı, 95/37, Kavaklıdere, mostly functions as an importer of Austrian ice axes, packs and stoves.

*Sırma Çanta*, Stad Oteli Bitis,iği 4, Ulus, are manufacturers of packs.

**İstanbul** *Decibel*, Valikonağı Caddesi corner Şekayık Sokağı, Nişantaşi. They deal mostly in soft goods such as parkas, vests and gloves.

*Yeşil Kundura* is out by the Topkapı bus stand, opposite a monstrous white modern building. They sell cheapish boots satisfactory for trekking, though certainly not state-of-the-art gear. They are supposedly contractors for the Turkish Army's mountain warfare corps.

*DA Sport* (tel 567 6427) Gümüşsuyu Caddesi, Dokumacılar Sitesi 42/1, Maltepe, Topkapı. You can get a direct line to the proprietor Mehmet Yücegilli by ringing 567 7333.

### TURKISH BATHS & THEIR ETIQUETTE

The *hamam*, or combination Turkish bath-and-sauna, is a national institution which the Seljuk Turks adopted from the Byzantines, who in turn had inherited it from the Romans. In medieval Turkey the concept of 'bath' reached a pinnacle of perfection, satisfying simultaneously the need to socialise, to keep warm during winter on the Anatolian steppe, and to stay clean according to the precepts of the Koran.

After a long trek there is nothing better than a visit to a *hamam*, but most visitors to Turkey are intimidated by the prospect and miss out on one of the more delightful aspects of travelling in Turkey. Perhaps they imagine that they will be propositioned, or worse, abducted into some modern equivalent of the harem, or subjected to some even more sinister medieval protocol. Protocol there certainly is, but of a harmless, comprehensible nature, and the following is intended to acquaint you with it.

Baths are sex segregated, with either separate facilities or by time schedules. If the sign on the outside which says *erkekler* (men) or *kadınlar* (women) is permanently affixed to the building, then that particular bath is probably devoted exclusively to the appropriate sex. If on the other hand the sign is movable, with *erkekler* and *kadınlar* inscribed on opposite sides, than the *hamam* is a double-duty one and you need to enquire about the appropriate hours. Our experience is necessarily limited to the men's baths but we cannot imagine that the other kind are radically different.

Upon entering you first visit the check-in counter, where you surrender any valuables (money, pocket knife, watch, etc). These are locked in a small numbered drawer and you are given the key, attached to a thong which you keep around your wrist for the duration of your bath. Next you are offered soap and sometimes shampoo (the latter is expensive – bring your own), and finally you're provided with a *peştamal*, a light-weight plaid towel which you keep wrapped around your waist at all times while in the inner bath area. It's considered quite bad form to let this drop and if you do any number of people will rush up and exhort you to cover up again.

Next you are shown to one of a number of changing rooms that are usually private, sometimes shared, but which rarely lock (hence the valuables drawer) and are often glass-fronted from waist height up. These rooms are usually arranged in a square around a sort of court, with often a small fountain playing in the centre and sometimes even a small çay-bar in operation. In each compartment, there's generally a nauga-hide cot to recline on after your bath. Here you undress and put on your *peştamal*, leaving your clothes on a free hook if it's a shared dressing-room. In addition to the *peştamal* you don *takunyalar* (wooden clogs) which, while ill-fitting, at least keep you from slipping on wet surfaces.

When ready you proceed through a weighted swinging door which leads first to the cooling-off room, the direct descendant of the Roman *tepidarium*. This is where you can take a break when the innermost quarter gets too hot to stand. Here also are the toilets and usually the *tıraşlık* or shaving stalls. Shaving is not allowed in the main bath. There is usually no mirror so bring your own.

At last you enter the main room through another swinging door. Depending on the age and design of the *hamam* this can be anything from functional to sumptuous. Almost all baths, though, are finished in marble up to waist height. Arrayed against the wall are many basins with hot and cold taps, each provided with a metal or plastic scoop. The trick is to fill the basins with water to a temperature of your choosing, douse yourself with a scoopful, soap down, then rinse. Don't make a big soapy mess in the basin itself. Also, washing your underside without taking off the *peştamal* is an acquired technique.

Conventionally it's one person to a basin, though bathing in full view of 10 or 20 other people may be the one aspect of a *hamam* that takes getting used to. If you want more privacy there are generally smaller rooms tucked into the corners of the building, with just four or three, or sometimes even two or one, taps.

In the very centre of things is the *göbek taşi* or 'navel stone', ideally positioned right over the wood-burning furnaces which heat the bath water. Here a number of bathers bask like beached seals on the marble, which can vary from lukewarm to scorching. Some establishments provide a small vinyl pillow; otherwise you can use your bath scoop as one as you admire the magnificent domes overhead, pierced with small round skylights through which the sunbeams play on the rising steam. There are always satellite domes over the corner rooms noted above and the distinctive lumpy silhouette created on the outside is one of the ways of finding a *hamam* from the street.

At some point your reverie may be interrupted by an enormous personage looming over you, inquiring vocally or in mime, '*masaj*?' This is the *tellâk* or masseur, who ambles around the bath looking for customers. If you submit to one it had better be on a half-empty stomach (baths go better that way anyhow), as the *tellâk* will manipulate you like so much Play-Dough, energetically exploring the boundaries between pleasure and pain.

He will also wield a *kese* (a mitt covered with an abrasive pile) to rub off all the dead skin and perhaps some of the live stuff too. When he is done you will definitely feel different. The *kese* session comes first, usually at your wash basin, with the *masaj* following on the *göbek taşı*.

Upon exiting into the courtyard again you'll need a dry *peştamal* (given to you or self-service from a pile of such), and you sling the by-now soaking old one into another pile or hamper. Again, observe the proprieties in switching them. There will either be a self-service stack of fluffy *havlu* (real drying towels), or one of the attendants will approach you, sit you down, wrap your head like a Bedouin's with one *havlu* and rub your trunk down with another. Except in a tourist-oriented bath there is generally no extra tip for this service.

Then you'll be asked if you want a *çay* or mineral water, which you can take out in the courtyard or in your dressing room, reclining on the cot.

When it's time to go you pay at the front counter and reclaim your valuables. Depending on the class of *hamam*, the price will be anywhere from US 50c to $US1.30 for the bath alone; a *masaj* will be as much again. Rates for these services and of course any refreshments taken are posted on a little placard above the counter. As you leave someone will probably say, '*Saatler olsun*' ('May it last for hours').

Top: Morning at Göcüklü Yayla, Bolkar Toros (MD)
Left: Çini Göl, Bolkar Toros (MD)
Right: Walking up from Maden, Bolkar Toros (MD)

Top: Top of Horoz Valley, Bolkar Toros (MD)
Bottom: Colchicum in the lower Narpuz narrows, Aladağlar (MD)

# Getting There

You can fly, sail, or go overland to Turkey – in roughly descending order of preference.

## AIR

Ankara is the capital, but as in the cases of Australian Canberra or Brazilian Brasilia, it isn't the international transportation hub. The majority of incoming flights arrive in İstanbul, though the airports at İzmir, Antalya, Ankara, Adana and Dalaman also have international status. İzmir's airport is being expanded in preparation for receiving a vastly increased number of charter and scheduled flights. Antalya and Dalaman are serviced mostly by warm-month charter flights.

The national flag carrier is Turkish Airways (Türk Hava Yolları), with service to most cities in Europe, North Africa and the Middle East. As yet their route network does not extend to Australia or New Zealand, but service to New York will start as of summer 1988.

### From Northern Europe

Only from cities with a high volume of travellers' traffic – London, Amsterdam, Paris and certain German cities (Berlin, Munich, etc) – will you find decent fares on scheduled flights. A good rule of thumb for London will be £120 sterling one-way, maybe £200 round-trip – at a minimum and in low season at that. Often Eastern European carriers such as JAT, Balkan or Tarom offer the cheapest fares (for decidedly no-frills service). Your best bet, though, especially during spring or early summer, is to visit a 'bucket shop' and find either a one-way or round-trip charter, in which case you should pay no more than £110 one-way, £180 round-trip. The exact figure will vary with the week of travel, your age and if you're a student or not.

Warning: Don't book a round-trip charter to Greece, visit Turkey, and then expect to use the return half of the charter! A Turkish entry stamp in your passport will invalidate it. It is, though, possible to fly to and from Turkey on charter service and visit Greece in the meanwhile.

### From Athens

This route is generally overpriced, but there are anywhere from two to four flights to İstanbul daily depending on the season. Olympic Airways leaves in the morning, THY in the early afternoon; the former is slightly cheaper. The usual Olympic fare is US$115 one-way, US$170 round-trip, but you can often buy *navtikó* (seaman's) tickets for about US$85 through travel agents. These tickets must be specially handled, though; they are not issued to you, but forwarded through Olympic to the airport counter. Sometimes the travel agent forgets to do so, or can't because it's a weekend. Mine was not waiting for me at the counter and I was almost thrown off the flight.

### From North America

This essentially means flying out of New York, and Pan Am, PIA, THY, JAT and KLM are the airlines most consistently offering one or two-stop service to İstanbul via selected European cities. Prices range from US$800 to US$1400 return, depending on company, season and exact routing. Charters, or discounted seats on scheduled airlines, are considerably cheaper and available through American 'bucket shops'. Even from the Pacific coast you can usually find this type of fare for US$800 to US$1000 round-trip. Check the Sunday travel pages of the *Los Angeles Times*, the *New York Times* or the *San Francisco Chronicle*.

### From Australia

All services from Australia to İstanbul are

routed via South-East Asia, one of the Gulf States, Athens, Frankfurt, London or another European gateway city. Neither are there any charters; count on spending A$1600 to A$1900 or more for a round-trip ticket to Athens, the closest point. The most direct service to Turkey from Asia is by Turkish Airlines out of Singapore or Kuala Lumpur.

## TRAIN
### From Northern Europe

Most services from Europe to İstanbul are geared to Turkish guest-workers returning for home visits. Second class is generally packed out, smoky and dilapidated, becoming progressively more so by the time either Yugoslavia, Greece or Bulgaria is entered. For any degree of comfort you would want to travel first class, and this will almost certainly cost you more than a plane flight.

It's only worth taking the train if one of the following conditions applies: you will be stopping at numerous spots along the way within the two months allowed in Europe; you are under 26 and so qualify for BIGE/Transalpino discounts or an Interrail pass; or you have a Eurail pass. The latter is not honoured within Turkey, so you'll have to pay a little extra to get to İstanbul. Make sure you do this before entering Turkey – if the Turkish conductors find you without a valid ticket, they'll dun you for something like US$15! It takes anywhere from 39 hours (Munich-İstanbul) to 57 hours (Paris-İstanbul) on the train.

### From Greece

This is a special case of dawdling; the 1400-km journey supposedly takes 30 hours, plus you must allow a few more for connections and unforeseen delays. It's suggested that you break the journey at Thessaloniki, a pleasant enough city some 21 hours (in theory) from İstanbul. Alternatively, you can take a domestic flight on Olympic Airways from Athens to Alexandhroupoli, 45 km from the Turkish border, and then arrange onward rail or

bus connection (see below). The flight-land combo to İstanbul will cost about US$68, and will save you a good 20 hours at an extra expenditure of perhaps US$35 (the through-train fare is about US$33).

## BUS
### From Northern Europe

Frankly, this is only for the masochist. The monetary saving, compared to the train or plane, is becoming less significant with each passing year, frequencies are often frustrating (it's easy to just miss the one weekly departure), and comfort can't compare with even the average train car. Beware of illusory savings in time and money – sure, that £70 bus from London to İstanbul might be £30 pounds cheaper than a one-way charter, but how many stopovers with hotel and food expenses will you have on the way?

### From Greece

The only instance where a bus can offer serious competition to a train or a plane is along the Athens-Thessaloniki-İstanbul route. The going rate for a 26-hour (elapsed time) itinerary is about US$40. Try to get a through-bus from Athens – if you are told to 'change buses' in Thessaloniki, you may find that the coach coming from Northern Europe is full and that you'll have to wait until the next one arrives.

## OVERLAND

It used to be that you could save a bundle by taking local transport within Greece right up to the frontier, walk across, and continue by local transport on the Turkish side, but not as of 1984. You must be given a ride on some conveyance across a 1500-metre military no-man's-land. The three official border crossings are Kipi (Greece)/İpsala (Turkey), Pithio/Uzünküprü (rail only), and Kastanies (Greece)/Kapıkule (Turkey).

Kipi is a one-hour, two-change bus ride from Alexandhroupoli. The frontier station is big and busy, and provided you show up during daylight hours you can probably finagle a ride across.

The northern crossing is a bit easier, since Kastanies is right on the domestic Greek rail line and only 5.5 km from Edirne. During the day the Greek guards are quite helpful about arranging a ride across for you, but after dark there will be little traffic and you'll probably have to pay US$8 for the 700-metre taxi ride to the Turkish post at Kapıkule. This is only two km from the first Turkish village of Karaağaç, which during the day has local bus service the final three km to Edirne, but again at night there will be no bus and anyway you'll not be permitted to walk to the village from the Turkish post. On request the guards will summon a taxi to take you to Edirne for US$5.

If all this sounds like too much hassle, compare it to the bother of a train or coach from Yugoslavia to Turkey across Bulgaria. A Bulgarian one-use transit visa costs US$10, and must be obtained in advance at a consulate; virtually all nationalities need them. Similarly, Yugoslav border guards have been known to charge a few dollars for transit visas that are issued for free at the appropriate consulate; citizens of the USA, Canada, Australia and New Zealand need these.

## SEA
### From Italy & Mainland Greece
If you're coming from Italy or Greece, this may be one of the more pleasant, if not always the cheapest way to enter Turkey. This section does not discuss specific companies – which pop up and disappear yearly like mushrooms in a cow paddock, except for Turkish Maritime Lines, which has had consistent weekly sailings linking Italy, Greece and Turkey – but rather concentrates on the most likely routes. Most services operate dependably only during the warm months.

From Venice, Ancona, Bari or Brindisi, boats ply from Patras or Piraeus (occasionally via Iraklion) to İzmir/İstanbul, or from Piraeus to İstanbul direct. Frequency varies from one to three times a week depending on the season. You in effect pay for a mini-cruise no matter what the distance; Piraeus to İzmir in spring, for example, will set you back about US$55. This compares poorly with the options below.

### From the Greek Islands
Most people sailing to Turkey from Greece go from either Lesvos, Hios, Samos, Kos or Rhodes, the major Greek islands just opposite strategic ports on the Turkish coast. Domestic ferry fares from Piraeus to each of the islands listed above are respectively US$17, US$12, US$15, US$18 and US$20 (figures approximate).

The Rhodes-Marmaris service is the cheapest of the international short-hop ferries, at about US$15 one-way; Hios-Çeşme is next at US$18; Lesvos-Ayvalik and Kos-Bodrum tie for third at about US$20 one-way, and Samos-Kuşadası brings up the rear as tour operators exploit the Ephesus-bound for US$25 apiece. Often substantial discounts apply to round-trip tickets.

From mid-June to the end of August, boats tend to cross four to six days a week, depending on the island. During the mid-May to mid-June and September periods, the frequency drops to two or four a week. During the rest of the year, departures may take place once a week, if at all, though the Samos-Kuşadası and Rhodes-Marmaris services never cease completely except in bad weather. The best way to obtain current information for the various short-hop ferries is to phone the *limenarheio* (port authority) on each island. Greek phone books (in Greek only!) list these numbers in a special governmental section at the start of each region/area code; *limenarehio* is prominently shown. If you can't puzzle out the script, ask the phone office employees to help you. Believe us, there is no other way to obtain this information on the mainland.

# Getting Around

This section covers the various long-distance, inter-regional means of transport within Turkey. With each hike write-up you'll find a Getting to the Trailhead section, which describes only the way to get from the nearest well-connected town, usually the centre of an *ilçe* (district) or a *bucak* (sub-district), to the village or roadhead where the walking actually starts.

## AIR

If you arrive in Turkey at İstanbul, as most people do, and have ambitions of trekking in the eastern half of the country, then you should explore the possibility of getting there by air. The Türk Hava Yolları (THY or Turkish Airways) network has expanded by leaps and bounds in recent years. It has more destinations and departures, and while no longer dirt-cheap, it is still good value for money on the long routes.

As an example, İstanbul-Van, via Ankara, costs about $US60 for 1400 km, and İstanbul-Erzurum, also via Ankara, is around $US56 for 1000 km. Summer (April to October) departures are four times weekly to Van and daily to Erzurum. Other flights of interest to trekkers are İstanbul-Kayseri (twice weekly), İstanbul or Ankara to Trabzon (daily), İstanbul or Ankara to Antalya (18 or 10 a week respectively), and İstanbul or Ankara to Dalaman (10 or 3 a week respectively). Frequencies and prices for return trips are identical. For further information contact a THY office in Turkey and get hold of their domestic schedule, a compact (9 cm x 13 cm) blue folder.

Be aware, however, that flights in summer are very popular and you need to book seats as far in advance as possible – three weeks before in the case of Trabzon flights, 10 days for Van flights. Planes usually leave on time although check-in can start only minutes before boarding.

Security checks of your person and hand luggage are usually thorough – a pocket knife, for instance, will be confiscated, so stash it in your checked luggage as it's tedious to hunt down at the other end. Like any other airline, THY does not allow butane stove cartridges in either your hand luggage or checked luggage. Since they are almost impossible to get in Turkey you might find some justification, as we did, in breaching regulations and sneaking them aboard. Checked luggage is rarely inspected. As a compromise in the interest of safety, only transport unmounted cartridges – once on the stove they do leak very readily under the stresses of carriage.

## TRAIN

For medium-range hops, such as going from Lake Van to the Toros, trains can be a delightful way to travel, as long as you avoid anything rated *posta* (mail) or *yolcu* (passenger). Stick to the expresses like the Vangölü (three times a week Tatvan-İstanbul via Kayseri and Ankara), the Anadolu and Mehmetçik (daily Ankara-Kars via Kayseri, Erzincan and Erzurum), the Toros (daily İstanbul-Adana via Ankara, Kayseri and Niğde), the Pamukkale (daily İstanbul-Denizli via Afyon) and the Marmaris (daily İstanbul-İzmir, initial leg İstanbul-Bandırma by pleasant ferry boat). Frequencies for the reverse itineraries are identical.

Take-away rail schedules are very hard to come by in Turkey and you must usually visit the nearest station and study the placards on the wall. The listed trains are only about 20% slower than a comparable bus, cost half as much or less, and sometimes follow very scenic routes. The main drawback is usually the lack of food service or even strolling vendors; at every stop of over 10 minutes passengers make a mad dash to the station *büfeler* and water taps, and then back to the train, which is quite ruthless about leaving people behind.

The good express trains are quite popular, especially the overnight trains with sleepers, so book as far in advance as you can, though three or four days ahead seems enough. The supplement per berth is about $US8, in line with European services, though sometimes (eg Vangölü Ekspresi) only 1st-class compartments are available and you are not allowed to share a compartment with strangers – they'll make you book the whole three-bed cabin at $US20 a pop.

## SEA

With the advent of the expanded air and road network, Turkey's coastal shipping services, run mostly by Turkish Maritime Lines, have dwindled in the past two decades. The Black Sea lines stop at Trabzon and no longer go up to the Soviet frontier; ports of call between Sinop and İstanbul are also now virtually non-existent. Even in the summer boats go only once a week each in direction (the day varies with the year), and cabins are immensely popular as it's something of a mini-cruise. In line with the government's new non-monopoly policy, a new private-sector company has began a Black Sea service as far as Giresun, perhaps on a different day than the TML departure.

The only other seagoing services of interest are those serving the islands in the Sea of Marmara (see the appropriate chapter), and the thrice-weekly (once in winter) 19-hour service between İstanbul and İzmir. This last is very popular, as it's an overnight, takes only about seven hours longer than the bus, and amounts to a budget cruise through the Dardanelles.

## BUS
### Long Distance Buses
The Turkish bus is a national institution;

they go almost everywhere (though sometimes with a relay of connections), at most hours, for about US 12c per 10 km (or less). Unfortunately they have few other virtues, and journeys of more than four hours are not recommended for the uninitiated or non-smoker.

For a start, only the driver's window opens and with half the bus smoking at any one time, the atmosphere soon becomes deadly and someone invariably throws up into a *torba* or bag provided for the occasion. You are a prisoner of the driver's taste in music, which is usually Syrian-influenced electric pop, and the numerous *molas* (hourly rest stops for tea of food) are also frustrating.

When you buy your ticket you might try asking how many rest stops there will be along the way – sometimes they'll tell you. But in estimating how long it will take to reach your destination, 60 km covered per hour is the usual pace, no matter what else you may be told. Every sizable town has either a specific bus station or a cluster of *yazıhanı* (offices) which handle ticket sales. Since bus companies in Turkey are private and competitive, ticket sellers have little compunction about telling you that they've the next departure, or the fastest service, when in fact they don't. Always take a stroll through the bus yard, look at the destination signs in the windshield and see who's got their motor running and their baggage bays open. For a short hop especially you can just hop aboard and buy a ticket once you're underway (note though that standing is often not permitted).

### Other Vehicles
Besides the Mercedes O302 vehicles there are two other classes of bus that are much handier for short hops of up to 100 km.

First there are the large, red-and-cream or blue-and-cream buses operated by the municipalities of outlying villages, which have the name of *Belediyesi* (municipality) painted on the side. These generally offer excellent, cheap service, with windows that open, clean luggage bays and brisk service.

Otherwise there are the swarms of smaller minibuses that ply routes between market towns and hill villages, or between two adjacent sizable towns. These are also usually less expensive than the long-distance buses, and generally have at least one window that opens, but seem to run only until dark. They are useful for getting to remote areas or when the big vehicles are sold out or otherwise not available. Minibuses used to be called *dolmuş* ('stuffed') but this term, with its connotations of discomfort, has fallen out of favour and indeed the little vans will often cruise half-full, picking up and dropping off such passengers as they find.

Sometimes even the minibuses fail you and then you'll have to hire taxis or tractors. If there are no minibuses, that probably means that the road is so bad that there will possibly be no taxis either, so prepare yourself for a bumpy (and expensive) tractor ride. Fares vary from US 50c per km to more than $US1.
It beats road-walking, anyway.

## HITCH-HIKING

Hitching over long-distances is difficult as a bus will probably show up first, and drivers of private cars know this. But in extremely isolated areas where vehicles of any sort are rare, begging a lift is quite acceptable, much more so for men than unaccompanied women. It is polite to offer a donation, and occasionally you may be asked to contribute to petrol costs, though it is usually not expected.

Trucks, large or small, are always the best bet, as they generally have ample (if none too clean) space for your backpack. Sometimes you ride in the back, sometimes you get the grand view from the cab. Conversation tends to be a bit more elevated, in all senses, than that in buses. Certainly what the drivers are up to tends to be more interesting. Once I got a ride in a truck that was driving 200 km to one particular village to pick up a load of what were supposedly the best peppers in Turkey; the next lift was with the man who delivered cooking fuel to the whole district. He smoked the whole way just the same.

Family from Eti Mesut, near Ankara

# Around the Sea of Marmara

This region of gently rolling hills and fertile fields, extending right down to the shore of the almost land-locked Sea of Marmara, is more famous as Turkey's bread basket than as a hiking region. Some of Turkey's best wine and dairy products come from the south Marmara coast, while both the Asian and European sides are famous for their peppers and tobacco. The best hiking is limited to the isolated summits of Uludağ, near Bursa, and Ilyas Dagı on the island of Marmara.

In ancient times the area was something of a backwater; the territory south of the Sea was variously included within Mysia or Bithynia, while the land to the north, then as now, was always eastern Thrace. The verdict of Herodotus, delivered on adjacent Aeolia, applies equally to the Marmara zone, today as in times past: 'The soil of Aeolia is better than [points south], but the weather is not as good.'

## ULUDAĞ OF BURSA

Uludağ ('Great Mountain') was in classical times the Bithynian Olympos, just one of the numerous peaks around the Aegean bearing this name. During the Roman era, with the rearrangement of provincial boundaries, it was referred to as the Mysian Olympos, possibly a better modifier since most of ancient Bithynia lay well to the east of the massif.

During Byzantine times the range was called Oros ton Kaloyeron, or the Monk's Mountain, after the many Christian ascetics who dwelt there. In the Ottoman era Muslim hermits and dervishes supplanted the Christian monks, and the mountain was known as Keşiş Dağı.

Uludağ dominates Bursa just to the north and indeed gives that city much of its delightful character. The Bursans treat the mountain as their backyard and playground, turning out in force on holidays and weekends, summer or winter, to create something of a circus atmosphere up in the alpine meadows and crowded campgrounds, and at the ski resort. Perhaps in recognition of this, Turkey's oldest (1961) national park was established here; it is also probably the only one with any marked or maintained trails, paltry as they are.

The tourist sites, however, are confined to the areas around the cable lifts and hotel complex. Away from these the range is still very wild – just a couple hours of walking will take you to a totally unspoilt cluster of alpine lakes just below Uludağ summit (2543 metres). The mountain can in fact be surprisingly dangerous. Because of its abrupt rise and proximity to the Sea of Marmara, the peaks act as traps for moist air; mists and day-long whiteouts are common, and one of us was marooned here for 36 hours in a violent July storm! Numerous unprepared climbers have reportedly died at the higher elevations, so bring adequate food and protective clothing, no matter what the season, even for only a day hike.

### Rating/Duration

These are easy-to-moderate outings. If you walked every marked trail in the park, including the way to the lakes, it would require about 12 hours, or two days. Given the limited opportunities for camping both comfortably and quietly, you might well consider using one of the less expensive hotels as a base. During the summer they are virtually empty, and prices drop to as low as $US15 to US$20 per person, with full board!

### Season

Since the weather is fickle, you may as well try anytime between May and September.

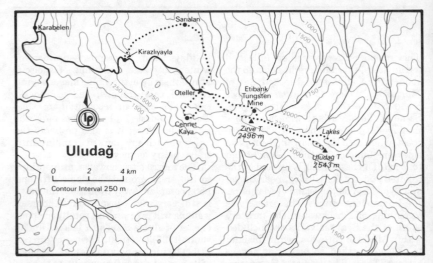

## Supplies

If you are not staying at one of the hotels, stock up in Bursa. At Sarıalan there are only some expensive items for picnickers.

## Map

Other than an inadequate sketch map handed out at the Karabelen gate, there are none.

## Getting to the Trailhead

If you wish to begin hiking at Kirazlıyayla, you need to take a *minibüs* up the 22-km road between Bursa and the Karabelen entry gate; the Kirazlıyayla trailhead is about 2.5 km beyond the entrance. The vehicles leave from Tophane in town, and some continue to Sarıalan or the hotels.

The best way to reach Sarıalan, though, is to take the cable lift (*teleferik* or *teferrüc*), which starts in the southeasternmost corner of Bursa near the university. *Dolmuşlar* to the lift depart from Ataturk Caddesi, next to the Kafkas Pastanesi. Avoid the cable cars on weekends, especially in summer, when you will wait for up to two hours in line. The lift is very cheap though, about $US1.25 one way, and the views on the 25-minute ride up are magnificent. The lift staff grumbles about backpacks but will eventually let you on, so it's best to keep your gear compact.

## Kirazlıyayla to *Oteller* via Sarıalan

Starting at the picnic ground at Kirazlıyayla, a good trail leads through the middle-elevation fir and beech forest to the contrasting mob scene at Sarıalan. This five-km stretch can be done in just under two hours. Next to the information booth in Sarıalan, signs point vaguely east toward Trail 1, 4.5 km up to the *oteller* (hotels), and Trail 3 to Çobankaya.

It will take you around 10 minutes to clear the sprawling picnic meadows, crammed with cars and day-trippers, and arrive at the actual Sarıalan trailhead, where there's another sign merely marked '3, 2565 m; 1, 4135 m'. For the next half-hour the path parallels some powerlines, up to another junction sign at '1215 metres', where you bear right for the hotels ('3385 metres').

The left turn leads to Çobankaya, 45 minutes walk away, where there are good views down the steep north face of Uludağ to Bursa, and also a large campground.

The path to the hotel continues along the right-of-way for the power lines, but at least it's not a road (of which there are plenty in the park) and it's well-marked with cairns and yellow arrows. It soon becomes a real trail through the forest, and about an hour out of Sarıalan you come to a brook and a meadow which would be ideal for camping if it weren't for the mosquitos. The path, which up to now has led south-east, veers south to parallel the stream. Next there's a stiff 20-minute climb up to Bozkurt Çeşmesi, only '1025 m' from the hotels. Unfortunately about 500 metres beyond this spring the trail is ploughed under some new bulldozer tracks, which lead up to the complex of about 20 hotels, two hours above Sarıalan.

### *Oteller* to the Lakes & Summit

Start on the paved street leading up from between the Ergun and Akkoçlar Hotels. After 100 metres bear left, then left again past the nameless ski hostel. Regrettably it's probably best to follow the obvious jeep track for 1½ hours from the hostel up to a tungsten mine managed by the Etibank. If necessary you can camp in the valley under the first ski lift encountered or in the empty valley just before.

There is plenty of water here but none higher up until you reach the lakes; moreover flat space is at a premium. The lift platform huts – eg No 4, a half hour past the hotels – tend to be unlocked in summer and make handy shelters. If neither this nor the campgrounds at Sarıalan or Çobankaya appeal to you, get an early start and camp at the lakes!

From the guardhouse of the tungsten mine it is a 30-minute walk along an increasingly clear path that climbs up to a small notch or pass in the main north-east/south-west ridgeline. Ignore for now the secondary summit 2496 (2487 metres on some maps) just to the west; instead veer south-east on the clear trail heading across bleak uplands, which drop away sharply to the north-east and south-west, and are enlivened only by wildflowers.

Çay time!

Just under an hour beyond the notch-pass the way forks. The right turning leads up the south-west slope of Uludağ summit and takes about an hour. The left, cairned fork veers east-north-east along the north-east flank of the 2543-metre summit. After a brief ascent, then a descent past a meadow usually tenanted by shepherds, the first lake, Aynalıgöl, comes into view on your right. No more than 30 minutes beyond the fork, a side trail leads down to it within 20 more minutes, for a total of just over two hours hiking from the tungsten mine. There are some dry, level campsites near the outlet and on the far side.

Karagöl, the second and most famous lake, is a 15-minute walk south-east of Aynalıgöl. It is almost round, with a maximum diameter of 200 metres and permanent ice floes from the glacier above it. The alpine scenery is spectacular but you must camp below and north of the lake.

The third lake, Kilimligöl, is well hidden up on a plateau some 25 minutes south-east of Karagöl. You cannot go up directly from Karagöl but must circle around north-east, then south; there are trails of a sort. It is not as impressive as the the other two lakes but there are a few more campsites. The fourth and fifth lakes are nameless and are said to be up in the crags above Aynalıgöl; bad weather prevented me finding them.

To vary the return, do not retrace the route to the tungsten mine but instead climb up to the ruined hut atop 2496. This peak is also known as Zirve or 'peak' even though it is the secondary summit. Then descend west until you intercept the path which rounds Zirve on its south slope, a couple of hundred metres below the hut.

This trail soon fizzles out but it at least gives you a start down the ridge, past the tops of the two ski lifts, to a saddle just above the treeline where you can rejoin the track for the last 20 minutes down to the hotels.

There's no need to see the ski lift scars and tungsten installations more than once, and the only reason the ridge route is not recommended for the ascent is because of the absence of a decent path. In fact, if the weather is holding, you could continue north-east along the ridge all the way to Cennetkaya ('heaven rock'), last and lowest of the series of peaks beginning with 2543. From this summit, just a treeline, a 2.5 km trail leads within 45 minutes down to the hotels.

# The Turquoise Coast

The south-western Turkish shore between Bodrum and Antalya has been dubbed the Turquoise Coast in recent decades, a tribute by visitors and local promoters alike to the allure of the blue sea and green pine forests. Tourism has grown by leaps and bounds in the past few years, particularly yacht or *caïque* tourism, and for most people, travelling in this region is synonymous with a cruise.

However there is some very good walking, especially on the Hisarönü (Loryma) peninsula, which is also a must on any seagoing itinerary. The hikes presented here have been selected to appeal to both the landlubber and those anchored near a trailhead. This superlatively beautiful part of Turkey includes what in former times was known as Caria and Lycia (pronounced Lykia).

## Ancient Caria & Lycia

The territory of ancient Caria corresponds almost exactly to that of present-day Muğla province, though this chapter concentrates on the pine-mantled south Carian coast between Köyceğiz Lake and the Gökova Gulf. Then, as now, the interior was populated by village people who claimed (probably correctly) that they were indigenous to the area, and who spoke a still imperfectly understood language only distantly related to ancient Greek.

Larger towns were confined to the coast, and they came under the cosmopolitan influences of the Greeks, Persians and Romans. However the backwater quality of Caria was never completely eradicated, and until just a few decades ago the Bodrum area was used by successive Turkish governments as a place of internal exile for political offenders.

Ancient Lycia was the territory lying south of a line connecting Antalya and Köyceğiz. This is mountainous, harsh country but has an austere beauty. The great limestone arc extending across the Aegean is distorted slightly, and the two parallel ranges of Akdağ (the ancient Massicytus) and the Beydağları (formerly Solyma) run from north to south. To the east the Alakır River separates these 3000-metre heights from the lower chain of Tahtalı (Lycian Olympos), and to the west the Eşen Çay (the Xanthus of antiquity) cuts off the central massifs from the Cragus and Anticragus group (today Baba and Mendos Dagı respectively). In ancient times, as today, only the coast and river valleys were appreciably settled, and thinly at that. However in every era the locals have fled the debilitating summer heat of the lowlands in favour of the mountain pastures, in spite of the perennial water shortages at the higher elevations.

The ancient Lycians are generally accepted to have been settlers from Crete and their unique language and alphabet, like that of the Carian, is still not completely deciphered. Their customs were considered peculiar by their contemporaries and Herodotus asserted that Lycian culture was an amalgam of Cretan and Carian cultures, and also claimed that they were matrilineal, which was unique among the known nations of the day. Their elaborate funerary customs have given us the greatest insight into Lycian culture, for today there are still thousands of the distinctive tombs, either sarcophagi or tombs cut into cliff-faces, which identify former Lycian settlements.

Foremost, however, of the Lycian qualities were the durable unions formed between their cities, rare in the ancient world, and an intense love of freedom and a desire to be left undisturbed. Outsiders generally obliged them in this regard, requiring only token submission, for the landscape effectively protected the Lycians from all but their own tyrannies. (Until as recently as 1980 there was no good road along the coast between Fethiye and Antalya.)

On two occasions,.though, the inhabitants of Xanthus found it necessary to demonstrate the importance of their independence by committing mass suicide rather than submit, first to the Persian, then the Roman armies besieging them.

Today the visitor will encounter no such desperation as the people here have become wealthy from cotton, tomatoes, citrus fruit and, increasingly, tourism, and the feeling of remoteness lessens with each year.

# Hisarönü Peninsula (Rhodian Peraea)

Between the Gulf of Gökova and the Bay of Marmaris an attenuated, split peninsula protrudes south-west into the Aegean. The long finger extending out to Datça and ancient Knidos is relatively straightforward, but the other portion, dangling claw-like in the direction of Rhodes, has the most convoluted coastline of any part of Turkey. This is the Hisarönü or Loryma peninsula.

While its many anchorages have long been familiar to seaborne tourists, the rocky and surprisingly mountainous interior is little visited owing to poor road links. This isolation, however, has had two happy side-effects: despite proximity to major tourist centres the villagers have remained friendly and open to outsiders, and extensive stretches of trail, some perhaps dating back to ancient times, are still preserved. The peninsula north of a line connecting the bays of Delikliyol and Çiftlik is heavily forested and has some groundwater; the best hiking is to be found here, though there are said to be a number of trails in the bare, dry south portion as well.

In ancient times the Loryma peninsula always formed the core of the Rhodian *peraea*, the term designating the mainland territory of the three united city-states of Rhodes. Although the area remained under Rhodian control from around the 6th Century BC until the 2nd Century AD, and despite the fact that the inhabitants of the peninsula were conferred full Rhodian citizenship, surprisingly few ancient remains, let alone full-sized towns, are to be found in the *peraea*. Of the half-dozen or so which George Bean describes in his guide (see Books in Facts for the Trekker), the trails outlined below visit three of them.

### Season
Best from April through June, or September through November. It is hot in mid-summer, and we were rained on in November but the days immediately before and after our ramblings had fair weather.

### Rating/Duration
You can mix and match the various legs to form itineraries of any difficulty and length.

### Map
The *Mavi Yolculuk ve Marmaris* brochure is sold in Marmaris (see Maps in Facts for the Visitor); pages C, E, F.

### Getting to the Trailhead
Several of the more important villages on the peninsula – namely Orhaniye, Turgut, Bayır, Bozburun, Selimiye, and Söğüt – have their own minibuses to link them with Marmaris. These depart in each direction approximately three times a day and any of the latter four services will get you to either Bayır or the Değirmenaltı *mahalle* of Turgut.

### DEĞİRMENALTI TO AKBAĞ
Değirmenaltı consists of seven or eight farms on the east side of the road, some two km south of 'downtown' Turgut (the

name 'Değirmenyanı' is also sometimes heard, but you may be misunderstood since there's a village of Değirmenyanı on the Marmaris-Datça road very nearby). *Değirmen* is Turkish for mill; the walk begins at the one watermill still in working condition. A wall plaque dates the building to 1810, and the present owner will allow you to look inside.

Walk east for 20 minutes, past two more ruined mills, to the *şelale* or waterfall where there are foundations of still more milling operations. The canyon here contains the swiftest stream on the entire

peninsula and so has traditionally supported watermills. However the mills have been abandoned one by one in the past few decades, since the tax department assesses the low-volume water mills at the same rate as the high-production electric ones.

The waterfall itself, while only four metres high, enjoys an enchanting setting and plunges into a wide, deep pool that is perfect for summer dips. It's known locally as the Kanlı Eğren or 'Life's Blood Swimming Hole', in memory of two soldiers who drowned here. Collect

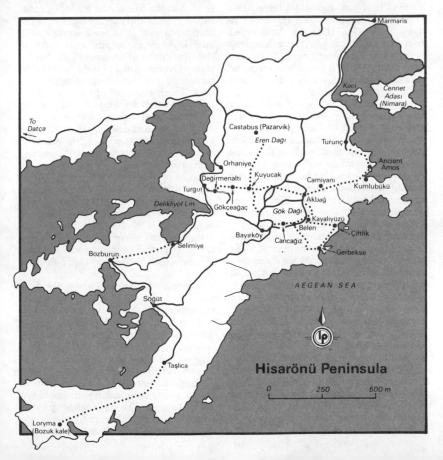

drinking water as this is the last for quite some time.

The trail is much improved and now easy to distinguish from the various sluices running every which way below the mills. It continues to the left (north) of the falls, and leads alternately east and north-east through a forest to the hamlet of Gökçeağaç, whose power lines and lowest house you should see after 70 minutes walking above Değirmenaltı.

Leave Gökçeağaç – where there is only well water – on the wide track heading east, then bear left onto the resumption of a broad trail just opposite a large field. Walk for 20 minutes along this track to where it meets the new back road connecting Kuyucak with Bayır; Kuyucak is only 10 minutes away from the intersection but it is possible to cross the road and follow traces of the old path most of the way to the hamlet.

Kuyucak straddles the auto road and is one of a dozen or so scattered *mahalleler* of the *muhtarlık* of Osmaniye, a name which under the circumstances is fairly useless when asking directions; you must specify the *mahalle* you want. On the right side of the road is a house with a blue metal gate; behind the house is the start of the onward trail to Akbağ. If you're not sure where to start, the friendly inhabitants will point you in the right direction.

Proceed east-north-east for 15 minutes to a meadow, then shun the obvious right turn in favour of the fainter left-hand trail which disappears near some beehives and a multiple intersection of new jeep tracks. Veer left at the beehives and get up to a long cow pasture; cross to its far end, where you should find the faint continuation of the path. This leads through more pine woods up to a pass of sorts, from where the sea east of the peninsula is finally visible. Below the saddle the trail becomes quite clear as it descends to Akbağ, another *mahalle* of Osmaniye, 45 minutes beyond Kuyucak. The total walking time from Değirmenaltı is 2½ hours.

## CAMİYANI TO TURUNÇ

A dirt road connects Akbağ with the *mahalle* of Camiyanı 1500 metres to the north-east. This is the central neighbourhood of Osmaniye, with its mosque and primary school; near these is a giant *çınar* (plane tree) marking the start of the trail leading north-east within 30 minutes to an obvious notch in the terrain. The path is enclosed within walls and skims close to the road at points, but always to the right (south-east).

At the saddle, the trail improves markedly as it descends away from the road. Nimara Island, the modern Cennet Adası, is constantly on the horizon as you drop to sea level. It's a one-hour walk, with no forks, through the pine and arbutus to the olive groves at the apex of the coastal plain of Kumlu Bükü (Sandy Bay). As the name suggests, there is a good beach to the right (south-east) end of the bay but the hitherto modest development will probably get out of hand within a few years.

After a swim and perhaps a snack, walk to the north-west end of the beach to continue the itinerary. The trail resumes next to the last restaurant on the shore; 10 minutes of effort will get you up to the saddle where you hit the new road coming down to Kumlu Bükü. Bear right to visit the ruins of ancient Amos, one of the three largest towns of the Rhodian *peraea*. Today there is nothing left except extensive stretches of polygonal wall and a theatre, both dating from the Hellenistic period.

Immediately beyond Amos the new road has destroyed most of the trail, and rather than try and rescue the remaining bits and pieces, which will surely disappear once the new 'vacation village' is completed, it is easier to walk for 10 or 15 minutes more to a high curve from where Marmaris is first visible.

The path re-emerges on the left near an orange power pole which you should not get too far past. The way snakes up to the base of a cliff, which initially seems odd since Turunç is lower than Amos, but you are immediately rewarded with superb views north over the straits between Keçi and Cennet islands. The trail itself has stone edging and is a joy to walk on.

After your first good look at Turunç, the route curves inland, descending steadily to an olive-treed saddle and the highest farmhouse facing away from the sea. The trail ends here and a track leads down to the beach, coming out next to the primary school, an hours walk beyond Kumlu Bükü. There are regular minibuses from Turunç to Marmaris throughout the day, though Turunç would make a good base if you wanted to explore more of the peninsula.

## AKBAĞ TO BAYIR VIA BELEN

From the highest houses of Akbağ, head south over rather open country until you link up with the main trail that initially heads east toward the Çiftlik Deresi. This traces the base of Gök Dagı; avoid the first prominent left turn down to Kayalıyüzü *mahalle*, then take a right some 50 metres after a weak *çeşme* (fountainhead). Circle Gök Dağı through the forest for an hour until you are headed west-south-west, and then drop briefly across some terraces to join up with the broad path linking Bayır village with Çiftlik Bay.

From the white farmhouse beside the intersection, it's 90 minutes via the *mahalle* of Kayalıyüzü, to Çiftlik. The trail is still in good shape except for the single instance where it is cut by the new road. At Çiftlik there is an anchorage, a beach and an island opposite, but unhappily the place has been spoilt by excessive development. It's probably best to admire its spectacular setting at a distance, from the forested slopes of Gök Dağı.

Most walkers will bear right (west) at the farmhouse and continue a few moments more to the saddle of Belen. Here you join up with the road, but for only 50 metres or so until, on the right, the walled in path resumes. This drops rapidly through the *mahalle* (this time

Bayır's) of Cancağız on a cobbled surface, passing just under a knoll still fortified by traces of polygonal wall; this is probably the acropolis of ancient Syrna, a small town known in ancient times for its sanctuary of Asclepius. You finally reach the *meydan* of Bayır, with its 200-year-old *çinar* (plane tree) and two teahouses, 1¾ hours after leaving Akbağ.

## BELEN TO GERBEKSE (GERBEKİLİSE)

Just west of Belen saddle proper, and immediately opposite the continuation of the trail down to Bayır, a track leads south to a lone farmhouse just under some powerlines. Bear left at the house until you find a dripping *çeşme* (fountain); here the trail begins unmistakably, leading south and up to an obvious pass 30 minutes above Belen.

There's a tiny meadow cradled in the rocks here, and the forest ends just below; keep straight and shun the trail on the left. The sea is now in sight, as is a second, larger pasture to which you descend. Some 15 minutes below the pass, bear left toward now-visible Gerbekse, a double cove separated by a tongue-like peninsula. The descent is quite precipitous but the trail remains evident, mostly because the locals continue to gather herbs in the vicinity.

At Gerbekse (a derivation of Gerbekilise) there are the ruins of several small Byzantine churches, with the most conspicuous one sporting columned windows. Swimming is better in the southern cove although most pleasure craft anchor in the northern one. It takes 90 minutes to reach Gerbekse from Belen, and another trail, steep but in good condition, links Çiftlik with Gerbekse within an hour.

## OTHER POSSIBLE WALKS

From Bayır, a red-dotted trail is said to head three hours north as far as the ancient sanctuary of Hemithea (today called Pazarlık) on Eren Dağı, above Orhaniye. The sanctuary was the centre of ancient Castabus, which despite a nearby theatre (in poor condition) was not really a town but a sacred precinct with periodic festivals. Hemithea was a mortal, favoured by Apollo, who became a healing deity; the ill would sleep in her temple at festival time and wait for her to minister to them in their dreams.

Roads, including the Bayır-Akbağ one, are said to cut the trail in at least two places but from Gökçeağaç onward the way is not disrupted. From the ruins at the summit you descend down to Orhaniye, where you can pleasantly spend the night.

Selimiye and Bozburun are connected by a path which takes about 1¼ hours and threads through a gully thick with oleanders. The road between the two is so bad that this is arguably a more pleasant way of going from one to the other.

Finally, there is reportedly a trail from Taşlica, south of Söğüt, to ancient Loryma, the present-day Bozuk Kale where there are seasonal restaurants, mooring for yachts and good (though cold) swimming, as well as extensive ancient fortifications.

# Around Dalyan

An easy dayhike links Dalyan, a town with one of the most unusual environments in Turkey, with Ekincik, a remote harbour with a good beach. Along the way you will have the opportunity to visit the remains of ancient Caunos at your own pace, without worrying about the schedules of hired boats, and to catch a glimpse of village life which carries on unimpeded just a stone's throw from growing tourist installations. Then there is the route itself, extremely scenic and with an excellent trail, from which you have superior views over large tracts of wild coastline.

Looking east to Dalyan en route to Ekincik

Top: Crossing from Cımbar to Narpuz, Aladağlar (EL)
Bottom: Family at Acıman Yayla in Yörük tent, Aladağlar (MD)

Top: 'Hand of God' ceiling fresco, Kokar Kilise, Ihlara Valley (MD)
Bottom: Upper Gorge, Ihlara Valley (MD)

## Season

Trekking can done year-round, though January to February will be wet and July to August roasting.

## Map

The *Mavi Yolculuk ve Marmaris* pamphlet is the only available map; page G.

## Getting to the Trailhead

At present, if you arrive by long-haul bus, you must get off in Ortaca and take a minibus 12 km further to Dalyan. These run every half-hour until 7 pm or so. There is talk of opening a new Marmaris-Fethiye coastal road which will run past the south shore of Köyceğiz Lake (instead of the north shore), very close to Dalyan, and if this ever happens you will be able to ride the bigger vehicles directly to Dalyan.

## DALYAN TO EKİNCİK

Dalyan is built on the east bank of the Dalyan Çayı (the ancient Calbis), which drains Köyceğiz Lake. It's a tidal river, with occasional saline intrusion as far up as the lake, and *kefal* and *levrek* fish swim upstream each season to spawn in the lake. For centuries the locals have taken advantage of this migration by erecting *dalyanlar* or fish-traps (thus the town's name) to catch them in large numbers as they come and go.

Below the town and the fishing installations, the river meanders through a giant swampy delta, which is home to a variety of wildlife. Oxbows and completely abandoned channels abound, and the silting process has left ancient Caunos stranded 3.2 km from the current shore, rendering its old harbour useless.

Back in town, however, the river is swift and canal-like, imparting an almost Venetian atmosphere to the place. For a good start to a hike, have breakfast at a *pansiyon* overlooking the water and the cliff-tombs on the west bank, while boats and waterfowl glide by.

In Dalyan town you must first cross the

river. The *geçit*, or rowboat ford, is right next to the new 40-unit *belediye* motel, at the end of the side street containing the *Özalp Motel*. Usually there is someone waiting on your side or the far one; if not, just whistle or holler until the boatman appears. There is no dock on the Dalyan side but on the opposite bank (part of the *muhtarlık* of Çandır) there is a small cement quay next to the *muhtar*'s house, and one of his relatives is usually 'on call'. The standard one-way fare is US 15c.

On the Çandır side head south-west on the only tractor track, past the rock-cut tombs and the modern *mezarlık*, to Caunos, 20 minutes away.

## Caunos

Caunos has been excavated sporadically since the last world war, and diggings in 1987 turned up some statues and precious metal ornaments. So in the future there will be more to see, not less as at some Turkish archeological sites being reclaimed

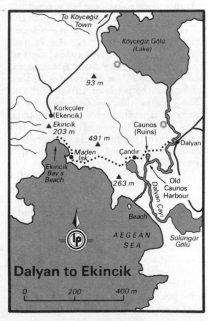

**Dalyan to Ekincik**

To Köyceğiz Town

Köyceğiz Gölü (Lake)

▲ 93 m

Kürkçüler (Ekencik)

▲ Ekincik 203 m

491 m

Caunos (Ruins)

Dalyan

• Maden Isk.

Çandır

Ekincik Bay's Beach

▲ 263 m

Old Caunos Harbour

Dalyan Çayı

Beach

AEGEAN SEA

Sülüngür Gölü

0      200      400 m

by the elements. However the elements are still very much in evidence here, and whatever is uncovered in the future will still be dwarfed by the magnificent setting.

Despite its vagaries the river has always been considered the boundary between Caria and Lycia. As a border city, ancient Caunos exhibited features of both cultures, and the Caunian language was an odd dialect of Carian – or perhaps vice versa. Caunos was first thought to be a Carian community, then a Lycian one, though the only evidence of Lycian influence is the complex of tombs opposite Dalyan town.

Caunos' inhabitants were scorned by their contemporaries as unproductive and listless rubes. A more charitable explanation for their lethargy is the incidence of malaria, which was endemic to the delta, and indeed the local anopheles mosquitoes were finally eradicated only in 1948.

From the rustic drink-stand at the entrance to the ruins, bear left to continue on the tractor track for 20 minutes to the village of Çandır; there is one obvious shortcut on the right. At the central *dörtyol*, or four-way crossroads, marked by a power pole heavy with transformers, bear left (south) for 15 minutes further walking to the *iskele* or village harbour. (This, unlike the adjacent harbour in Caunos, is still usable.) The tractor track ends at the cement wharf but the onward path itself begins 100 metres before, immediately opposite the last farmhouse.

The trail snakes up the right side of a small gulley and is obscured by pine needles for the first 15 minutes walk. You'll hit a brief, clear, rocky stretch and a momentary descent, and then after some more progress through pine woods you climb a sloping meadow. Always keep a west-south-west bearing, without veering down or right.

Thirty minutes above the harbour, near some beehives, the trail joins a bend in a faint track; the sea is visible ahead. Head

right (north-west) along the track for perhaps five minutes until you find a small *mezarlık* (graveyard) on the saddle above Çandır. From the graveyard there are two trails you can take.

The best trail, though not marked, continues from the south-west corner of the graveyard. Initially it descends on a stretch of *kaldırım* (cobbled trail), and after 30 minutes it reaches a meadow at the bottom of a ravine. The trail fizzles out temporarily but just walk past some beehives and a shack to the base of the bluff in front of you, and find the obvious resumption of the trail. Within a few moments you link up with the marked route at a point where a red arrow points right. Do not follow it, but continue left toward the sea.

If you would rather follow a marked route, the first of these leads you north-west away from the graves, in between two barbed-wire fences. Hang an immediate left through a gate and pass a shed with a spring-fed, stock-watering trough; this is the only water en route. The painted red dots follow a course designed to make sure walkers don't lose any altitude. The route takes you over a wall next to a rockslide, then to another large group of sheds amongst some olives trees, 15 minutes past the first shed, down to the bed of a ravine some 45 minutes past the *mezarlık*, and finally 10 minutes more up to the junction with the 'real' trail, where the aforementioned red arrow points against you.

Proceed on the joint route towards the sea. The path, very well engineered now, skims some 150 metres above the water level. It is still used by villagers travelling between Ekincik and Çandır, and it seems likely that the path was originally built in Ottoman times by Greek woodcutters active in the area.

Take one last look at the magnificent view before reaching a hilltop shed, from where the way plunges down sharply toward Maden İskelesi. There is only one luxury restaurant in Maden, catering to the yacht trade; the turnoff left is 45 minutes beyond the ravine bed. Once past Maden the path broadens and briefly rises very steeply inland to a dry *çeşme*, and then skirts some wire fence and parallels the sea once again.

The final 20 minutes of the 2¼-hour walk from the *geçit* takes you over a final ridge and down to the east end of Ekincik beach. At the far end of the bay a cold-drink stand operates seasonally and there's the possibility of simple food, and perhaps a *pansiyon*, nearby.

The only bad thing about the walk is that fact that Ekincik is something of a dead end; there is a daily minibus out to Köyceğiz town, but the 40-km road is horrendous and it is faster and easier to take the seasonal shuttle boats operated by the Ekincik Cooperative. These depart from near the drink stand and will take you back to either Caunos or Dalyan for a fee that is reasonable as long as there are others about to share it with you. Failing this, or in the off-season, you will have to retrace your steps to Dalyan.

# Around Fethiye

The Fethiye area, the centre of the tourist explosion which has taken place on the Turquoise Coast, might not immediately strike one as a base for rewarding dayhikes. But there are at least two half-to-full-day excursions through the pine-forested hinterland behind, and it is worth exploring a landscape which most visitors only see at a distance, from the deck of a yacht or recumbent on a beach.

The first hike begins in Fethiye town itself, and follows a mostly intact cobbled way to Makri (Kayaköyü), the largest Greek ghost town in Asia Minor. From there you've a choice of onward routes to either the shore opposite Gemile (Aya Nikola) Island, where the yacht denizens will stare at you in disbelief, or to Ölü Deniz, the stereotypical Turquoise Coast

paradise which appears on many a Turkish travel poster.

The other hike begins in Ovacık, on the road between Fethiye and Ölü Deniz, climbs up to the saddle between Mendos Dağı and Baba Dağı, and then drops down to the village of Dip in the Eşen Çay valley before ending at the village of Minare, whose name is a corruption of that of the nearby ancient city of Pinara.

## FETHİYE TO GEMİLE/ÖLÜ DENİZ VIA KAYAKÖYÜ

### Rating/Duration
An easy dayhike if done in the direction described.

### Season
Year-round, except that June to August will be very hot and January to February very wet.

### Map
*Mavi Yolculuk ve Marmaris Rehberi*; page H.

### Route Directions
Climb to the castle above Fethiye town and take the road running behind it up into the woods. After 15 minutes you'll come to a spring; facing it, turn left to pick up the beautiful old *kaldırım* rather than continue on the new (1987) dirt road bulldozed to facilitate tour buses.

A half-hour above the spring, the cobbles are again ploughed under the ugly new right-of-way. At the summit of the joint road, there is a peculiar domed *sarnıç* (cistern) on the left; 15 minutes after this landmark the ruins of Makri come into view, at the far end of a giant fertile bowl ringed by hills. Here the old way re-emerges gloriously on your right, for a 15-minute descent to the end of the cobbles next to another cistern at the edge of the valley.

It's a total of two hours to the village of Kayaköyü, where you've a choice of three eateries for lunch! There are also now two modest *pansiyonlar* here, and rumours of at least two foreigners renting houses long-term.

Hopefully the eerieness and solemnity of the 500-plus ruined dwellings on the slope to the south will dwarf any crass development in the future. In its heyday Makri was a strong third to the nearby insular Greek centres of Meyisti and Symi, to whose architecture it displays a strong resemblance.

The village became so prosperous from timber export and the produce of the still-fertile plain that the roof tiles were supposedly imported from Marseilles. Now the only roofed structures left are the two large churches with their pebble-mosaic courtyards. In the westernmost one there was until recently a rather poignant graffiti: 'My parents were born here' – then a date in September 1979 and the signature of a native of Nea Makri, a refugee community near Athens.

In the charnel house of the same church the bones are limited to various femurs and tibias; the 3000-odd living Greeks took the skulls of their ancestors with them when they left in 1923. Very few houses have been appropriated by the Turks, who live on the fringes of the ruins, nearer their fields, because they believe that the Greeks cursed the place before leaving.

From the westernmost basilica you can climb to the obvious saddle, flanked by two old chapels. The well-defined trail from there leads within 90 minutes to the bay opposite Gemile (Aya Nikola) Island, which is covered with Byzantine-era ruins. It may be possible to continue from there along the shoreline to a farther bay opposite the small island of Karacaören, but in either case you will have to walk back out or hitch a ride on a passing yacht.

Most will want to continue to Ölü Deniz. For this path you need to find the less conspicuous saddle closest to the eastern basilica. Red dots on the corners of

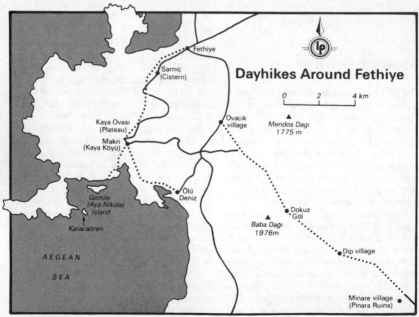

ruined houses lead up to this pass and continue almost all the way to your final destination. This trail is faint in spots and you will appreciate the waymarking.

Some 20 minutes beyond the ridge, you come upon a great view over Karacaören and Gemile Islands. Below the vista point, the path, now buttressed switchbacks that are occasionally even cobbled, is in its own way as much of an engineering marvel as the old Fethiye-Makri *kaldırım*.

After another 25 minutes you should reach a square cistern in the middle of a pasture. Here you begin the progressively more treacherous descent which ends in a gully dotted with various shapeless ruins, cisterns and lean-tos. The trail is briefly ambiguous but the north shore of the Ölü Deniz lagoon is not far.

Pick up the track paralleling the water for the final stretch to the grounds of the *Motel Meri*. The total time is two hours to the motel from the pair of restaurants and fountain on the main access road to

Kayaköÿ. From the motel it's a matter of minutes down to the resort of Belçeğiz, and a swim. Minibuses run regularly back to Fethiye until well in the evening.

Note that there is no fresh water along the way from Makri, and with the usual heat a reverse hike is not recommended. Nor is it a good idea to be en route at dusk – the hills are full of wild boars.

## OVACIK TO PİNARA VIA BABA DAĞI
### Rating/Duration
This is an easy to moderate excursion, but you need at least seven hours (including rests) from Ovacık to Pinara, plus a couple of hours more for the ruins. The main Eşen-Fethiye road passes five km below Minare, and you won't find any buses in either direction after 8 pm.

### Season
Best done in a relatively cool, long-day season (May to early June); the weather is also cooperative in September and

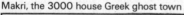
Makri, the 3000 house Greek ghost town

October but you may run out of daylight.

**Map**

None.

**Route Directions**

From Ovacık, a fast-growing tourist centre on the Ölü Deniz-Fethiye blacktop (bitumen road), begin walking on the driveway marked by a yellow 'Yasemin Pansiyon' sign, and take an almost immediate left onto a narrower track.

After 20 minutes you'll come to a *sarniç* (cistern); bear right at the adjacent fork. Some 40 minutes out of Ovacık, you're in forest. The trail is a clear gravel way between pines and scrub oak, and Baba Dağı is always before you to the south-east.

At the only major intersection, bear right onto a bigger track running briefly along the edge of a gulley. From here on the path may be double, ie two parallel tracks. After one hour, you hit the forest road for the first time; cross it. Next there's another cistern and a junction with a wider, non-vehicular track, which you should take.

Eighty minutes above Ovacık take a left fork below a rock outcrop. Just under two hours along, the trail ends at a group of goat pens and a cistern with drinkable water, despite appearances.

From here you must follow the forest road uphill for 40 minutes, with a couple of trail shortcuts, to the large Dokuz Göl plateau, just north of Baba Dağı ridge. In summer there are sometimes villagers from Ovacık tending crops or cattle; they can bring you water from a distant spring and point you along the way.

The track crosses the *ova* in 10 minutes, passing one cistern (definitely emergency fare) on the right. At the far end of the field you come to a faint right fork. Bear left instead, then after 150 metres bear right, just before some goat pens, to resume the footpath down to Dip. Initially there are some cedars, as on the Ovacık side of

Dokuz Göl, but most of the descent is through a low maquis. On a clear day there are fine constant views of the Eşen Çay valley and Ak Dağ to the east; Dip is plainly visible below as well.

From Dokuz Göl it's 1¾ hours to the spring above Dip, and a full two hours is needed to clear the village. The canyon above the spring, situated in a mulberry and *çınar* grove, is another possibility for exploration if you have time – it leads up the south flank of Baba Dağ, which itself is a dull climb according to the crew of the fire watchtower on top.

Thirty minutes down the road from upper Dip, you come to the lower neighbourhood of Dip and a second spring. Bear right onto a wide country lane which gradually veers to a southerly bearing. After clearing a saddle with power poles and gravel pits, the track quickly dwindles to a real trail for a sharp descent through pine forest.

Finally you wind along a stream bed and past olive groves to the highest houses of Minare, some 45 minutes walk after leaving the second spring at Dip. Continue through this friendly village (*not* on the road passing the school) until you see the little yellow sign pointing the way uphill to Pinara. But first a beer at the little teahouse just beyond!

You need to allow substantial time for the detour up to Pinara as the driveway up is about 3 km long. There may be a more direct way up from the stream bed, and I saw at least one rock tomb overhead, but this cannot be counted on. The site is, appropriately, as untamed as the country just traversed.

A spring-fed stream runs through the ruins. In ancient times the source was a bit higher and fed an aqueduct leading to the Roman baths. Built into a slope beyond the baths are the ruins of a theatre and on a hill to the west are traces of temples to Artemis, Apollo and Athena. But the real business of Pinara is tombs – reputedly 1200 of them in various shapes and sizes. The prize exhibit is the *kral mezar* or king's tomb, with its elaborate bas reliefs on the lintel and sides.

# Beydağları

The Beydağları, the ancient Solyma mountains, run in a 50-km line from north-east to south-west on the west slope of the Alakır Çay valley. They begin above the ruins of Termessos and culminate in the 3070-metre cone known as Kız Sivrisi or the Maiden's Point.

Unfortunately hiking opportunities here are limited. Bakırlı peak at the north-east end of the range has been converted into a ski resort, and the slopes above 1900 metres are treeless and waterless, as is typical for limestone ranges around the Aegean. Also there are few villages to stop at or stay overnight.

The one recognised outing is the dayhike up to Kız Sivrisi, but in retrospect we feel bound to comment that it is only worthwhile if you have your own transport, or if the forest service puts you up for the night. We cannot even compare the view from the top with that from Tahtalı, as we were enveloped in thick mist as soon as we reached the peak!

### Rating/Duration
A moderately strenuous full-day hike.

### Season
Spring (May in a normal year), when the remaining snow provides some additional interest, as well as some water above the springs.

### Supplies
Supplies can be bought in Elmalı or Finike.

### Map
None.

### Getting to the Trailhead
Twelve km south of Elmalı on the Finike-bound road a sign indicates the side road for the cedar research station at Çamkuyusu, 11 km away. (These cedars are the same kind as found at Tahtalı.) In fact we saw no research station, only extensive logging of the trees, some of the larger of which are said to be 800 years old.

### Places to Stay
Of interest to the hiker is the *Orman Bakimevi Misafir Hanesi* (Forest Service Guest House) at Çamkuyusu, where it is possible to overnight with the permission of the Orman Müdürlüğü in Elmalı. Their office is a two-storey building on the north side of the road running into Elmalı town centre from the Elmalı-Korkuteli road.

As part of their hospitality they will give you a ride up to the guest house in their truck, usually in the late afternoon. There are cooking facilities in the guest lodge, which is very sumptuous, but you must bring your own food. Alternatively, the forest rangers live in several houses just below the lodge and if you show up they might just allow to use the facilities.

Barring this, there is a campground among the trees just in front of the guest house; you get water from a well down in the meadow beyond the forest rangers' houses. This meadow is in fact completely ringed by untouched stands of cedar, and is probably one of the more attractive spots in the Beydağları.

### The Tahtacılar
Çamkuyusu, where the walk begins, is a summer residence of the so-called *Tahtacılar*, a secretive and much-misunderstood group. From May to September they dwell at the edge of the meadow in the semi-permanent huts, which in fact belong to the Forest Service, who hire the Tahtacılar on a year-to-year basis to fell timber – hence their name, which means 'the loggers'.

The ones we spoke to came from Arıf and Çatallar, villages in the nearby Karasu River valley, though there are

Tahtacılar villages from İzmir/Manisa all the way to Adana, with a particular concentration in the middle Toros. Any one clan has no idea which grove they may occupy in the following season as it seems to depend on the whim of the Forest Service.

The Tahtacılar are in fact Alevis, a sect of Islam closely related to Shiism and more specifically the suppressed Bektaşi dervish order. They are descended from the remnants of the defeated army of the general Shia Shah Ismail, who rebelled unsuccessfully against Sultan Selim the Grim during the early 16th Century. After the collapse of the revolt the stragglers retreated to the mountains of southern Turkey, where they took up the calling they are now known for.

It is becoming increasingly harder to distinguish the Tahtacılar from other Turks. Their sense of religious cohesiveness and observance began to die out two generations ago, although there is still a seminary at Narlıdere near İzmir. One institution which still persists is the institution of *kankardeşlik* (blood brotherhood) – both men must be married and are sworn in a ceremony to defend each other to the death.

## ÇAMKUYUSU TO KIZ SİVRİSİ SUMMIT

Set out from the guest house or the campsite on the road going up into the forest. After 40 minutes the forest ends and a vast upland studded with *yaylalar* begins. Leave the dwindling road at a cement cistern and angle up the ridge to your right.

After about an hour, some faint trails all converge at a spring above the highest *yayla*. (This is the last dependable water.) Another half-hour brings you to the base of the ridge to the south; choose its lowest point and toil for 75 minutes more up to the ridge line.

Next, bear north-north-east toward the visible Kız Sivrisi; it's another half-hour to the slight dip into a pass separating you from the summit. From the floor of this

base the easiest ascent continues, still going north-north-east, until the base of the mountain proper is reached and the climb begins in earnest.

It's another 45 minutes up to either of the two marked summits: the north-eastern one, with a wood altitude marker stuck in cement; and the western one, painted with the initials of the İstanbul University Mountaineering Club. There is supposed to be a sign-in register buried in a canister on the west peak but we didn't find it. You should allow five hours, including rests, from Çamkuyusu to the top.

Returning to the lodge or campsite requires just over 2½ hours, assuming you descend from the pass down into the gully which spills over the south-west flank of the peak. (Not recommended going up – incredible amounts of scree!)

# Olympos National Park

### THE CHIMAERA (YANAR) OF LYCIAN OLYMPOS

Some five km north-west of the ruins of ancient Olympos, and 250 metres up a hillside, there is a perennial natural flame which has burned since antiquity. Called *yanar* in Turkish, its appearance has changed over the centuries, but the flame remains inextinguishable – it will re-ignite itself a few moments after quenching. Depending on the number of active vents, it is also visible far out to sea at night. Because of this nearby flame, the chief patron of classical Greek/Roman Olympos was Hephaestus/Vulcan, deity of fire and the forge. The medieval buildings just below the *yanar* are built on the remains of the sanctuary of this unusual dedication.

In ancient times this hill was called Chimaera, after the fire-breathing monster that Bellerophon, on his winged horse Pegasus, was sent to destroy. However the monster was reputed to dwell in the west of Lycia, near present-day Fethiye; so the

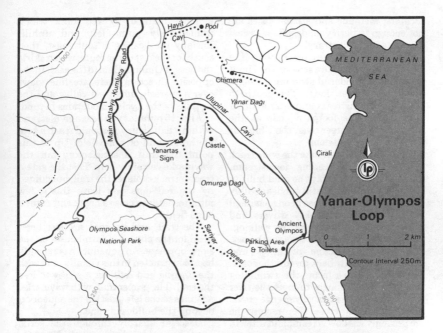

Map showing the Yanar-Olympos Loop, including Mediterranean Sea, Chimera, Yanar Dağı, Ulupınar, Castle, Yanartaş Sign, Omurga Dağı, Çıralı, Olympos Seashore National Park, Sarıvar Deresi, Ancient Olympos, Parking Area & Toilets. Contour Interval 250m. Scale 0 1 2 km.

transference of the name to the other end of the province seems due solely to the fact that the mythological beast breathed fire.

### Rating/Duration
Easy to moderate depending on whether you extend the basic walk or not.

### Season
Year-round, except for mid-summer when it's too hot and January to February when it's rainy.

### Map
None.

### Getting to the Trailhead
Approximately 33 km north-east of Kumlaca on the Kumlaca-Antalya highway, there are respective turnoffs for Olympos (12 km) and Çıralı (7 km). All big buses will leave you there. Once daily in the afternoon there is a minibus from Kemer.

### Route Directions
At the north end of the Çıralı coastal plain, a narrow track veers left (west) off the main shore road at a point where a red arrow is nailed to a pine tree. After 500 metres the side track ends, and cairns and more red dots mark the start of the 20-minute walk to the first cluster of vents on a bare slope. The medieval buildings, including a church, are just below; otherwise there is no sign of the old Hephaesteum.

Another 20 minutes of well-marked trail brings you to a second, smaller cluster of vents at the top of a ridge from where you have fine views up to Tahtalı (north) and the sea (east). It's easy to see how, when in full spate, the vents would constitute a natural nocturnal beacon. Be cautious about applying matches/lighters to possible hot spots – the flames from the escaping methane and ethane gases are hot enough to burn you, despite classical accounts to the contrary!

The path continues down from the ridge for 20 minutes to a stream, the Hayıt Çayı, and a wonderful swimming trough about 12 metres long. The footpath continues downstream and after another 20 minutes, the footpath ends at the junction with a larger river, the Ulupinar Çayı, as do the red dots.

Cross the river and take the wide track on the far bank, heading downstream. The track was probably the road built to lay the pipeline which still gurgles audibly here and there; now it has been reclaimed by the grass and donkey drivers and makes for perfectly satisfactory walking.

The way curves south, then south-east, through a landscape of pines and oleanders, en route back toward the coast. Some 45 minutes below the swimming hole, the track plunges to meet the river near a small house in a tiny orange grove. Just beyond you cross, then recross the surprisingly shallow stream, and after 15 minutes more through a second orange grove you intersect the main seven-km track running between Çıralı and the Kumluca-Antalya highway. A small sign on a tree reads 'Yanartaş', pointing back the way you came.

From here it's a four-km road walk to Ciralı, slightly longer to the river mouth just below the ruins of ancient Olympos. If possible, arrange a ride for this distance. Time permitting, you can also visit the remains of a castle overlooking the road down to the beach. To do this, turn left at the Yanartaş sign and walk some 200 metres along the road until you see a large red dot on a rock to the right. This is the beginning of the 30-minute, waymarked path up to the crumbling fortifications.

If, and only if, you are staying at one of the two campgrounds *upstream* from the site, then you may want to consider extending your walk as follows.

Cross at right angles to the far side of the road from the Yanartaş sign, then find a path marked by red dots which immediately point left and uphill. Initially the bearing is south-east, then south for the rest of the route, which skirts the base of Omurga Dağı to the east. In the opposite direction there are fine views over a sparsely inhabited valley and the foothills of the Lycian mountains beyond.

After 15 minutes you pass a rivulet, and within a half-hour you should reach a gate at the far end of a hayfield. Up to this point the trail is satisfactory but the waymarks certainly help. Past the gate a tractor track replaces the trail, but guided by the red dots you leave this a few minutes later to cross a creek and enter a huge field.

The trail, and its dots, are lost here; head for the cluster of farmhouses on the slope opposite. An aqueduct has recently been constructed in this vicinity, and with the digging and refilling it's easy to lose the trail. The proper trail, with waymarks, resumes to the left (east) of the aqueduct, beyond the bulldozed zone.

Descend sharply through the scrub until, just over an hour past the Yanartaş sign, you arrive at more fields, plastic greenhouses, and unfortunately a bulldozer track which has destroyed the old path for the final 15 minutes to the side road connecting the main highway and ancient Olympos.

From the junction there's no way to avoid 45 minutes of road-walking east and north-east down to the ruins and campgrounds; total elapsed time is just over two hours, about the same as following the Ulupınar Çayı down to the beach and then walking along the sand to the archeological site. Again, try and get a ride for this last leg. However, we noticed a prominent track going up the Sarıyar Deresi just before reaching Olympos, and were told that it lead back up to the main road.

It is highly likely that it's the tractor track mentioned above, and by following this once through the gate rather than the marked trail you might save yourself considerable time and so complete a truly circular loop connecting the *yanar* and the Olympos ruins.

## TAHTALI DAĞI (LYCIAN OLYMPOS)

At least 20 mountains around the Aegean were known in ancient times as Olympos, and the name is possibly a Dorian or Phoenician word for 'mountain'. Usually a city was associated with a nearby Olympos or guardian mountain, and this is the case with Lycian Olympos, today called Tahtalı. It is situated at the very eastern edge of ancient Lycia, near the frontiers with Pamphylia and Pisidia.

Originally this area was not considered to be part of Lycia, which was reckoned to stop at the Alakır Çay valley, the present location of the old Kumluca-Antalya highway via Altınyaka. To add to the ambiguity, 2366-metre Tahtalı/Olympos is actually closer to the site of Phaselis with its triple harbour than to its namesake ancient Olympos, 16 km south. This led to a great deal of confusion even in such sources as Strabo: perhaps Olympos was present-day Musa Dağı, a hill above the ruins of Olympos town, and Tahtalı was Solyma of the Termessans up in Pisidia? The current theory is that Tahtalı is old Olympos, the Bey Dağları is Solyma and Musa Dağı is identified with Phoenicus.

Despite its modest elevation Tahtalı is a beautiful mountain for hiking. The name itself means 'wooded', an accurate description as the lower slopes boast several species of pine (duly exploited) and the zone just below the treeline at about 1900 metres is home to great stands of *Cedrus libani*, the famed cedar of Lebanon. The local name is *katran*, which also means 'tar' in Turkish, because the villagers still extract pitch from the wood to use as a salve for livestock wounds. A rare endemic plant, called simply *Tahtalı çay* and vaguely similar to dittany, can also be found on the highest crags.

For a limestone massif, Tahtalı is well supplied with water and the trails are in reasonable condition. But Tahtalı is a favourite with Turkish and foreign hikers largely because of the magnificent view from the summit, from where a 'living map' of eastern Lycia spreads before your eyes.

### Rating/Duration

This is a moderate trek and takes two days at most (assuming entry from Altınyaka, overnighting in Yaylakuzdere, exit next day to Beycik). For a dayhike you're best off starting from Yukarı Beycik; from there uphill to the saddle should be no more than 3 hours.

### Season

The best time is in spring or autumn. Although there would probably still be plenty of water in summer, the heat would be considerable then.

### Supplies

Supplies can be bought in Kemer or Kumluca.

### Map

Oddly enough, the best map is a navigation chart – *Antalya Körfezi* published by the Seyir, Hidrografi ve Oşinografi Dairesi, and sold in yachting shops in Marmaris, Bodrum or Antalya. The scale is 1:100,000 and it goes inland almost as far as Altınyaka.

### Getting to the Trailhead

Starting from Antalya, there are at least three ways to approach the range. The most straightforward involves taking a bus to Kemer, a rather gross resort on the coast south of Antalya, and hiring a tractor for the bumpy 23-km ride up to the hamlet of Yaylakuzdere. The road is beautiful but horrendous, and you will soon see why the going rate for the trip is a minimum of US$36! If need be you can stay the night at Yaylakuzdere with the hospitable villagers; some 15 families live here.

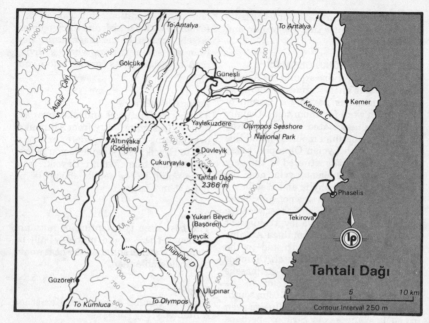

A more economical approach, and one that will give you an extra four hours of hiking, is to take a bus from Antalya to Kumluca and then another up the Alakır Çay valley to Altınyaka, from where a well-established trail heads east to Yaylakuzdere.

If you're merely after a dayhike on the mountain, the most feasible access is from Beycik, just seven km off the new Antalya-Kumluca highway; the turnoff where the bus will drop you is about 20 km south of Kemer. There does not appear to be any bus service up to Beycik so you will have to walk the remaining distance, hitch it, or get a taxi in Kemer to begin with.

### ALTINYAKA TO BEYCİK VIA TAHTALI SUMMIT

From Altınyaka (shown as Altınkaya or Gödene on some maps), a straightforward trail heads east, threading its way through the obvious pass between Güzelkatran Tepe (2145 metres) and Dazkır Tepe (2014 metres). This is probably the easiest way to get to Yaylakuzdere, and anyone in Altınyaka, an attractive place with ample water, will point out the way to you. There is also reportedly a direct trail from Altınyaka to the summit area, but this is faint and not as frequently used.

At a slow pace it will take you no more than four hours to reach Yaylakuzdere. Although you do not have to enter the hamlet proper to continue up toward the summit, it is best to do so, to keep your bearings as well as to meet the villagers.

From Yaylakuzdere retrace your steps west on the main trail out for 15 minutes to the highest of the rather messy cluster of bulldozer tracks above the last houses. At this point the right fork leads back to Altınyaka, so you take the less conspicuous left turning, often blocked with a thorn barrier. If you're not sure about the place, there's a major creek here.

After another 15 minutes on the proper way you should come to a fenced hazelnut grove known as Körmen. From here you climb on a faint but steady path surface up the ridge; the creek and meadow with the nut grove falls away to the left.

Some 10 minutes further, ignore a left fork; for the next 15 minutes the trail threads its away above and to the right (west) of a giant landslide erosion zone. If you're in it, or can't see it, you're too low/high respectively. Just over an hour along you pass through a gate, and after 10 minutes you come out of the trees and onto the *yayla* of Düvleyik, one of the most beautiful spots on the mountain. There's a rushing stream at its top end where you should fill up.

The north flank of the summit cone and the west-to-east saddle abutting onto it loom just above Düvleyik, but getting up there is not as simple as it looks. It is possible, just by following the tree line, to slip through the 'notch' directly overhead, but it's steep and the scree makes it inadvisable to attempt with a full pack.

Instead take the less direct route via the spot called Çukuryayla. To get there leave Düvleyik by the gate on the slope to the west; a trail of sorts meanders along for a few moments, apparently in the wrong direction, before ending at the base of a relatively low and manageable bluff.

Once over this you should see the flat, oval expanse of Çukuryayla just below you. There is an extremely cold spring emptying into a trough at its top (south) end; the faint trail up from Altınyaka reportedly passes near here as well. But since the *yayla* belongs to Beycik, a very good trail starts just upslope from the spring. This eventually ends in Beycik but

for now follow it uphill for about an hour to the top of the saddle, some 400 metres west of the treeline and the base of the peak proper.

Leave the trail here and deposit full packs in the highest trees. From the treeline it's 90 minutes to the top. The first 40 minutes are the worst – this involves reaching the main south-east/north-west ridge, after which it's a pretty easy climb along its length to the peak with its many broken-off altitude markers.

Weather permitting, you'll have magnificent panoramas west to the Beydağları; east over Phaselis and its triple cove, and Tekirova with its tomato/cucumber hothouses; and south over the Çıralı plain to Çavuş Burnu and Gelidonya (Taşlık) Burnu, the nemesis of ancient mariners. From this promontory you can trace the coast west as far as Finike; looking north of Phaselis you can see as far as Antalya if it is not too hazy.

From the top it's just over an hour down to the treeline. Once you pick up the established trail again, it's a 45-minute descent to a spring and a treehouse picnic platform built into an old *çınar*. This is an excellent spot to rest from the rigours of downhill switchbacks. The fine cedar forest ends just above the spring and from here it's another 45 minutes down through pine forest to Yukarı Beycik, also known as Baş Ören. (There is a lower Beycik, a cluster of houses about five km lower on the way to the main highway.) Some 50 to 60 families live in the higher settlement; they are friendly enough but somewhat used to walkers, so it's best not to count on being able to stay the night.

# The Toros (Taurus) Ranges

The Toros mountains (or Taurus, as they are traditionally spelled) extend from the lake district around Burdur and Isparta all the way to the headwaters of the Fırat River beyond Malatya. At their western extreme they steer well clear of the Mediterranean, leaving a fertile coastal plain some 80 km long by 20 km deep. This was the classical Pamphylia, settled by Greeks fleeing the Dorian invasion of the Balkans in the 12th century BC.

Beyond Alanya the range swoops down to approach the sea, resulting in a rugged landscape which produces little other than lumber and (until recently) brigands of legendary stature. This was the 'Rough' Cilicia of the ancients, notorious for its pirates in Roman times.

Once past Silifke (the modern rendition of Cilicia) the peaks recede again, leaving in their wake another agricultural lowland, the cotton-rich Çukurova, which straddles the deltas of the Seyhan and Ceyhan Rivers. Around Malatya the countryside subsides and it is tempting to pronounce the Toros finished, but there is one final limestone irruption, the Munzur massif of Erzincan, almost up by the Black Sea. If the Munzur group is included, the aggregate length of the Toros summit ridge is close to 500 km, making it Turkey's longest mountain chain; their geological homogeneity supports treatment of the various mountains as a unit.

Although the southern Toros serves as a formidable barrier between the central Anatolian plateau and the ocean, there have always been caravan routes linking the two, taking advantage of a limited number of north-south passes or river valleys, some of exceptional beauty. The first of the treks approximately follows one of these, and trekking in the Munzur consists mostly of negotiating the lengths of long canyons passing from one side of the range to the other. Gazing up at the heights of the Bolkar or Aladağlar, however, a hiker may be excused for believing that the Toros are genuinely impenetrable.

## Western Toros

At its western extreme the Toros range forms a formidable barrier between the historical regions of lake-studded Pisidia and the coastal plain of Pamphylia. In this area, however, the main ridges all run from north to south, as do the rivers, and the east-to-west barrier is not so impassable as elsewhere, so that communication between the Mediterranean region and the high inland plateau occurred (and still occurs) along the lengths of the river valleys.

The Aksu River Valley was in former times the main north-south artery and sections of a fine, paved Roman road – today called the *Kral Yolu* or Royal Way – still exist between Adada, an ancient town near Sütcüler, and the better-known Perge near Antalya.

However the relatively wide, flat and fertile Aksu Valley will soon be disfigured by a dam near Çandır, so the best remaining trek in the area is the one concentrating on the headwaters of the adjacent Köprü River. These are walled in more closely by two ranges known on the government map (but to few others it seems) as Kuyucak Dağı and Dede Göl Dağları.

### KÖPRÜSU RIVER VALLEY TO SELGE
The trails in the upper part of the watershed are in good condition and for the first two days you'll get a good feel for the village life and topography of the middle Toros. Thereafter a vehicle transfer is necessary to get you over a hot,

dull, flat section, but the trek finishes in a satisfactory fashion at ancient Selge, an isolated site on the borders between the two classical regions of Pamphylia and Cilicia.

### Rating/Duration
This is a tough, three-day trek which presupposes well-broken-in boots and good physical conditioning.

### Season
Definitely spring – this is a hot hike even then, and with the uncertain water supply beyond Çaltepe it would be unwise to try it after the end of May.

### Supplies
Supplies can be bought in Eğridir or Kesme.

### Map
None known.

### Getting to the Trailhead
From Eğridir, the town at the south end of the lake of the same name, you catch an afternoon bus (around 2 pm) to the village of Kesme in the south-west corner of Isparta province. The southbound bus stop is on the lakeshore road, just past the Kontaş office, in front of a small metal shed serving as a depot for the numerous small village transport cooperatives.

It's nearly a three-hour ride to Kesme via Kasımlar and Ayvalı. There is no hotel in Kesme, so you must look into using the forest service guest house or rely on village hospitality (*köy odası* or private homes).

### Stage 1: Kesme to Kuzdere
Although Kesme is the end of the bus line you should proceed the next morning eight km further to Cukurca, where the trail begins. From here it's 45 steep minutes down to a bridge over the Köprü River, and once on the other side an equally steep hour up to Beydili, a seasonally inhabited hamlet of perhaps six houses which has been largely abandoned in favour of nearby Çimenova because of the lack of a road. However for hikers the lack of vehicular access is a blessing, as the three-hour onward trail going up and down over lightly forested ridges is still in good condition.

At Çimenova, which is the last place along the way to pick up any substantial supplies, you should follow the inbound road from Sütcüler some 500 metres beyond the village going south to the first *yayla*. Here the trail resumes on the left (east) side of the track, passing another *yayla* within a few minutes, before starting gradually downslope toward Kuzdere village through an attractive landscape of pine and juniper.

About a half hour out of Çimenova you'll come to a spring, after which the path veers south-east, and after another 30 minutes down some switchbacks you enter Kuzdere itself. If you don't wish to accept the villagers' offer of hospitality there is a meadow about 10 minutes east down the canyon which is ideal for camping, but collect sufficient water for the night at the village spring.

### Stage 2: Kuzdere to Değirmenözü
The second day of trekking begins with a rugged 40-minute climb to a view east over the rest of the tributary canyon running down to the Köprü River, on the far side of which is the (in spring) snowy summit-ridge of the Dede Göl range.

Immediately below your vantage point lies the *yayla* of Sorkul, which has the only water for the next couple of hours. From Sorkul it's an hour of more gradual climbing through virgin forest to another vista at the second highest point of the day. Here the route stops paralleling the eastbound gorge and heads south, roller-coaster style, through a reasonably thick forest of pine, oak and cedar. Next there's a meadow, then a steady climb to the top of a pass, behind which is the *yayla* of Belova, reached some 3 hours or more after leaving Kuzdere.

Belova is populated in the warm

months by about 25 people who will be happy to provide you with well water and perhaps some milk or cheese. To continue on your way, put the biggest bluff in the area to your back and then turn left (east). The track is not initially obvious, so get the Belovans to show you the way for the first few hundred metres up and out of the high meadow.

Next there's a descent into a horrid karst dell; keep to the north (left) side, and on the faint path. After another 30 minutes or so you should come out onto a saddle from where Değirmenözü should be plainly visible. From here on, the path is clear but that's small consolation during the next 2½ hours of descent – with few switchbacks to break the grade – over perhaps the rockiest path in Turkey.

Finally you arrive at the highest fields of Değirmenözü, where you turn right, before reaching the river, onto a meadow sheltered between two rock walls. Proceed counterclockwise around the easterly bluff, passing some cave-tombs overlooking a bend in the river, for 30 more minutes until reaching the recognised ford of the Köprü Çayı. This is thigh-deep, but you can do it if you're not too heavily laden.

The alternative is to stay on the west bank of the river for 25 more minutes until reaching a bridge some distance upstream from the village. Allow at least 3½ hours from Belova to Değirmenözü, including the fording and final procession into the village ('procession', because you will most certainly be accompanied by the curious at this point). As at every community along the way, there is no formal accommodation; your choices are either the *köy odası* or traditional hospitality.

### Stage 3: Değirmenözü to Selge
Below Değirmenözü the river valley opens open into a wide flood plain which is very fine for crops but not particularly enticing trekking country. So it's advisable to catch either the one daily minibus or the twice-weekly full-sized bus, which both run between Değermenözü and Serik on the coast, as far as Çaltepe some 11 km downriver.

Çaltepe lies on the west bank, and is joined to the main road on the opposite side by a fine old bridge. You resume walking from this bridge, bearing left (away from Çaltepe) and up past a vegetated bluff on a very faint goat trail which after 2½ hours gets you to Ballıbucak, a rather small, poor village with only well water. From here the route veers south roller-coaster fashion over forested ridges for four-plus hours to Altınkaya or Zerk, the two modern names for the village adjacent to the ancient city of Selge.

Like Ballıbucak, Zerk has a severe water problem; the ancient aqueduct which supplied the classical and Roman city of 20,000 inhabitants has fallen into ruin, though the contemporary settlement has barely a hundredth of that population. The ancient site had never been excavated, and only the theatre is conspicuous among the unsorted rubble. The villagers have, however, conducted informal archaeology for years, carting off column fragments, relief work and water troughs to be incorporated into their homes and gardens.

From Zerk it's 14 km along an atrocious jeep road down to the 'highway' leading to Serik (note spelling difference!), but on foot there are some shortcuts possible, either via the various washes leading down to the Köprü River (the ancient Eurymedon), or along surviving stretches of an ancient road consisting of transversely placed stone blocks.

Any of these alternatives will bring you out near the two Roman bridges spanning the torrent, still sturdy enough to be part of the jeep road and the focus of the much-ballyhooed 'Köprülü Kanyon Milli (National) Park'. Unfortunately the coach-tour companies have discovered the site and the character of a famous treehouse-type restaurant has been drastically altered. So after a look at the

Top: Ruined Byzantine church, Vıranşehir, Hasan Dağı (MD)
Bottom: Mt Erciyes NE Glacier from shelter area (MD)

Top: The larger outer caldera lake, Süphan Dağı (MD)
Left: Kurd girl at İbrahim Kara, Ağrı Dağı (EL)
Right: Ascent to Camp 1, showing typical group bunching, Ağrı Dağı (MD)

bridges and a swim just upstream under two artesians gushing out of the riverbank, it is probably best to move on. The nearest village with public transport is Beşkonak, three km below the bridges.

# The Bolkar Toros

This massif is the second highest in the entire Toros range, and while not nearly as spectacular as the Aladağlar on the other side of the Gülek Pass it offers enough to interest the trekker who would like a modest four-to-five day tramp. The name means 'abundant snow', although we saw little of it during our late-summer visit.

Water is less of a problem here than in other parts of the Toros, and there is plenty of reef limestone (just as porous as karst but less sharp) and a handful of fantastic panoramas. Even if your immediate surroundings are featureless (which they tend to be), there is always the horizon, studded with peaks of grey, tan and purple. This is not to say that there isn't magnificent scenery at your feet – the lakes of the Bolkar are as beautiful as any in Turkey, and the approaches to or exits from the villages described are a pleasure – but the landscape is more subtle than points further east, such as the Kaçkar.

## DARBOĞAZ TO HOROZ VALLEY

This trek seems to be the classic traverse, judging from conversations with mountaineers and coverage on the available map. This is in no way the only possibility of the area; Aydos Dağı, technically the centre of a separate group to the west, and the huge forbidding wilderness to the south of the main watershed would suggest themselves for further exploration. If you are intrigued you should try and secure a copy, in English or German, of Dux Schneider's specialist volume *Bolkar* (see Books in Facts for the Trekker).

## Rating/Time Course
This is a moderately difficult trek spread out over five days: Days 1 and 2, Meydan or Kara Göl; Day 3, Yalaklar; Day 4, Göcüklü; Day 5, Horoz and beyond.

## Season
Views, and water supply, are most dependable in early and mid-summer. However there were plenty of both in early September, and Meydan is sufficiently low to make a comfortable spring or late summer campsite.

## Supplies
Adana or Niğde.

## Map
*Bolkar Dağı*, scale of 1:25,000, prepared by Bozkurt Ergör.

## Getting to the Trailhead
The first order of business is to get to Ulukışla, an important rail junction and automobile crossroads just north of the Bolkar range. A train leaves Adana daily at 9.30 am, reaching Ulukışla just after 1 pm.

The Toros Ekspresi, leaving Adana at 5.30 pm, is less convenient because of its late-night arrival, but coming from the Ankara/Niğde side is ideal since it arrives in Ulukışla before noon. There are daily short-haul trains from Konya or Niğde/Kayseri as well. Bus service is of course even more frequent since this is one of the major north-south highways in Turkey.

In Ulukışla you may have time to peek into the historic *han* (tradesmen's hall) before catching the minibus which leaves for the village of Darboğaz at about 2 pm.

## Stage 1: Darboğaz to Meydan Valley
From the centre of Darboğaz, a rather rustic settlement at 1250 metres, walk south to an immediate Y-forking, and bear left onto a walled-in track winding through apple orchards which are heavy with fruit in September. Keep left at the next junction, shortly after which an aqueduct crosses your track; follow it,

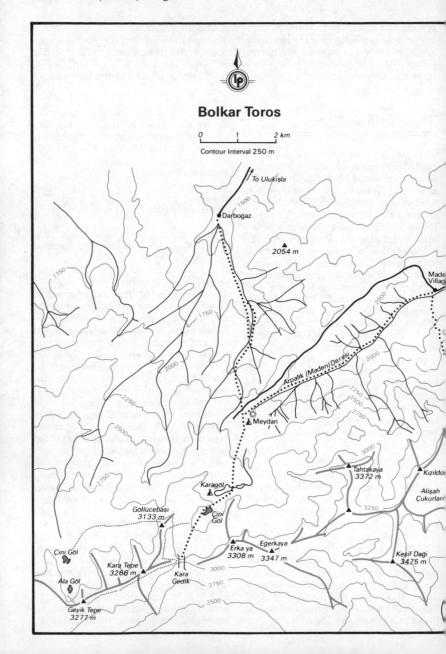

**Bolkar Toros**

0        1        2 km

Contour Interval 250 m

To Ulukışla

Darboğaz

2054 m

Maden Village

Arpalık (Maden) Deresi

Meydan

Karagöl

Tahtakaya 3372 m

Kızıldo

Alişah Çukurları

Göllücebaşı 3133 m

Çini Göl

Çini Göl

Erka ya 3308 m

Egerkaya 3347 m

Keşif Dağı 3475 m

Kara Tepe 3266 m

Kara Gedik

Ala Göl

Geyik Tepe 3277 m

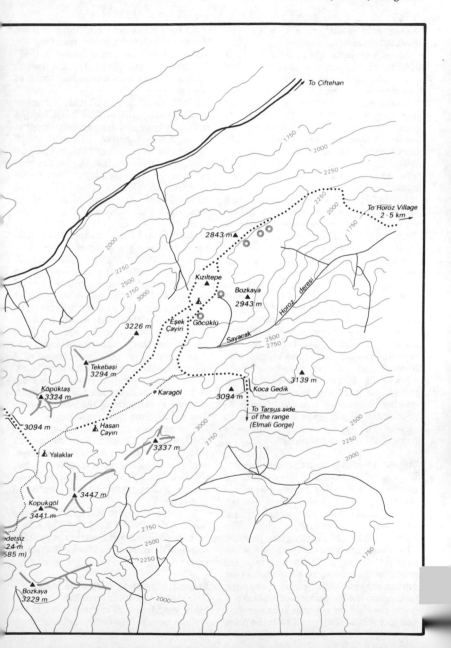

taking still another left when the opportunity arises.

About one hour along, a small path heading right from the apparent main path, just under a giant hogback to the left (running north-north-east), gives access to a stream bed with perennial water. This secondary trail stays on the left (east) bank of the stream until it divides into two brooks. Adopt the path paralleling the right-hand or westerly brook, and you should reach Deli *yayla* (1900 metres) some 45 minutes after leaving the larger track.

Above Deli the path crosses a jeep road just at the point where the stream divides yet again; this time choose the left-hand draw. Following this up 45 minutes from Deli, or a total of 2½ hours out of Darboğaz, will bring you (over an often trailless surface) past Calıl Pınar to yet another dirt road which borders the Meydan valley. Coming over the ridge you'll have your first, if modest, close-up look at the Bolkar summit-ridge.

On the floor of the valley itself (2290 metres) many springs well up in the turf beyond an unfinished alpine shelter, and Meydan makes a good camp-base for the Kara Gedik dayhike. The one big minus, though, is the presence of the road, making unattended tents vulnerable to ill-intentioned visitors in automobiles. In view of this, you may wish to press on to Kara Göl if daylight permits.

### Stage 2: Meydan to Kara Gedik via Lakes

It's a 45-minute walk to Kara Göl (2650 metres), at a leisurely daypack pace, via the trail going south-south-west through the narrows at the south end of Meydan. The lake here is large, clear and surrounded by perennially green pasture. There's more private camping here at the base of Gölkaya (2950 metres), the prominent spur plunging down from as-yet unseen Erkaya (3308 metres). Swimming in the non-weedy portion of the lake is quite possible on a warm summer day, and more than likely you'll have the place

to yourself, since both Meydan and Kara Göl were declared natural reserves, off-limits to small grazing animals, in 1985. There is, though, a herd of wild horses at the lake, which adds a romantic touch to any stay here.

It's 15 minutes, and 50 metres, further up the drainage to Çini ('tile') Göl, hidden in a rocky bowl and deep and aquamarine as its name suggests, but still warm enough for frogs. From this spot it's 90 minutes of walking, initially on the trail heading for Kara Gedik but later cross-country, to Göllüce Başı hill (3133 metres), with its comprehensive views west over the balance of the Bolkar range.

Geyik Tepe (3277 metres), the flat-backed peak in the distance, overlooks a basin containing Ala Göl and a second Çini Göl, but this valley is too remote to reach as a dayhike unless you've camped at Kara Göl and started early. A look at the map suggests that you might get there by following the ridge which connects Gölüce Başı with nearby Karatepe (3266 metres) and then continues to Geyik Tepe. Your alternative, possibly mandatory if sheer walls separate Geyik from the lakes, would be to traverse in a straight line from Göllüce to the lakes via the hummocky country at the base of the various spurs descending from the named peaks.

The panorama to the east, taking in as it does Erkaya, Gölkaya, Tahtakaya (3372 metres), and Koyun Aşağı (3426 metres) peaks, is arguably more spectacular, but with the exception of Tahtakaya these summits are reserved for technical climbing.

Vary the return to Karagöl by looping down to the obvious Kara Gedik pass for a look south into the wild terrain beyond the watershed, uninhabited for kilometres on end.

### Stage 3: Meydan to Yalaklar via Maden

Yalaklar is the traditional base camp for hikes up Medetsiz, highest point in the Bolkar group. However, getting there directly from Meydan is all but impossible so you'll have to take the slightly roundabout but enjoyable route through the village of Maden (not to be confused with Meydan).

The Arpalık (Maden) Deresi leads straight down from Meydan to the village in 1 hour 45 minutes. Stick to the stream and shun the trail high above which merely meets the road into Meydan after a while. Paths of sorts parallel it on both banks, but the north-west (left) side is preferable, as there's more spring water (the creek's not so good to drink) and there are imposing views of the mountains on your right. The last 45 minutes of the descent are especially beautiful, with views over the village and its bean fields and orchards; weather permitting, you can see the Aladağlar on the horizon.

Maden itself is a friendly place, with a single *çayhane* (teahouse) and one simple store. The name, meaning 'mine' or 'metal', comes from the numerous tin, lead, uranium, copper, gold and silver mines (27 in all, claim the locals) in the surrounding hills. These are currently abandoned but had been worked since antiquity, and supplied the Ottoman Empire with much of its coinage silver. As recently as 1939 the Germans were set to re-exploit the diggings but when war broke out they suspended their efforts, leaving now-rusty equipment everywhere. Lately there have been newspaper reports that a South African firm is preparing to reopen some of the gold works, so the wealth of the Bolkar is apparently not yet exhausted.

Today Maden functions mainly as a summertime retreat and *bahçe* (garden annex) for the people of Pozantı and Çiftehan, and is also noted for its cherries (sweet and sour), walnuts, and green beans which are purportedly the best in central Anatolia. Buses out along the 12 km to Çiftehan on the main road are scarce, taxis somewhat less so; most people will wish to continue the itinerary as follows.

To continue up to Yalaklar, use (as unlikely as it seems at first glance) the drainage heading south and up from the bed of the Arpalık Deresi, just above the last pines, between Köpüktaş Tepe (3324 metres) and the ridge which culminates in Kızıldokot. Any of the older villagers will point out the first few minutes of the way; there is even a definite trail, once used by camel caravans but now falling into disrepair.

After 45 minutes of zigzagging up through scree, the path slips between two giant boulders and the grade lessens and the surface improves briefly. Next you head south-south-west up along the east side of what is now seen to be a giant tributary of the Maden Valley below. The improvement is short-lived, since the trail is soon intermittent again as it toils up the cruel slope at the base of a rock wall on the left, heading for the upper reach of the canyon and a pass of sorts to the south-east. Just below the pass, 2 hours 15 minutes above Maden, you'll see a turfy spot; this makes an acceptable emergency camp for one tent, with water available into September from a nearby snowbank.

Beyond this patch of green a long boulder-slide zone leads to a cleft in the rock; squeeze up through this, then follow a path of sorts. This climbs to the pass (75 minutes above the turfy spot), which is actually the first of two. Here you'll get your first look at the rather bleak, hummocky limestone badlands beyond, an intimidating sight particularly if night is approaching.

The way continues briefly left, then right (south) within 15 minutes more to the second pass at about 3000 metres, from where you can see all the Bolkar summits between Keşif Dağı to nameless 3447. Bear left (south-east), avoiding the depression of Alişah Çukarları, unless it's early summer, when there will be a populated *yayla* and dependable water.

From the second pass it's an hour-plus to Yalaklar, 'the basins', at the foot of nameless 3447. The name refers to the natural sinkholes in the terrain which herald your approach to six or seven artificially scooped-out basins at the foot of an all-year snow bank. These are just south of and below two roofless rock shelters which provide the closest flat camping spot to Medetsiz.

### Medetsiz Summit

Medetsiz, meaning 'good-for-nothing' in the vernacular, is in fact good for one of the best views in south-central Anatolia. Try and get up top within three hours of sunrise, no matter what the season, as the haze tends to rise after that. From Yalaklar, head south-west around the base of Kopukgöl Tepe (3441 metres – no need to climb it) until, 45 minutes along, a fan-shaped false summit comes into sight.

Traces of hiker traffic are evident going up and around to the left; follow your predecessors and come out onto the ridge right next to a deep vertical cave. The real, pointed Medetsiz looms before you; the remaining distance is an easy walk-up, with the summit just over 90 minutes above Yalaklar at a moderate pace.

As always in the Bolkar, it's the long view that impresses; Hasan Dağı to the north-west and the entire Aladağlar to the north-east are easy to pick out, and Erciyes will be seen due north, visibility permitting. To the south, you see nothing but the vast, uninhabited, semi-forested river valley system leading down to the Mediterranean. There used to be a climbers' register in the summit cairn, but it went missing in 1985 – who know's if or when it'll be back? The altimeter elevation is officially 3524 metres, though a few maps insist on 3585 metres. The return to Yalaklar takes an hour at most.

### Stage 4: Yalaklar to Göcüklü

Proceeding east-north-east, you descend for 45 minutes through typical Bolkar reef limestone dells to Hasan çayırı (3000 metres), with good flat camping if necessary and a tiny permanent spring

oozing out of a green spot west of the flats. A *yayla* operates here until mid-summer.

On the slope just north of the meadows here a trail commences and leads directly to the *yayla* of Göcüklü, via Eşek çayırı; we didn't use it but instead took another, fainter 25-minute path to (yet another, small) Kara Göl (2900 metres), which dwindles to a murky puddle by late summer. Next you've a 20-minute climb up to a pass of sorts overlooking the head of the Horoz Deresi, followed by a *steep* (350-m altitude change), virtually trailless, half-hour descent to the intersection with a prominent path crossing the head of the valley.

Looking right, this thoroughfare leads visibly up toward Tırnaklar Tepe, then over the Koca Gedik pass, and eventually down through the Elmalı gorge to a roadhead on the Tarsus side of the range; the tenants of Göcüklü use it frequently and will be pleased to fill you in on details.

For now, bear left onto this trail and ascend north for one hour to Göcüklü, a Turkmen *yayla* set near a running stream at 2850 metres on the slopes of Kızıltepe. (Avoid the temptation to dip into the terrible 'hanging meadows' of Sayacak to the north-east; the gorge at their far end is impassable, even assuming that you fight your way through the maze of step-like drops separating the various meadows.)

The three families here hail from Alibeyli and Göcük villages near Tarsus, and have been coming up to this same pasture since 1973. They are very friendly and hospitable and since they are living astride the main route out of the Bolkar going north-east, it's hard to refuse an invitation to make camp here rather than at one of the meadows just beyond.

### Stage 5: Göcüklü to Horoz

Set off, with a north-easterly bearing, on the trail threading between Kızıltepe and Bozkaya Tepe. Soon you pass a first spring on a slight slope and then, about 45 minutes out, you get your first glimpse of

Horoz Köyü: for now only road's end and a couple of houses, but at least it gives orientation to your rambles.

Proceed north downhill to the next meadow and the intersection with an alternate trail coming clockwise from around Kızıltepe. Bear right and slither down a gully path to a broad meadow with a spring, overlooking the Horoz Deresi and reached 90 minutes after leaving Göcüklü.

Another 15 minutes suffices to clear this pasture, going over an apparent 'edge' and continuing east-north-east past still another spring. This is the last campsite above Horoz. As you may by now have concluded, the route does not dive off the fearsome drop into the Horoz valley to the right, but tackles the tree-tufted ridge just ahead.

Once onto this ridge you negotiate 45 minutes worth of messy switchbacks down into the thick of a mixed cedar/juniper forest; then there's another hour on an improved, straighter trail through increasing numbers of pines, to a link-up with a bigger, descending path near the edge of the gorge. From the junction it's another hour down to the village, with the last 45 minutes through orchards and gardens even more attractive than those above Darboğaz. If you turn around you'll have a fine picture of the territory just traversed; somewhere in here the cover shot for Dux Schneider's *Bolkar* was probably taken.

The total elapsed time from Göcüklü to Horoz is 4½ hours. The elongated village, with many shady *mahalleler* (neighbourhoods), straggles for almost 1500 metres along the side of the valley, with one sleepy *çayhane* and one store at the far end of things.

The inhabitants are not too helpful in terms of finding the rather elusive transport out. Minibuses from Pozantı or Tarsus *arrive* at about 2.30 pm; it was difficult to get a straight answer as to exactly when they return (probably in the morning), so it is perhaps wisest to walk

without delay down the six-km side road to the main highway. Buses can be hard to flag down at the lower turnoff and you may have to hitch to Pozantı, where there are some roadside restaurants and gas stations and buses are more likely to stop.

# The Aladağlar

The Aladağlar range is the loftiest in the Toros chain and the most popular one with both Turkish and foreign rockclimbers and trekkers. The mountains are compact – occupying barely 200 square km – and rear up suddenly when seen from the fertile plains to the west, north and south. Nonetheless an intricate topography of narrow gorges, intersecting valley systems and sheer pinnacles makes route planning a challenge, and once underway the area seems large enough, especially if you get lost!

The landscape consists almost exclusively of naked karstic limestone, sporadically stained red or black and moulded into the savage outlines typical of this rock. These contours are softened by forests only in the south and east quarters of the Aladağlar, and the strata dictate prudence at all times in regard to water use and collection. But the shapes of the peaks, the unexpected dash of colour and amazing light conditions at dawn and dusk make up in some ways for the severity of the terrain.

Along with Ağrı Dağ (Ararat) and the Kaçkar chain, this is one of the few alpine areas in Turkey that receives any attention from overseas or İstanbul-based trekking companies. We used their various itineraries as a guideline for our own wanderings and discovered many laughable route errors promulgated by promotions staff who had obviously never left their desks to visit these mountains. The most serious omission, though, was the total neglect of the southernmost valleys of the Aladağlar, which are far greener, majestic and open than the popular northern systems. We ourselves only stumbled into this zone unintentionally, and briefly, but this is where we will return next time and where we would urge you to do any further independent explorations.

We also suggest that you try and lay hands on a copy (easiest in İstanbul) of Haldun Aydingün's new, detailed guide to the entire Aladağlar (see Books in Facts for the Trekker).

## Rating/Duration

An itinerary with the following camps, as we did, would be a strenuous undertaking:

Day 1 – Arpalık
Day 2 – North base Demirkazık
Day 3 – Sokullupınar
Day 4 – Çelikbuyduran, after a detour
       to Emlı
Day 5 – Barazama
Day 6 – Acıman

By visiting Cımbar and Narpuz only as daytrips, and shortening the hiking day, the trans-Aladağlar trip can be rated as a moderate outing:

Day 1,2 – Arpalık or Sokullupınar
       (dayhike base)
Day 3 – Yedigöller
Day 4 – Soğukpınar
Day 5 – Büyük Çakır
Day 6 – Bostanlık Deresi
Day 7 – Acıman or beyond

## Season

July is perhaps best – there are wildflower displays and water is still plentiful, while the heat is moderate. In June you may encounter a bit of a snowpack in the average year but a visit then is not out of the question. Early August is perhaps the worst time, with roasting heat and shrinking lakes, though the handful of snowmelt springs don't dry up until later.

Late August and early September are marginally better, with reduced temperatures but also reduced water supply. Thereafter the locals not unreasonably consider it to be 'winter' and indeed Aladağlar nights are chilly in any month. If you venture into this range in late summer, pray for a high cloud cover to buffer temperatures and reduce your need for water.

## Supplies

Best one-stop store is *Baykan Supermarket* in Niğde, 200 metres south of the Niğde Seyahat ticket office.

## Map

*Aladağlar*, 1:25,000, prepared by Bozkurt Ergör; various sketch maps in ADB news bulletins. On all maps, coverage extends only from Çukurbağ to Hacer Boğaz, going west-to-east, and from Cımbar to the Avci Veli pass going north-to-south.

In the Narpuz Valley

## Guides

If you'd rather go in a group, we can provisionally recommend Doğan Şafak, Paşakapı Caddesi Bal Apartman No 10/4, Niğde, tel (483) 12117. Doğan was born in Çamardı, knows the Aladağlar intimately, and is certified as a guide by the Turkish Mountaineering Federation. He also acts as a subcontractor to *Nouvelles Frontières*, the prominent French agency, and speaks good English as well as French. You can form a group in Turkey, and contact Doğan, or he can try and fit solo clients onto one of the French tours. His standard price for a 5½-day excursion is $US125, from Demirkazık Köyü to Adana, including porterage, tents, meal service and necessary minibus transfers.

If you begin trekking in Çukurbağ, then you should get in touch with villager Mehmet Taşyalak. Although he speaks no English, he is said to really take good care of mountaineers and comes highly recommended by the ADB. Even if he cannot accompany you he will brief you on the area you propose to enter, put you up for the night, supply pack animals, and/or send his son along as an escort.

## Getting to the Trailhead

In Niğde, there are a handful of bus companies running services to the vicinity of the village of Demirkazık, the preferred trailhead. However, very few buses actually enter Demirkazık – most let you off at the turnoff from the main highway, four km from the village, and then continue past Çukurbağ en route to Çamardı.

The municipality of Demirkazık has one of the few direct services, departing Niğde at 12.30 pm daily. The Çamardı *belediye* operates a vehicle at 2 pm, but this only goes to that town, merely passing the turnoff. Niğde Seyahat, with offices at the end of Yeni Çarşı Sokak, has departures at 7.30 am, 2 pm and 6 pm, but again stays on the main road all the way to Çamardı. All services leave from the new bus station (*yeni terminal*) in the

northern half of Niğde, even in those cases where the company has a sales office downtown. Reserve seats at least a few hours in advance – these particular lines are popular.

It takes about an hour to cover the 55 km to the Demirkazık side road, and another hour should be allotted to walk the final five km to the village, although rides are not hard to find.

## Places to Stay

At the far end of Demirkazık (elevation 1550 metres) you'll find the *Dağ Evi* or mountain inn. These very luxurious and well-designed facilities are continuously staffed, and while food service is not yet available you can prepare your own in the huge kitchen. The building has 15 bedrooms containing anywhere from two to 10 beds each, both with and without bath, for a total capacity of 85 guests; prices per person run from $US3.50 to $US12 depending on the room. It's good to know about the Dağ Evi if you have started late.

## TRANS-ALADAĞLAR TREK

### Stage 1: Demirkazık Köyü to Arpalık

Leave the Dağ Evi on the donkey/tractor track, going south and parallel to the property line; after 300 metres bear left and uphill at a three-level trough spring. The trail is rudimentary here but your destination (also known as Arpa Çukuru) is marked by a prominent red splotch on the lower flanks of Demirkazık peak to the east-south-east; the campsite itself is for now hidden at the base of the mountain.

Angle gradually up and left to some green bushes – rare enough to be a landmark – on the flank of a knobby hill, and intersect an increasingly good trail with a view of Demirkazık's west flank. The path runs parallel to a ravine on the left as you continue up toward the red patch, which is probably iron oxides leaching out of the rock. The valley containing Demirkazık and other scattered hamlets, all noted for their cultivation of

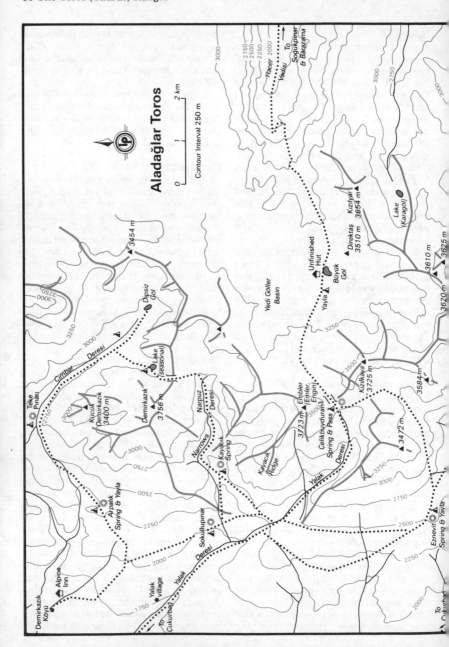

**Aladağlar Toros**

Contour Interval 250 m

0    1    2 km

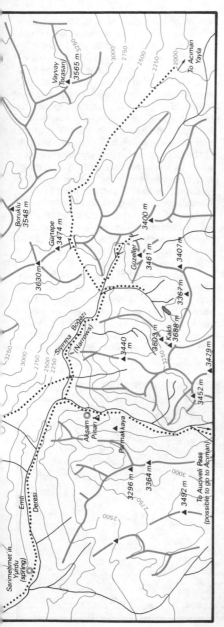

apples and *nohut* (chickpeas), is revealed behind you to the west.

An hour after leaving the mountain inn, you reach the top of a shallow side ravine; turn left to continue on to Arpalık (keeping straight leads to Sokullupınar, reached easier from Çukurbağ). Total walking time to Arpalık, a small plateau overlooking the lower reaches of the Cımbar valley at about 2000 metres, is just under two hours. There are campsites for a maximum of six parties, a good if somewhat camouflaged perennial spring, and usually a half-dozen tents of a shepherd family from Demirkazık village.

### Stage 2: Arpalık to Cımbar Valley

Leave Arpalık, going north, by the higher, right-hand (easternmost) trail. Avoid the incline down to the head of the gorge – actually the lowest reaches of Cımbar – on the left (west). Once clear of this, your course up to Cımbar proper is obvious; rock walls on your left and right (the latter actually the base of Kuçuk Demirkazık) hem you in. After about an hour you come to a pass; the trail slips through a gallery on the right and descends to the spring of Teke Pınarı. The vegetation around it is the only sign of life in the limestone wilderness all around; there's space for three or four tents here should you wish to camp. This is also the last reliable water in Cımbar, so fill up.

Proceed up the valley for another hour to a point where a prominent side canyon, and a pass just to the left (east) of big Demirkazık, come into view. Here you must choose whether to bear up toward the pass or move on to Dipsiz Göl (2900 metres) at the head of the main valley. This lake, 45 minutes away, belies its name, meaning 'bottomless', in August and September when the bottom is all too apparent, and it probably dries up by summer's end. Still, this is probably the cleanest water source in the upper Cımbar, especially for those camping at some green patches about 20 minutes before the lake. The scenery, too, makes the excursion up here worthwhile, if only for a dayhike.

We turned right and headed up toward the base of Demirkazık. This course makes the most sense if you intend to get over to the Narpuz canyon the following day. A half-hour suffices to reach a minimally´reliable lake (elevation 2900 metres) at the base of the pass. Only puddles remain in the lake bed come August, and these cavities are jammed with tiny red hatchlings, whether fish or insect we couldn't tell, but they don't seem to effect the potability of the water. There are two or three level but rocky campsites a couple hundred metres before reaching the lake bed.

### Stage 3: Demirkazık Pass to Sokullupınar via Narpuz Valley

Many hikers will want to skip the complete loop back to the Çukurbağ side of the range as outlined below, for reasons which will become evident, and instead visit the Cımbar and Narpuz canyons on dayhikes from Arpalık or Sokullupınar. For those who insist on hauling a full pack over the rugged terrain to Sokullupınar,

we emphasise that this is Class 3-plus climbing, and that a rope, while not mandatory, will be put to good use.

From the seasonal lake at the foot of Demirkazık it's 90 minutes up to the first 'lip' visible from below. Avoid both the exposed rock face to the far right and the rotten-mud palisade to the left, closest to the pyramid of snowmelt above the lakebed. Instead try to find a natural ramp of sorts which takes off from the top of the talus slope coming up from the lake area. In its worst moments, this 'ramp' acquires low walls on either side for grabbing on to and keeping your footing. Now there's another miserable 75 minutes inching up the couloir to the true top of the pass (around 3400 metres); you must hug the rock wall on the right and lever yourself up, since the scree – tons of it – offers no secure footing.

For those who have ropes and feel that they haven't had enough before lunch, the top of the pass is the jump-off point for some Class 4 climbing, namely the ascent of the east-south-east face of Demirkazık itself. We did not do this ourselves but reliable accounts allow two hours to the

Demirkazık ridge seen from Kayacık Pınarı

top, one-way, along the south-east face which consists of slabs and shallow gullies. Because of its size and confusing layout it's easy to get lost on the peak, so it is also suggested that you adhere to the junction of the south-east and sheer north faces going both directions.

Most people will descend directly from the pass, whose view extends only as far south and east as the ridges enclosing Narpuz; the northern Aladağlar tend to be rather concentrated. An hour is required to get to the valley floor as you slide down giant talus piles which, while safer than the terrain on the north side of the pass, would be infinitely more tiring for an ascent.

Once in Narpuz, a very faint trail leads down-valley for 45 minutes to a greenery-flecked cliff face at the top of the Narpuz *Boğazı* (Narrows). The place looks like it ought to have year-round water but doesn't after mid-summer. It takes another 45 minutes to clear this tight spot, going downhill; with some two- and three-metre drops along the way, it's tricky if there's a lot of water about and the narrows are probably impassable before 15 June in an average year. We saw cairns marking a possible alternate route above and to the north but after our morning over the pass we took what seemed to be the path of least resistance.

Where the Narpuz Boğazı ends (fairly abruptly), a trail commences and, adhering to the south-east bank of the widened watercourse for 30 minutes, you'll reach Kayacık Pınarı (2500 metres), an all-year spring at the base of Kayacık Tepe. There's flat space for up to five tents if necessary, but it's better to continue 45 minutes further down through the last gorge of Narpuz to Sokullupınar (2250 metres). These narrows, visible just west of the spring, are much easier to negotiate than would appear at first glance, and the rock walls enclose a magical place with wildflowers, two gushing springs, and two caves to stay in if necessary. Sokullupınar, with its grassy expanse and trough spring

conveniently close to the best tent space, is fine enough but it's the last set of narrows which lifted our spirits after a gruelling, 6½-hour walking day.

Trekkers pressed for time may wish to skip much of the foregoing by starting in Çukurbağ, from where a trail leads up the Yalak Deresi, past Yalakköyü, to Sokullupınar within 2½ hours. Sokullupınar is also accessible from Demirkazık Köyü, but this stretch takes three hours.

## Stage 4: Sokullupınar to Yedi Göller Basin via Çelikbuyduran Pass

From Sokullupınar, rather than drop immediately down into the bottom of the Yalak Deresi, you can retrace your steps (assuming you came that way) some 400 metres back up toward Narpuz and then head south-south-east over sloping grazing land. After about an hour you'll hit the bed of the Yalak Deresi, considerably narrower and shallower here where it exits from between the wall formed by Kayacık and Embler on the north-east and a longer ridge system coming down from Kızılkaya to the south-west. You can also reach this spot directly from Kayacık Pınarı, without going down to Sokullupınar, via an obvious trail starting at the former and cutting south-south-west across the nearby pastures. At this point you also have the option of making a side trip, or more extensive treks, into the Emli Valley (see Detour to Emli Valley).

Continuing to Yedi Göller, it's almost three hours from the time you join up with the faint route along Yalak until reaching the spring just below Çelikbuyduran. This is the only water source in the canyon, so fill up when leaving either Sokullupınar or Kayacık Pınarı. Just above the spring, which can partially freeze at night even in summer, there are level campsites for three parties.

The pass proper (3450 metres) is only 20 walking minutes above the spring. From there you have fine views of the Yedi Göller ('seven lakes') basin, though most of the lakes are still out of sight.

More compelling is the opportunity to climb Mt Embler (Engin Tepe on some maps), immediately to your left (north-west). It's a two-hour maximum round-trip up the third-highest peak in the Aladağlar, but the attraction of this easy walk-up is the fine view north to Demirkazık rather than the altitude. Kızılkaya, on the opposite side of the pass, cops second place – barely – at 3725 metres, but is strictly a technical climb.

A maximum of one hour's walking separates the pass from the single *yayla* of the Yedi Göller valley (3000 metres), inhabited (partly by Yörüks) from June to September. They enjoy the company of the numerous trekking and climbing parties who stay nearby but complain about the *öşek*, something similar to a jackal, but bigger, which wreaks havoc among their sheep.

A snowmelt-fed spring in the vicinity usually runs until late September. Although the big lake at the foot of unmistakable Direktaş ('column rock') is year-round (the only such in the valley), its water is a swimming spot for animals and humans alike. Visitors tend to camp near the lake, or slightly higher up near the shell of an unfinished alpinists' shelter.

### Stage 5: Yedi Göller to Barazama

The main way out of the Aladağlar toward the east starts just below the half-built mountain hut at Yedi Göller. After clearing the base of Direktaş to the right of the hill with a triangulation point, you'll log 2½ hours of downhill until reaching the highest trees on the floor of the Hacer Boğazı (about 2500 metres). The path is clear though the descent is initially accomplished by sharp jumps and later on switchbacks with some scree.

Soon after meeting the first clump of trees, the trail becomes a jeep track, and you should walk no more than an hour along this before reaching an unsignposted side road leading right to Soğukpınar.

Two clues to finding the turnoff are a crude corral five minutes before the turnoff, and the local woodcutters' habit of stacking lumber at the junction.

At Soğukpınar, 10 minutes up the side road, there's a spring, as the name suggests, space for a few tents, and a summertime *yayla*. The spring is snowmelt, however, and can dry up by the end of the summer, so don't count on it. If while on the main road you pass a giant meadow with beehives to the left of the road, you've passed the detour to Soğukpınar; back up five or 10 minutes.

Below this *ova* (meadow) the forest, hitherto strictly pine, begins to exhibit deciduous specimens, mostly *su kavağı* (white poplar). The jeep track becomes a bit frustrating to follow, winding this way and that, and often seems to go in the wrong direction. There are many shortcuts, consisting of sections of the old path and known only to the locals, but there is a very prominent one, marked by a roadside cairn, which will save you about an hour of walking.

Without using any of these it's 90 minutes from the giant meadow to the first overlook of Barazama village. Almost immediately after, hang a left onto a huge path which crosses the road diagonally. This heads straight down to the village within an hour, with the halfway mark being the environs of a spring near which you can camp. Total elapsed walking time from Yedi Göller is just over six hours.

Barazama, at an altitude of 1550 metres and officially named Ulupınar, has few facilities other than a single *bakkaliye*; if you wish to spend the night the *muhtar* (headman) will arrange something. Those needing or wanting to end their itinerary here can take a morning minibus out to Yahyalı, the first substantial town in Kayseri province.

### Stage 6: Barazama to Şelale and/or Acıman

From the village houses, descend to the

poplars on the west bank, (ie the same bank the village is on) of the nearby stream and pick up the trail heading south, parallel to the water. After 45 minutes cross on a bridge to the opposite bank; the path continues, some 200 metres above the river, through a pine wood, then descends through a field and past some shacks.

After about two hours the trail gets progressively more chewed up as you approach the junction with the road coming from the other bank. Shortly after the wood bridge, trails of any sort disappear completely, and you pass through the village of Kapuzbaşı.

Fifteen minutes of downhill road walking separates you from a giant rock face on the right, where countless waterfalls (şelale in Turkish) erupt from the cliff. It's an impressive sight but staying the night in the immediate surroundings is difficult; there's only a simple teahouse on stilts wedged into an overhang, intended for road maintenance crews. Instead keep going another 15 minutes down the road to the turnoff for the partly Yörük settlement of Büyük Çakır.

This is a delightful place, an oasis of mulberry, walnut and other fruit or shade trees supported by a surging artesian well and one, big, final cascade on the upper outskirts. There are several interesting watermills, similar to some further up the canyon but more accessible, and most of the houses are built on stilts to take advantage of the coolness afforded by the trees; one of these is kept free as a shelter for guests.

The inhabitants are curious but friendly and eager to show you around what is in fact the summer *mahalle* (annex) for the actual village some two km further downstream. At an elevation of only 950 metres the heat here can be considerable in summer, but the nearby river and torrents are perfect antidotes.

It's possible to get directly from Büyük Çakır to the Acıman highlands, and

trekking companies operating in the area occasionally do it, but the altitude change is considerable (Acıman is at 2100 metres) as is the minimum elapsed walking time (seven hours). To start in Büyük Çakır, choose the right-hand track (not the one going over the stone bridge), proceed south-west for some 1500 metres, and then adopt the riverbed trail when the tractor track veers up and left. We feel it's only fair to warn you that we didn't follow this route the whole way, and that there are no maps for the immediate area.

Most expeditioneers will opt to return to Barazama from the Şelale area, or skip that excursion altogether in favour of the more conventional – and easier – approach to Acıman described as follows.

Leave Barazama on the main road heading south past the lone store and the forestry post. After five km, you'll come to a hairpin turn in the road next to a yellow government sign and some beehives. Various tracks head to the right and up the Bostanlık Deresi, toward an obvious saddle on the horizon; pick the oldest of these thoroughfares, which dwindles shortly to a trail.

There's abundant water at the beginning – for example from a *çeşme* (fountain) flanked by two *çınar* and a *dut* (mulberry) – but this gets scarcer as you climb. After passing a forest watchman's white tent, you slip over the saddle and skirt the base of a bare rock bluff to the right, which is actually the eastern end of the Torasan/Vay Vay group in the south-east corner of the Aladağlar.

A lone Yörük tent has in years past been pitched just before the knoll of Yedigözler (2200 metres). On the far side of this is Acıman, a Yörük *yayla* of about a dozen tents, five walking hours above Barazama. If you visit the Şelale, then backtrack almost to Barazama to pick up the road leading to the Bostanlık Deresi trailhead, you're proposing a nine-hour walking day from the waterfalls (and that's assuming you spent the night there!). You should probably break up this journey with a camp beside the spring with the *çınar* and mulberry.

Acıman offers marvellous views over the Toros in all directions and level campsites for large parties. It is most famous, though, for the *Acısu* (bitter water), an extremely sulphurous/medicinal-tasting spring some 20 minutes below (not to worry, there is more or less normal water up by the *yayla*). Strangely, the lower source is a big attraction and weekend picnic spot for scores of villagers who, convinced of its tonic properties, guzzle large quantities of the stuff after driving up an appalling road.

Tractors congregate here too, with half an eye out for trekkers willing to pay $US12 to US$15 per head for the 40-km transfer downhill to Karsantı, the first proper town encountered in Adana province. This takes 2½ hours and can be compared to sitting on a jackhammer for a similar amount of time. In Marc's experience it ranks right up there with a 10-hour ordeal in Pakistan hanging on to the roll bars of a jeep or a 30-hour marathon dust wallow on a Peruvian bus from Cuzco to Ayacucho. Finding a tractor on the spot is a chancy business anyway, and unless you're going on to the Bolkar as we were, you should seriously consider leaving the area via Yahyalı.

Should you make it to Karsantı, you'll find two hotels, three restaurants, and one to three daily buses down to Adana (Sunday is the light day, with only dawn service). The trip to Adana takes three hours via Imamoğlu, where there's a short tea break.

## DETOUR TO EMLI VALLEY

The Emlı Vadısı (Valley) and its extension the Sıyırma Boğazı comprise roughly the southern half of the Aladağlar, and is arguably the most attractive. We wandered into this territory strictly by accident, which turned out to be a mostly happy one, and we thought enough of our day there to present it here as an alternate route up to Çelikbuyduran.

You can get to Emlı fairly easily from the point in Yalak Deresi where the routes from Sokullupınar and Kayacık Pınarı drop down to the canyon bed (see stage 4 of the Trans-Aladağlar Trek). Yalak can appear to some – as it did to us – to be too insignificant here to really be Yalak, so thinking this it's easy enough to continue up 45 minutes to a low point on the ridge to the south.

Cross over for 45 minutes of downhill-to-level progress until meeting up with a main trail paralleling the very broad Emlı basin on its north-eastern edge.

As you lope along, passing above an unknown *yayla* with a spring, you can look across the vast expanses of pasture sloping up to the tree-tufted base of the bare ridge opposite. Eznevit spring and its *yayla* just beyond lie some 45 minutes still more up this trail. The *yayla*, consisting of about a dozen *obalar* (tents in this sense), is home to a clan from Çukurbağ who spend winters there weaving rugs; 'winter' means, as it seems to throughout these mountains, any time after mid-September.

Emlı is more usually and properly entered by a well-used trail starting in Çukurbağ, which wends its way below Eznevit closer to the gorge running down the centre of the valley. In terms of point-to-point trekking, as opposed to peak-bagging, there are reportedly only two onward routes, with semblances of trails, over passes that are feasible to a lightly laden backpacker.

One route heads due south past the distinctive Parmakkaya ('finger rock') to the Avciveli *geçidi* (pass); precisely where you'd end up once on the other side is uncertain.

The other way out involves entering the Sıyırma gorge and finding an unconfirmed pass said to exist between Kaldı Dağ (3688 metres) and Gürtepe (3474 metres). Should you get over this ridge, you would be within striking distance of the Acıman plateau and the end of the verified itinerary written up in this guide.

It is probably thanks to the problematic

Top: Typical crowd at the summit, 8.30 am, Ağrı Dağı (MD)
Bottom: Afternoon at Camp 1 with the summit in the background, Ağrı Dağı (MD)

Top: Büyük Deniz Lake, Kaçkar Range (MD)
Bottom: Wildflowers below Caymakçur Pass, Kaçkar Range (MD)

nature of routing in the southern valleys of the Aladağlar that the trekking companies have left this part of the range alone.

After a visit to Eznevit *yayla*, most trekkers will be interested in getting back onto the main west-to-east 'highway' through the Aladağlar. Short of retreating back to the lower reaches of the Yalak valley on the west flank of the mountain, there is one other solution.

Being careful not to lose any altitude, leave Eznevit going east-north-east on faint trails traversing a scree-laden bank until, 45 minutes away, you reach a broad rocky incline leading up to apparent passes on the left and right. Aim for the scree pile at the base of the right-hand one and slog up some 45 minutes more. Once atop this heap you'll discover that this nameless pass, indicated on most maps as a relatively gentle grade enclosed by peaks

3589, 3550 and 3473, is in reality a double one, with the second pass at the far left-hand corner of a high cirque delineated by the summits noted.

You in fact face a total of two hours of climbing from the bottom of the first couloir to the top of the final gap, from where you should see the flank of Embler to the north and the Yalak valley yawning at your feet. The fun's not over yet, as you've another hour of descent, then ascent, up to Çelikbuyduran spring, where you'll most likely have to camp – a chilly proposition.

Starting at Sokullupınar, the above transit adds up to a seven-hour hiking day. The territory beyond Eznevit is not that difficult or dangerous, but rather tedious because of the scree and the necessary minute-to-minute route-finding. It's only fair to note that the elapsed time would be little different if you returned from Eznevit to Yalak the way you came and then proceeded up to Çelikbuyduran.

Child spinning, Eznevit yayla, Emli Valley

# The Munzur Group

The Munzur mountains are difficult to classify; geologically they are an extension of the Toros, and at the same time are the north-western-most Turkish alpine area inhabited by Kurds. This compact (30 km by 25 km) range is located between Erzincan and Tunceli, with the Fırat (Euphrates) River curling around it to the north and west before being impounded in the Keban dam to the south.

In general the topography consists of grassy high-altitude basins, the products of glacial action, suspended above interconnecting valley systems which are surprisingly shallow. Because of the relatively high elevation (1500 to 2000 metres) of the canyon floors, altitude gain is modest when climbing toward the twenty-odd 3000-metre peaks in the region.

Once up above the gorge systems you will find that the high plateaus have ample water to support both *yaylalar* and campers. Inclines up to the peaks proper are gradual and you can pass from one ravine system to another via gentle passes, but the attraction for most Turkish trekkers at least seems to be the feasibility of point-to-point traverses from one side of the Munzur to the other, using the valleys as thoroughfares.

## Warning

We were personally unable to visit the Munzur in 1987, but have furnished the account below anyway to give you an idea of touring possibilities in this relatively unknown massif. The information given is based solely on an article in the 1983 ADB bulletin and a brief synopsis from the Tourism & Culture Ministry's Mountain Tourism planning office. There may or may not be an actual trail along the route indicated, but there will at least be a cross-country course to get you to your destination. You should check with the authorities in the towns of Kemah or Ovacık before setting out, for the latest news on any troubles or restrictions in the area, and you might want to hire a local guide in these places.

## Rating/Duration

Alp-Ovacık via Kurik Deresi will require three days, two nights, with time allowed for dayhikes around Gedik Direği Çanağı, and seems slightly easier than the moderately difficult Acemoğlu traverse, for which you should allow four days.

## Season

Mid-June to mid-September.

## Supplies

Erzincan or Tunceli; last-minute topping-off in Kemah or Ovacık.

## Map

Sketch map in 1983 ADB bulletin.

## Getting to the Trailheads

Itineraries start either on the north-west slope of the Munzur or on the south-east flank. To get to the north-west side, you can take a train directly to the village of Alp, 30 km south-west of Erzincan; the two eastbound express trains on this line pass through in the early morning and around noon. Alternatively, buses plying between Erzincan and Kemah pass through Alp.

Gözeler, the most frequent jumping-off point from the south-east, is most easily reached by taxi from Ovacık, in turn linked by minibus with Tunceli.

## ALP TO GÖZELER

From the train station, find the narrow entrance of the Kurik Vadisi to the south-east, 165 degrees on a compass. The initial elevation is 1200 metres. Begin walking south-west up the valley to Kurik *yayla* at approximately 2400 metres, and then continue on over a 2900-metre saddle to the Gedik Direği Çanağı basin, reportedly a 5½-hour march from Alp. There is water here and the turf is level, making it a good base camp for excursions to the nearby peaks.

It is possible to proceed south-south-west, via Herdif *yayla* and the Karagöl pass, to the head of the Karagöl canyon which leads down to Ovacık, but the most popular route heads south, then south-east with a slight climb, skirting a small lake before reaching Kırkmerdivenler ('the forty ladders'). This is at the head of the Aksu River canyon, into which you drop to follow the watercourse to Gözeler village.

## KEMAH TO OVACIK

From Kemah take a taxi to the *karakol* (gendarme post) of Derebaşı *mahalle* and trek east-south-east until entering the Güvercinlik Deresi. Then follow this valley south-east to the 2900-metre plateau mentioned in the first section, and take your pick of either the Aksu or Karagöl ravines to finish out in Ovacık.

The village closest to the mouth of the Karagöl Deresi is called Köseler (not to be confused with Gözeler!).

## ALP TO OVACIK VIA ACEMOĞLU VALLEY

Enter the mountains 3.5 km east of Alp at the mouth of the Acemoğlu Vadısı and start walking due south-west. Four km along, the valley splits, with the broader Şoran canyon (of which there are no reports) veering off to the south-east. The confirmed route up the Acemoğlu takes you past two side valleys, the Çivikdere and the Kulkul, reputed to be exceptionally

beautiful. You can camp at the head of the Kulkul Vadısı, and the next day negotiate the pass between peaks 3331 and 3370 to reach Gedik Direği Çanaği.

Alternatively you can exit Acemoğlu via the Memo Çayırı at the extreme south end of the valley, camping at Kepir *yayla* and descending to Gözeler via the Harami Deresi.

Of course all of these options, especially traverses via the Aksu ravine, can be reversed by starting in Gözeler, and this is apparently done quite often by Turkish trekkers.

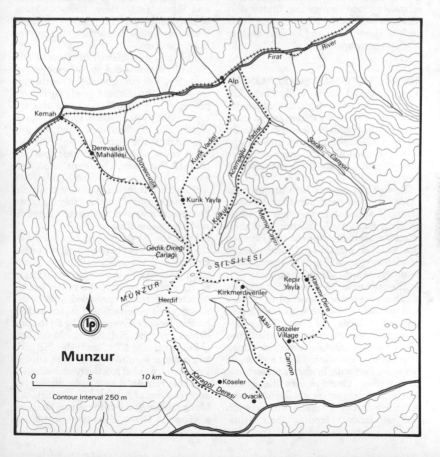

# Central Anatolia

Trekking in central Turkey means volcano-scaling or walking through landscapes which are largely the result of volcanic activity. Most people associate volcanoes with the 'Ring of Fire' around the Pacific, but tend to forget that the Mediterranean basin is also a place where the earth's crustal plates collide, resulting in similar hot spots. The Anatolian steppe is certainly not the Mediterranean, but in geological terms the African plate is relatively close, burrowing under Asia Minor as well as the Aegean, with vents such as Hasan Dağı and Erciyes Dağı to mark its presence.

## IHLARA (PERISTREMA) VALLEY DAYHIKE

This delightful short walk along the length of the 11-km Melendiz Suyu gorge, including visits to the important group of early frescoed churches found in its walls, will be a welcome change for anyone who is disillusioned with the commercialism prevailing at Göreme 75 km to the north-east.

Though the murals here are in most cases in poorer condition than those in central Cappadocia, they are of equal religious and artistic interest, and their effect is magnified by the contrast between the level of culture and achievement which they represent and the superlatively beautiful natural surroundings.

The canyon varies in width but its floor is almost everywhere cloaked in poplars and willows, and alive with the song of millions of birds and frogs. The whole setting is reminiscent of landscapes deeper in central Asia, with the added attraction of the warm-toned rock walls honeycombed with laboriously hewn-out monasteries, churches, dwellings and stables. Contemporary village life is also much in evidence; for much of the way you will see farmers tending their fields, women laundering, and (of course) curious children.

Melendiz Dağı to the south-east cradles a high valley rich in springs, a rarity in central Anatolia. These unite to form the Melendiz Suyu, which on its way to dissipation in the salt expanses of Tüz Gölü to the north-east, has carved a gorge through the relatively soft tufa commonly found between elevations of 1200 and 1500 metres in the vicinity of both Erciyes Dağı and Hasan Dağı. Here, though, except near Selime and Yaprakhısar villages, there are no pinnacles or fairy chimneys as in Cappadocia.

The area was ignored in classical and Hellenistic times due to its remoteness, though it was considered the south-west corner of the Roman and Byzantine province of Cappadocia. Local modern roads pretty much follow Roman rights-of-way, one of which connected Aksaray (then Archelais) with Niğde and Seleucia via a track which passed near, but not through, the valley. Thus Peristrema, as it was then known, was both relatively secluded but sufficiently close to the main pilgrimage routes to the Holy Land to become a favoured monastic centre in mid-Byzantine times.

From the 7th to the 10th centuries AD, the shifting border between the Byzantine Empire and the Arab caliphates to the south-east was always within virtual sight of Peristrema, so that the many nearby frontier garrisons provided additional security for the hermits and monks in their hidden redoubt. Even after the Byzantine defeat by the Seljuks at Manzikert (Malazgırt) in 1071 and the Seljuk's subsequent dominion over Cappadocia, Peristrema was left relatively undisturbed, and this remained true even during the depredations of Anatolia by Timurlane's Mongols during the 13th century. Indeed, a vigorous Greek Christian population persisted in the valley's villages until the exchange of populations under the terms of the Treaty of Lausanne in 1923.

There are reputedly 150 churches in the entire canyon between the villages of Selime and Ihlara, but of these only 11 have any substantial wall decoration left. The remaining frescoes date from the 7th century AD until the end of the 12th century, well into the Seljuk era, and are clearly divided into two groups representing the endpoints of this time period. The earlier cluster at the south end of the valley displays a marked similarity to Coptic, Syrian and so-called 'Paleo-Christian' decorative art, hardly surprising since at least some of the painters were probably refugees from the Arab caliphates. This group, with its often Gnostic or Apocryphal subject matter and naive style, is clearly distinct from the later, northerly group which adheres more strictly to Byzantine iconography.

Three of the earlier churches – Ağaç Altı, Yılanlı and Sümbüllü – are fairly obvious, since they are nearest the tourist pavilion north of Ihlara village and also because they have maintained steps leading up to them. Finding most of the others, though, is something of an Easter-egg hunt, involving scrambling up scree piles to the correct one of perhaps half-a-dozen promising-looking entrances in the cliff face.

The accompanying map shows the approximate locations of the other eight painted churches, but your chances of finding them will be improved even more by possession of the one excellent, literate guide to the valley, entitled simply *Churches of Ihlara Valley*. This appears to be a pirated English edition of *Nouvelles eglises rupestres de Cappadoce* (Paris, 1965), as the title page is conspicuously absent, and the sole publication information available is 'Okan Kitabevi, Yakıcılar Sokak 10A, Sıhhiye, Ankara', and 'Ihlara Vadisi Turistik Tesisi', (the tourist pavilion), presumably the only two points of sale.

If you wish to start the dayhike from Selime or Yaprakhısar as described below you might have to do without the book, but guide or not, the most important piece of equipment will be a powerful flashlight, as almost all the churches are dimly lit inside.

**Rating/Duration**

This is an easy three-hour outing. If done going upstream, this walk fits in nicely with the ascent of Hasan Dağı (see next section).

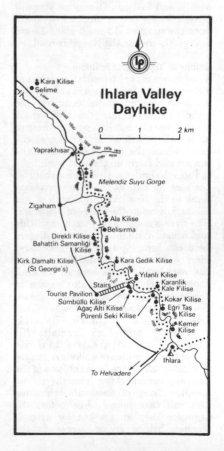

### Supplies

Opportunities are limited in Selime, only somewhat better in Ihlara, so you may want to stock up on snacks in Aksaray.

### Map

Included with *Churches of Ihlara Valley*.

### Getting to the Trailhead

From Aksaray to Selime, Yaprakhısar and Ihlara villages there is at least one daily bus at around 11.30 am, though there may be another midday vehicle since there are two in the reverse direction at 6.30 and 8.30 am. Otherwise you will have to hire a taxi or hitch 25 to 35 km from the signposted turnoff some 13 km east of Aksaray on the Nevşehir road.

### Selime or Yaprakhısar to Ihlara

The narrows of the Melendiz Suyu start at Selime, an interesting enough village with at least one monastic complex (no paintings) hewn into the cliff which overshadows it, but it is perhaps best to start walking below Yaprakhısar, at the point where the auto road crosses the stream and starts up the west bank.

From the bridge it's less than an hour on the east (or left, as you face upstream) bank to the first frescoed church of Ala Kilise, just before the village of Belisırma. The river is not potable – too many fields and houses drain into it – so the villagers here can bring you water if necessary. Here you should cross the footbridge to the west bank, partly because the trail there is much better and also because of the presence of two pure springs ahead, but mostly because three of the four other later churches – Direkli, Bahattin Samanliğik and Kırk Damaltı (St George's) – are on that side of the river.

Another hour-plus of walking separates the Belisırma bridge from the base of the stairway coming down from the tourist pavilion, though of course with sightseeing you will take longer. Just before the staircase keep an eye out for a small wooden bridge giving access to the

opposite bank and the enormous Yılanlı Kilise; the trail on this side continues some 25 minutes more to the Eğri Taş church but is thereafter swamped by the stream.

At the top of the cement stairs which enter the valley between the Sümbüllü and Ağaç Altı churches, you will find a tastefully conceived restaurant/drinkstand with excellent views over the area. You can buy the *Churches of the Ihlara Valley* guidebook here.

To re-enter the gorge from this point you will have to pay an admission fee, as the entire canyon from Belisırma upstream is a national park. Camping is not allowed in the park, but the helpful staff at the pavilion may rent you one of a limited number of simple beds at a reasonable price (they are really intended for staff). Otherwise your alternative is to continue through the valley to Ihlara village, where there are a couple of simple *pansiyonlar*, restaurants and a campground.

Returning to the bottom of the park entrance stairway, adopt the west bank trail, which passes under the Pürenli Seki and Kokar churches after an hours walk to the south end of the Peristrema valley. This is marked by a giant boulder wedged in between the cliffs at a particularly narrow point to form a natural bridge between the two neighbourhoods of Ihlara village. But the trail itself never quite makes it to that point, being forced up to the village by the increasingly steep terrain a few hundred metres before.

## HASAN DAĞI

The conical Hasan Dağı does not dominate the landscape in the same way as its cousin Erciyes to the north-east. Furthermore, some geographers dismiss it as merely the western appendage of the larger (though lower) Melendiz range, to which it is physically linked by the intermediate peak of Keçikboyduran.

Yet in its own way it is a beautiful mountain, less forbidding than Erciyes and more accessible to the casual hiker.

The flanks of the volcanic cone drop steeply to a relatively flat apron to the south, west and north-west, with a more gradual series of plateaus and ridges to the north and north-east, where most of the best campsites are to be found. Also on the north slopes are occasional patches of forest, summer *yaylalar*, and strangest of all, the ruins of several Byzantine churches, absolutely the very south-westernmost in Cappadocia.

Wildlife is also much in evidence. We saw marmots, hawks and millions of migrating – or mating – ladybugs. Wolves can be a nuisance to the locals; as summer progresses the wolves leave their habitual haunts in the low-altitude oak forests and climb closer to the high pastures to bag the odd sheep.

### Rating/Duration
This is a moderately difficult two-to-three day trek. We suggest that you start either from Yenipınar or Sütlü Kilise, make an appropriate camp for two nights, and then descend to Helvadere via Vıranşehir, which really merits a visit.

### Season
Although permanent water is available on the mountain at the points detailed, a late spring or early summer visit (mid-June at the latest, late May after a mild winter) is advisable because some snow provides for hiking interest and wildflower displays. The *yaylalar* are inhabited after snowmelt, and the caldera lakes are then uncovered as well, but the summer heat is a factor to contend with.

### Supplies
Buy supplies in Aksaray; Helvadere will have basic staples only.

### Map
None known.

### Getting to the Trailhead
If you are coming from a dayhike through the Ihlara valley, you should hire a tractor or a taxi in Ihlara village (tractor available from the storekeeper) for the 15-km transfer to either Yenipınar or Helvadere village. (Consult the route descriptions below to decide where you want to start.) A tractor ride to either village will cost about US$8 and will save you at least a half-day's walking. For a couple of dollars more, the driver (tractors only!) will take you a few km further above Helvadere to the end of the rutted track at treeline, just below the Sütlü Kilise.

If you are not coming from the Ihlara valley, there is a morning bus from Aksaray to Helvadere (and back as well); if you miss it there are taxis and just possibly an occasional minibus. Helvadere itself has one restaurant and several simple stores, but you would have to sleep in the *köy odası* (travellers' lodge).

It is also possible to approach the summit from the village of Gözlüköyü; you get there by taking any bus going from Aksaray to Taşpınar and then arranging transport the five or so km east to the village.

### Sütlü Kilise Route
From the last oaks at the end of the tractor/jeep track, round the bend of the hill until you see the Sütlü Kilise or 'Milky Church'. The two apses of this double-naved sanctuary are buried to half their height in rubble. From this point, though, a fairly clear trail leads within two hours, up the ridge behind, to an exposed *yayla* on a saddle at the foot of a higher hill to the north-west.

This hill is called Bozboyun, and is important for two reasons. On its summit are the remains of yet another church, the Han Kilise. The name is perhaps derived from its narrow, hall-like dimensions, visible today only in some knee-high foundations. Of possibly more interest is the fact that in the giant ravine at the base of Bozboyun there is a year-round running spring, one of the few on the mountain. A path leads down to it from the saddle *yayla*, and you can see another trail

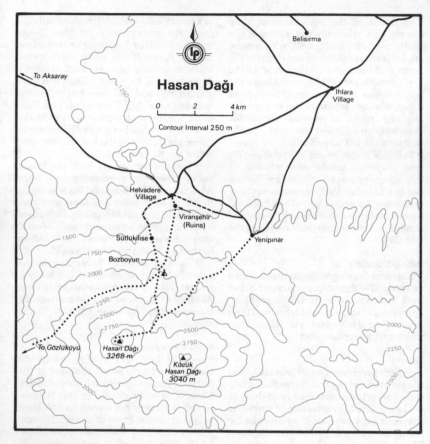

Hasan Dağı

0    2    4 km

Contour Interval 250 m

To Aksaray

Belisırma

Ihlara Village

Helvadere Village

Viranşehir (Ruins)

Sütlükilise

Bozboyun

Yenipınar

To Gözlüköyü

Hasan Dağı 3268 m

Küçük Hasan Dağı 3040 m

traversing the opposite scree bank of the ravine. The spring is just at the spot where the paths meet; this is also incidentally the way you would begin skirting Hasan Dağı to get to Gözlüköyü.

Twenty to 45 minutes above and to the south-south-east of Bozboyun is a series of three grassy meadows, plus one more clearing to the north-east of the middle meadow. These all have their advantages as base camps for the summit approach. The largest, lowest one is a working *yayla* after snowmelt, and is the most protected if the wind is up. The topmost one has the

best view, but you may be most interested in the lone one off to one side. Here an ingenious culvert system channels the snowmelt and drains into a huge cistern which holds water all summer long. There are several holes to get water from, including a large entrance with steps down if you haven't got a bucket.

From this cluster of meadows, it's three-plus hours up, first on a south-easterly, then a southerly, bearing to the anonymous peak 3268 (10 or 15 metres less on some maps). It should be emphasised that the peak which you see from the north is the lower, secondary summit, even though it, and not the true summit, has a flag planted on it! You should still climb it, however, in order to circle the crater zone in a counterclockwise direction en route to 3268. One of the tributaries of the Melendiz Suyu begins in the high valley just to the north-east of the secondary peak, and after snowmelt is complete, a three-metre-deep well is reportedly exposed in this area.

The summit caldera is double, with the higher but smaller caldera to the south at the base of peak 3268, from which you have the sort of magnificent vistas one would expect from an isolated peak of this elevation. In summer each of the craters contains a lake, but they are both quite unpotable, even sterile, owing to the amount of sulphur dioxide bubbling up through them.

### Vıranşehir Route

From Helvadere itself, a conspicuous trail climbs up from the back of town through a notch in the ridge behind. After 20 minutes you come out onto a vast meadow, with the extensive ruins of a Byzantine town on your right. The landscape is studded with vaults and walls; most obvious are two impressive churches a few hundred metres further up the meadow. The first church still has two arches, some walls, a crypt or cistern, and a separate chapel intact; it was built on an east-west axis with the now-shattered apse facing east.

The other church, about 200 metres directly south, is in better condition but is currently used as a goat pen. Its character is considerably diminished by bricked-in arches, a padlock and thornbush goat-proofing. Both the churches and the town probably date from the same 7th to 10th Centuries AD period which saw the flourishing of nearby Ihlara.

The main trail up to the alpine zone from Vıranşehir continues on the other (east) side of the long meadow. It is fairly heavily used, so you should have some company at least part of the way. Once out of Vıranşehir meadow, the trail wanders up a series of narrow pastures flanked by oak-tufted ridges. From here you should see two wooded and two bare hillocks to the south-west, with the secondary peak of Hasan Dağı just behind them. The proper trail proceeds to the right (north-west) flank of the first wooded hillock, then climbs onto a small flat area to the left of the second hump before disappearing in the oak-leaf litter.

You must now ascend the ridgeline of the second knoll. The route eventually flattens out, pleasantly, between two hogbacks, to continue on a very straight course for some minutes. At treeline, go just left of straight ahead to continue up a series of valleys and tiny meadows, with a very occasional trail, until you reach the *yayla* with the giant cistern on the Sütlü Kilise route. The total time up from Helvadere will be almost five hours.

Coming down from the cistern pasture, you should get to Helvadere in about 3½ hours. Looking from the cistern you might first familiarise yourself with various landmarks. The reservoir just to the north of Helvadere is plainly visible, as is the series of long, narrow meadows just below the oak woods (Vıranşehir is out of view). You want to avoid a large, round meadow to the east. The hillock at treeline, with its two parallel hogbacks, is also in sight.

### Yenipınar Route

Our information on this approach is second-hand, but we do know that above this village you would have to cross through thick forest before reaching, after at least five hours, a cluster of *yaylalar* similar to those above Helvadere. These would be somewhat lower in altitude than the latter, making for a longer ascent to the summit area the next day, but in compensation the grade up the river canyon to the saddle joining Kücük Hasan Dağı (3040 metres) with the secondary summit would be gentler.

### Bozboyun to Gözlüköyü

From the spring at Bozboyun you could climb out of the giant ravine and march along the north-west base of the volcanic cone, but you would have to avoid the heads of a half-dozen successive ravines – none as large as the first – on your way to the above-named village. It would be rather dull going, too, for five hours; the only pluses would be a possible detour to the church of Bozdağ, visible from Bozboyun, such *yayla* life as you would encounter, and easy exit from Gözlüköyü.

### Gözlüköyü to 3268

This could just barely be feasible as a dayhike – seven hours up, four down – around the date of the summer solstice. This is not much shorter than the approach from Helvadere and it might be wise to break up the ascent with a camp at a *yayla* above Gözlüköyü. Overnighting in the village itself would involve relying on traditional Turkish rural hospitality.

### ERCİYES DAĞI

Erciyes Dağı, Mt Argaeus of the classical era, dominates the skyline to the south-west of the city of Kayseri, and while high enough at 3917 metres, it seems even higher since, like few other peaks on the Anatolian plateau, it rises suddenly and solitarily from the flat country around it. In ancient times the peak was an important focus of Zoroastrian worship.

Erciyes is an extinct volcano, similar in appearance to other mountains of this type (particularly Mt Kenya and certain peaks in Mexico and South America), but is a particularly harsh mountain, with little vegetation to soften its symmetrical contours. A girdle of secondary cones (also extinct) guards the approaches to the mountain from the north and west; to the south and east the landscape is much less complicated.

In summary Erciyes, with its perpetual snowcap and jagged summit, is a more tempting target for the technical climber or cross-country skier, but there is one

recognised traverse route which will give you a good look at the peak from two angles, as well as a healthy hike, if you're not inclined or equipped to tackle the top.

### Rating/Duration

This is a moderately strenuous two-to-three day outing which can be allotted in a number of ways. Our strategy was to camp at the recommended campsite above Tekir Yaylası, at about 3000 metres, make the ascent of 3917 as a dayhike, and traverse the following day all the way to Söğütlüpinar (though in retrospect it might have been wiser to make another camp in the vicinity of the two mountain huts).

Alternatively you might overnight at the Kayak Evi, reach the pair of shelters at the end of a very long day (assuming a day hike to the summit), and descend to Hacılar the next morning. If you've no tent, not too much time, but perhaps some money to spare, we suggest you hire a jeep-taxi in Hacılar up to the old mountain shelter and make a one-day traverse east to the Kayak Evi, then do a dayhike up to the top the following morning.

If the lack of public transport out of Söğütlüpinar is daunting, it's quite possible to do the traverse in reverse; the altitude gain/loss is the same though there's a somewhat better chance of getting lost. You would follow the ravine from Aksuyurdu up to the *yayla* below Süt Donduran, thus skipping the area around the alpine huts entirely.

In Kayseri the terminus for the Hacılar buses is on Nazimbey Caddesi, in the north-west part of town, near the Hotel Erdoğan. There is only one morning service to Seher Paşa Durağı.

### Season

Because of the apparent shortage of springwater on the mountain, and because snow provides much of the interest – and challenge – on this traverse, this is a good outing for late May, June or early July. Ice axe and gaiters are strongly recommended even if you're not planning to bag the peak – the snowfields are extensive and, as the weather warms up, progressively mushier.

## Supplies

The Kayseri bazaar is fun but rather time-consuming as you must go to the various specialty shops to assemble your menu. The quickest one-stop source is the *Beğendik Supermarket* in the city centre, right next to the Sahibiye Medresse.

## Map

The Tourist Office hands out a really excellent map, at a scale of 1:80,000, drawn up by Dr Bozkurt Ergör, head of the local mountaineering club. This is a reduction of a 1:25,000 large-format blueprint which is not as readily available.

## Guides

If you would like to speak to Dr Ergör (German or Turkish only), his office is at Millet Caddesi 17, tel 21-513. An associate, Tekin Kücüknalbant, speaks some English; his number is 13-393.

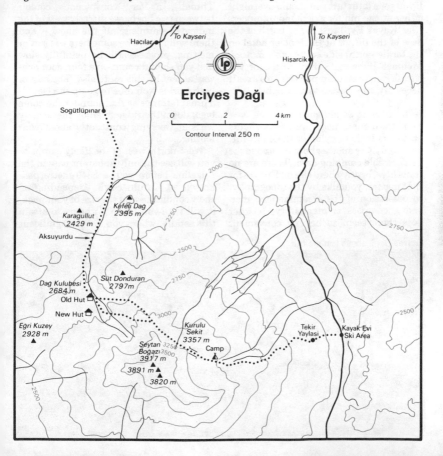

### Getting to the Trailhead

The hike described below starts from the Kayak Evi ('Ski House') at Tekir Yaylası, a plateau 26 km south of Kayseri at an altitude of 2150 metres. A taxi will take you up there for a flat rate of about $US8. There is bus service as far as the village of Hısarcık, 16 km below the ski centre, but a taxi from here on would probably cost as much as from Kayseri anyway, so this strategy, entailing an extra three hours of road walking up to Tekir Yaylası, is only for the impecunious.

There is no accommodation at Hısarcık. If you get a late start you should overnight either at the inn for skiers/mountaineers (the 'Kayak Evi') just to the north of the base of the lift, or at the fancier hotel on the far (ie south) side of the cable motors. Mehmet Babayiğit, the warden of the Kayak Evi, rents crampons and ice axes if necessary and speaks some English.

### Tekir Yaylası to Söğütlüpınar

From the mountaineers' inn it's two hours up to the highest pylon of the chair lift, and from there another hour beyond to the first feasible camping area. There are no trails here, or anywhere else on Erciyes for that matter; you hike by the topography, so possession of the recommended map and a compass is mandatory. Neither does there seem to be any convenient springs in the alpine zone, though we did see a rather dilapidated, frozen-over aqueduct in the gully just to the north of our campsite as indicated on the map.

From this base camp there are perhaps three routes – two accepted, and one questionable – up to the nameless peak 3917. The easiest, but perhaps least efficient approach involves following the long, continuous ridge which encloses the high alpine bowl where you've camped; this would take at least 4½ hours.

The most direct route is through the aptly named Şeytan Boğazı ('Devil's Throat'), a very conspicuous couloir between two hogbacks directly west of the indicated campsite. If the snow – and there will always be some here – is soft or melting, progress will be painfully slow and you should count on a four-hour one-way ascent by this route also. The best of both worlds would be to go up the Devil's Throat (strange as that sounds) and come back down the ridge to enjoy the scenery without worrying constantly about your footing.

West-north-west of the likely campsite you will see the only apparent pass in the ridgeline before you, a 3340-metre pass known as Kurulu Sekit. Depending on snow conditions and the size of your pack, it will take you 1¾ to 2½ hours to attain this saddle, where you have magnificent

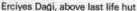

Erciyes Dağı, above last life hut

views over the country behind and ahead of you. There is a hogback leading south-west from here up towards 3917 and it is tempting to take this route to the peak, but the rock looked crumbly, there appeared to be some traverses past unprotected sheer drops, and we therefore cannot recommend it with confidence.

Assuming that you have brought your full pack up to Kurulu Sekit, it's another 75 minutes to the next, lower saddle at the base of 3261, somewhat south-west of the hill designated as 3061. Another hour-plus of walking (for a total of four since quitting the campsite) should put you over the spur plunging down from the summit area to the satellite cone Süt Donduran ('Freezes Milk') – 2797 metres.

You should see a *yayla* in the hollow at the foot of 2797, but you don't want to dip that low unless you want to skip the stop at the mountain shelters. One of the shelters is actually in sight from the ridge above Süt Donduran, but is a lot further away than it looks – an hour if you aim correctly across the descending ridge system, 90 minutes distant if you drop too low toward the *yayla* and have to climb into and out of a couple gullies.

The shelter, at an altitude of 2684 metres, is in extremely dilapidated condition and is actually more useful as a landmark than anything else. There is good early summer camping in the meadows just beyond it, and most of all superb views of the snowfields and glacier adorning the north-east face of Erciyes.

There is a new hut under construction some several hundred metres south-south-west of the old one, at an altitude of 2711 metres, but as of this writing only the foundations have been completed. As at the campsite above Tekir Yaylası it seems one would be dependent on snowmelt for water near either of the huts.

To complete the traverse to Sögütlüpınar, leave the old hut by the jeep road heading initially north-north-east. Shortcuts across the bends are possible, and at one turn a proper old trail heads straight down

toward a water pumping/filtration plant along the aqueduct which has erupted suddenly from the hitherto bone-dry mountain. An hour-plus of walking should suffice to get you from the old mountain shelter to Aksuyurdu, as the water plant is locally known.

The trough-shaped ravine just above Aksuyurdu in fact leads relatively gradually up to the *yayla* at the base of Süt Donduran, and is the preferred access to the alpine zone if you're climbing Erciyes from the Sögütlüpınar side (see Rating/Duration). Facing downhill once more, skirt the largest cistern below the water plant and adopt a pleasant track down through green meadows until rejoining the main road.

After threading your way through a rocky gorge and seeing perhaps your first tree in a couple days, you arrive after 90 minutes at a quarry with a spring – the Sögütlüpınar – just below it, recognisable by the adjacent lone pine tree (though the name means Willow Spring).

From the area around the quarry you've a panorama of the attractive high plateau, studded with poplars, known as Sakar, which functions more or less as the garden suburb of Hacılar, the nearest major town. The older buildings at Sakar feature curious vaulted annexes which are either stables or crop storage cellars, of a type not seen elsewhere in Anatolia.

Keep to the main, partially cobbled route, taking the left fork below the quarry and shortly after passing another weak spring and a turnoff to a sandpit. A half-hour below Sögütlüpınar you'll come to the shelter for the marked Seker Paşa Durağı bus-stop, from where there is service daily only at 5.30 pm. If you've missed it, you must continue another 30 minutes, until just past Yeşil Durak bus-stop, and turn right (east) at the right-angled intersection. Another 30 minutes of walking over the ridge before you gets you to Hacılar, which while it has no restaurant or hotel does have some stores, and buses every 30 minutes to Kayseri.

# Around Lake Van

The shimmering expanse of Lake Van, the largest in Turkey, is the centrepiece linking the scattered peaks of this corner of the country. The other common factor is the predominately Kurdish population in the hinterlands of Ağrı, Süphan and the Cilo-Sat Dağları. The main trunk road to Iran notwithstanding, this is some of the highest, wildest and least developed terrain in Turkey. When the government agreed in 1981 to accept some 14,000 Kirshiz and Uzbek refugees from Afghanistan, it chose the Van basin as the region most resembling their homeland and resettled them there.

Much negative publicity has been broadcast of late about the ongoing conflict between the Kurdish guerrillas and the Turkish government. This is not the place to comment on the merits and demerits of their respective positions; we will only say that things here don't necessarily work as they do in western Turkey, and to keep your ear to the ground. What may be allowed today may be restricted tomorrow – and (hopefully) vice-versa.

## The Cilo/Sat Dağları

The Cilo/Sat range is tucked into the extreme south-east corner of Turkey, in the province of Hakkari. This joint chain is oriented along a north-north-west to south-south-east axis, with the portion north-west of İştazin village and the road through it being referred to as the Cilo group, while the massif lying in the opposite direction is known as the Sat.

A total of eleven peaks in the region exceed 3500 metres, with the Cilo area sporting the highest points of Uludoruk (Gelyaşın, Reşko) at 4136 metres and Buzul (Suppadurek) at 4116. They are by all accounts the most spectacular mountains in Turkey and provide some of the best trekking.

The range exhibits a rather jagged profile, owing to the ongoing action of the largest remaining glaciers in Turkey and the many swift streams in the area. In mid-summer the snow and ice cover recedes to the 3000-metre level, leaving in its wake high, level plateaus ideal for camping and *yayla* life. There are a number of glacier-fed lakes, abundant wildlife including mountain goats and larger birds of prey, and even some Stone Age pictographs discovered some years ago near Sat Gevaruk.

### Warning

Unfortunately during the past 20 years the area has been closed to outsiders more often than not, owing to the unpredictable activities of the PKK separatist guerrillas. If you attempt to leave the main roads in the area you will be turned back at army or police checkpoints, and even if you were successful in eluding them you could count on an unfriendly, possibly fatal, reception from any guerrillas you might meet.

It follows therefore that we have not personally been to Cilo/Sat, but as in the case of the Munzur we have translated material from ADB bulletins and the files of the Tourism Ministry's mountaineering desk, and present it in the hope that at some point in the near future the region will once again be open to trekkers.

The same caveats set forth for Munzur apply here: trails are implied but in fact may be only cross-country routes, elapsed walking-time reports are second-hand, and above all check in with the *local* authorities before setting off into the hills. Under the circumstances an encouraging or discouraging signal from an official in Ankara or İstanbul is fairly meaningless.

It might be worthwhile to hire local escorts and pack animals in Hakkari, Yüksekova or İştazin.

The Cilo/Sat are inhabited mostly by Kurds, and place names below are given first in Kurdish, with the Turkish alternate (if any) following in parentheses. It is helpful at the outset to know that der (deri in the genitive) means pass and zoma is the Kurdish equivalent of yayla.

### Season
Most practical season is from mid-June to early October. Rain is not likely during this time, but there will be a considerable snowpack early in summer after a severe winter.

### Supplies
Get them primarily in Van, especially if you're not going all the way to Hakkari, though it and Yüksekova should have staple foodstuffs.

### Map
None confirmed.

### Getting to the Trailheads
The aspiring trekker has several choices. From Hakkari town you can take a minibus or full-sized one 20 km north-east toward Van and disembark at the Zap Karakolu (jandarma post). Cross the river Zap which parallels the highway, and then begin walking along the left (north-east) bank of the Avaspi (Beyazsu), a main tributary of the Zap.

Starting from Yüksekova, board a local minibus headed for Oramar (Dağlıca) but get down at the stop for İştazin village (about 1½ hours along) and walk north-west (away from İştazin) toward the village of Serpil. Another option would be to take a taxi from Yüksekova to the hamlet of Orişa and then trek west along the north side of the Cilo watershed toward Deri Cafer pass.

To reach the Sat mountains, take the

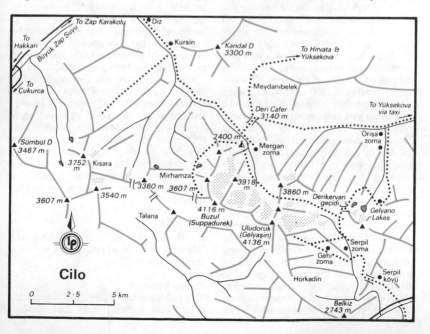

bus to İştazin junction as described above but this time cross the river going south-south-east *toward* İştazin village, which you will pass through on the way to İştazin *zoma*.

## CİLO TREK
### Rating/Duration

This is a rigorous but rewarding trek if you are lucky enough to be permitted into the backcountry here. Suggested camps are as follows:

Day 1,2 – Mergan *zoma* (with dayhikes)
Day 3 – Meydanıbelek or Orişa
Day 4 – Gelyano lakes
Day 5,6 – Serpil *zoma* (with dayhikes)
Day 7 – İştazin junction

### Route Directions

Avaspi, the name of the stream which you follow south-east from the Zap gendarme post, means 'whitewater' in Kurdish, as does the Turkish alias. After passing the villages of Diz and Kursin, you will encounter two tributaries coming down from the right (south-west); stay on the left bank in order to follow the main watercourse to Mergan *zoma*, where you will make the first night's camp. This lies at an elevation of 2400 metres, and is six hours in from the trailhead. With this as a base camp you can undertake enjoyable dayhikes to the bases of Uludoruk (Gelyaşin, Reşko) and Buzul (Suppadurek), but the ascent of their actual summits from this side is a Class-5 endeavour requiring full ice-climbing and rock-climbing gear.

From Mergan retrace your steps toward Zap for one km, and then climb north-east toward the Deri Cafer pass, one of the few breaching the ridge above this bank of the Avaspi. The grade is reportedly very steep but even so there is still a trail suitable for mules. Once over the top you descend to Meydanıbelek, a flat, green meadow which could serve as a contingency camp. Otherwise you would continue to Orişa for

the second camp, 5½ walking hours from Mergan. If you want more privacy, you might try staking your tent at the *zoma* above Orişa. In emergencies you can also end the trek prematurely by exiting from the village to Yüksekova via taxi.

From Orişa, the trail heads due south along the stream bed up toward the Gelyano lakes, which while slightly off the trail would seem a good place to make a third camp if you were not pressed for time. The main route veers west-north-west at the *zoma* below the lakes, and after crossing a minor ridge tackles the main watershed via the Derikervan pass. Descend south from this to Serpil *zoma*, on the south-west bank of the stream draining this valley.

This is the classic base camp for Class 3 ascents of Uludoruk (Gelyaşin, Reşko). You can get there from the *yayla* by either heading over a pass to the west, or by repositioning three km downstream opposite the mouth of the side valley leading up to Gehi *zoma*. The summit is reportedly eight hours away via Gehi, if carrying daypacks, but we have the impression that this applies only if you camp near the entrance to the Gehi valley rather than further up at Serpil *zoma*.

From the latter you can also take a dayhike up the main valley to the saddle between peak 3860 and Uludoruk (essentially meeting the point attained on a dayhike up from Mergan). Finally, you will leave the valley in the opposite direction, heading south-east over the pass separating the *zoma* of Serpil from the village of the same name, from where it's a brief trek out to the road at İştazin turnoff.

## SAT TREK

If you are up for more trekking the following can be appended nicely to a traverse of the Cilo.

### Rating/Duration

The full itinerary as proposed is probably a bit more difficult than that through

Top: Old bridge above Çat, Kaçkar Range (MD)
Bottom: Deniz Gölü showing lone campsite, Kaçkar Range (MD)

Top: Knitting at Pişenkaya Yayla, Kaçkar Range (MD)
Left: On the track out of Barhal, Kaçkar Range (EL)
Right: Yayla Amaneskit, Kaçkar Range (EL)

Cilo. Suggested nightstops would be as follows:

Day 1 – Dehi *zoma*
Day 2,3 – Sat Başı *zoma* (with dayhikes)
Day 4 – Sat Gevaruk *zoma*
Day 5 – Bay Gölü
Day 6 – Sorinki *zoma* area
Day 7 – Piskasir/Yüksekova

### Route Directions

From İştazin village itself continue south-east and upstream past its *zoma* and that of Dehi. If you are caught short by nightfall, the latter could be your first camp. Otherwise tackle the pass ahead to reach Sat Başı *zoma* and camp by the numerous lakes nearby, which are reached 6½ trekking hours above İştazin. You should budget two nights' camp here to allow exploration of the basin.

From here our route bears south-east, crossing another route or trail going from south-to-north over a pass between Sat Başı summit and peak 3396. Skirt the spur plunging north from the latter, and get over the ridge just to the east to drop briefly into the watershed south of 3396. Do not lose much altitude but head for a pass to the east which gives access to the valley containing Sat Gevaruk *zoma*. Once on the other side there is possibly a proper trail the rest of the way to Sat Gevaruk, where you can camp by the south end of the lake. Total elapsed hiking time between Sat Başı and Sat Gevaruk should not exceed 5½ hours.

You could ask the inhabitants of the *zoma* where the *kaya resimleri* (pictographs) are, and if they understand you they should point you in the right direction or possibly even take you there. Time permitting, the Samdi Dorukları peaks to the south are said to be worth a visit.

When you are ready to leave Sat Gevaruk, cross the stream and find the pass north-north-east of the lake and north-north-west of Terazin summit

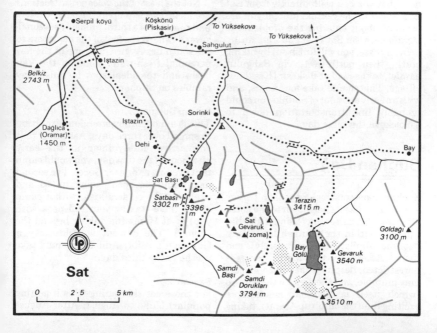

(3415). Once you've put this behind you, you face yet another one to the north of an intervening valley; approaches to both passes are likely to be scree slopes. After attaining the second gap, you need to find, somewhere below you, a major junction on the main trail/livestock route linking Bay village and Sorinki *yayla*. Veer south-east from this point, on a trail or otherwise, to recross the ridge bounding this valley on the south, and then head south-south-west to Bay Gölü, thus completing a virtual circle around Terazin. The lake, some six hours on foot beyond Sat Gevaruk, is famous for the many glaciers overhanging it and the riotous wildflower and summer turf growth.

To conclude your trek, backtrack to the big intersection on the Bay-Sorinki route and follow such paths as there are west-north-west to the latter. Camp above this *zoma* near the confluence of two streams, where you should arrive some 5½ hours after quitting Bay Gölü. (It is only fair to note that you can walk directly from Sat Başı *zoma* to the Sorinki area, if you are hesitant about entering the problematic terrain between Sat Başı and Terazin.)

In any case, you will finish out by hiking north, then north-west, via Sahgulut hamlet, to the road at Piskasir (Köşkönü) village. This should take four hours, and with an early start out of Sorinki you could probably find transportation down to Yüksekova the same day.

# Süphan Dağ

Suphan, the second highest peak in Turkey after Ağrı, is like its neighbour to the north a volcano (though extinct), and it also lies squarely within the Kurdish homeland, but the similarities (fortunately) end there. Access to the alpine zone is unrestricted, despite what some villagers may mumble, and the view on the way up (which itself is not that much more exciting than the climb up Ararat), taking

in as it does vast portions of the Lake Van basin, is arguably more spectacular than that to be had from the top of Ağrı Dağ and certainly more dependable. Hearing of this, an increasing number of foreigners are coming to hike each year and on any given summer day there is likely to be at least one climber somewhere on the peak.

Seen from the standard automobile approach routes, Süphan doesn't look like much – a broad, flattish mountain that isn't notably higher than its surroundings, the 1720-metre-high Van basin. But unlike the discrete cones of Ağrı, Erciyes and Hasan Dağlar, it's something of a Chinese puzzle box: layer after layer of ridges and false summits that make it easy to miss the true peak. Even the cartographers are a bit vague about Süphan's maximum elevation; the standard figure of 4434 metres does not jibe with the value of 13,314 feet (or just over 4300 metres) listed on British and American military maps.

Not the least of the volcano's attractions are its lakes – two up in the outer caldera and rumours of a third, probably seasonal, lower down. At the foot of the mountain to the south lies Aygır Gölü, one of the few perennial fresh-water lakes in the Van basin and the ideal spot to finish any rambles on Süphan.

## Rating/Duration
This is a moderately strenuous excursion to spread over three days. Assuming that you arrive at Aydinlar in the early afternoon of the first day, you would camp that evening at or near Göcer. The second day would be spent going up to and exploring the caldera area, with a camp either there (taking your full pack with you) or at Horaz (dayhiking beyond the couloir). The descent to Yıldız, Aygır Gölü and possibly Adilcevaz would take up the entire third day.

## Season
For those not ski touring (this is getting popular), June to August. After August

water is not so much a problem as is severe weather (snow, cold) sets in.

## Supplies
Tatvan or Van are the best places; Adilcevaz is a bit primitive in that respect.

## Map
None.

## Getting to the Trailhead
In Van town, minibuses to Adilcevaz, the closest major town to Süphan, leave from beside the Emlak Kredi Bank building in the Beşyol area. Signs on the vehicle will say 'Erciş/Ahlat/Adilcevaz'. However it's easier to get to Adilcevaz from Tatvan, where you'll have a choice of big buses run by long-distance companies or the more frequent minibuses leaving from in front of the post office.

For the minibuses inquire at the 'Erciş Seyahat' *yazıhanı* nearby. Some of these continue the 30 extra km up to Aydinlar village (shown as Kazık on some maps), the classic base for ascents of Süphan from the east, and it is worth staying on your bus for the final leg of the journey, even though the driver will probably overcharge you, rather than hunting around for another conveyance in Adilcevaz. The total fare for the distance Tatvan-Aydinlar should be no more than $US1.75.

## Stage 1: Aydinlar to the Summit via Göcer Yayla
Aydinlar itself is not a very prepossessing Kurdish village and the curious and undisciplined children can be extremely annoying. It is best to leave as quickly as possibly rather than drawing attention to yourself, stopping only to collect water from the highest *çeşme* (fountain).

Exit Aydinlar by going west on the track aiming directly at the peak; you will almost immediately intersect the vehicle

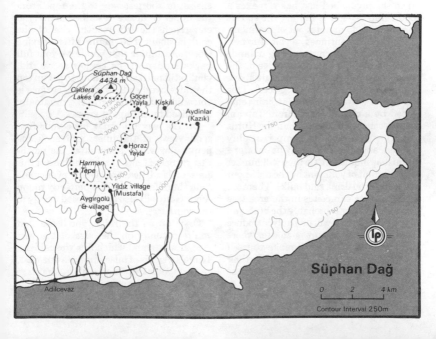

Süphan Dağ

road going up to the village of Kışkılı and a phone relay or radar station. On the high side of the road you should quickly find another 'spring', actually a hole in a pipeline coming down from the mountain. (This may come in handy, as some of the younger villagers are disinclined to even tell you where their fountains are!)

Proceed up the road for about an hour until turning left onto a prominent track which appears a few hundred metres before Kışkılı. Soon there's another fork, with a final take-out hatch in the aqueduct; bear right. The track, still well-defined but narrowed and impassable to vehicles, climbs along a plateau between two ravines.

Dead ahead the east flank of Süphan displays a prominent couloir, full of snow until late in the summer. The track shortly veers right (north) to slip through some narrows at the top of the right-hand ravine; some rank vegetation in the gully marks the location of a slow spring. A sand pit in the ravine bed just below makes a good camp if night is falling; the spot is some 2 hours 45 minutes out of Aydinlar.

The track continues a bit further, veering west again onto slanting uplands at the base of the outermost ridge of the crater zone, before ending 3½ hours above Aydinlar at the *yayla* of Göcer. This consists of a dozen or so goat-hair tents owned by a clan of Kurds from Tatvan. They are more hospitable than the Kurds of Ağri – permission to camp is readily granted, and sheep milk may be on offer – but just as inquisitive (ie they will hunker down in front of your tent by the half-hour and watch you drink said milk). There are other possible campsites in the area (see below) but Göcer is probably the best, and since the shepherds will probably introduce themselves at odd hours no matter where you tent you may as well make yourself known right off and benefit from their intimate knowledge of the mountain as well.

There is no spring at Göcer, only snowmelt. If you don't camp at the *yayla*

there is one obvious place, flecked with green well into August, just to the left of the ravine leading down from the couloir. It's some 45 minutes above Göcer, and some basins have been scooped out of the turf to catch the snowmelt. However before coming up here you should decide which side of the couloir you're going to climb, as the routes end up in different places.

The most direct way to the peak involves starting from Göcer, going up to the next level pasture some 30 minutes above it, and then attaining a still higher plateau on the right (north) bank of the couloir. This in turn gives access to an almost-level ridge leading to the gentlest ascent of the summit mass – a blunt, reddish cone with many jagged edges. On one of the more southerly peaks you'll find the altitude marker, reached some three hours above the *yayla*.

Going up the left bank of the couloir is perhaps more interesting but is not the easiest or shortest way to the top. From the upper campsite described above you can reach the left (south) rim of the couloir about two hours after leaving Göcer. Assuming that you leave your full packs hidden in the couloir as we did, you'll still need another hour to get up top the ridge overhead. The hiking surface is volcanic sand and gravel, minimally stabilised by clumps of grass.

On the way up you'll have your first good views of the inlet, and enclosing peninsula, which punctuates the north-east corner of Lake Van; at the base of this claw of land lies Arin Gölü, even more soda than Van itself. The perfectly round Aygır Gölü will also be glimpsed briefly to the south.

Once up on the ridge, you'll see that you're actually on the edge of the vast glacial wasteland which fills the caldera. There's a series of false summits due west, and at your feet is the main drainage leading out of the caldera area. From this point the true peak cluster, on the right, looks deceptively insignificant; between it and the secondary spur to the south is a snow-clogged valley. Proceed up this until the terrain breaks up into a series of hummocks and a large glacier comes into view on the left.

The hummocks soon resolve into a discrete ridge and some 75 minutes after leaving the top of the couloir's left bank you should get your first look at the larger, green caldera lake, to the right (north). It is permanently glacier-fed and is also reputed to contain pieces of an airplane which crashed in it some 50 years ago. Almost immediately after you'll see the smaller, second lake to the south-west, considerably shrunken at summer's end. If you climb yet another secondary knoll to the west of the larger lake and look back, the primary summit cone will appear obvious and symmetrical above the far shore.

## Stage 2: Summit Area to Aygır Gölü via Yıldız

All this is about 4½ hours above Göcer, assuming a daypack only from the couloir on. You could do far worse than to camp in the caldera area; there are flat places not only in the bed left by the smaller lake as it recedes but also by the large lake and next to the main runoff exit south-east of the snowy valley. It would be quite a long day to visit both the summit and the lakes as a dayhike.

Once you've committed yourself to the left (south) rim of the couloir, the next relatively easy cross-over point between the two routes is at the top of the snow-clogged valley, where the glacier becomes evident and just before the lake overlook. Here bear right across a level area in the noted hummocks to the base of a horrible scree and rockfall slope leading up to 4434.

This climb together with the described look at the lakes will eat up around five hours one-way, plus you must allow three hours to return to the couloir where you will have probably left your pack – a dayhike to consider only for long summer

days. Even then you will have to start thinking about a campsite. Fortunately there is quite a good one, Horaz Yaylasi, just over an hour south of the couloir bank and plainly visible from there.

No change in altitude is needed to reach this green spot with stone rings on the far bank of a dependable torrent. This is the roughest thing you'll have to traverse getting there; collect all the water you'll need for supper and breakfast as there's no water at Horaz proper. On the way you can take a last long look over the Van basin in the late afternoon.

In the morning continue coming off the mountain toward Yıldız village (marked as Mustafa on older maps). It's a 2½ hours descent from Horaz over some rough sand-and-gravel slopes; there's no trail. Once atop the ridge just south of Horaz you merely use Aygır Gölü for navigation. Yıldız is a friendly, helpful village that will correct any negative impressions left by Aydinlar. It's 15 km from Adilcevaz by road; there's no bus service but some shortcuts exist. Water may be a more immediate concern, and Yıldız is very proud of its four springs. Two of them, channelled in from four km to the north-west, are highly mineral but tasty.

Occasionally climbers begin the ascent of Süphan Dağ from Yıldız. In that case you must first head up past the primary source for the mineral fountains to Harman Tepe, which abuts a ridge leading (steeply!) up to the summit zone. There is reported to be plentiful snowmelt in an adjacent canyon well into August.

Keeping on with the more common itinerary, leave Yıldız on the auto road. Just past the first bridge encountered a donkey track shortcuts right and down to the shore of Aygır Gölü. Where this track meets the shore is a good place for a swim – the water is a bit sweet but perfectly drinkable and indeed there are plenty of small but edible fish in the lake. The locals assert that it's bottomless and in fact the drop-off is quite sharp.

Willows and green fields at the north end

of the lake, perhaps 15 minutes from the bottom of the donkey track, hide the tiny village of Aygırgölüköy. The occasional taxi plies the last nine km to Adilcevaz, and it's worth waiting for it or another car, if necessary camping in the greenery near the village.

At the very most, walk around the lake along the ring road to its south end, where several roads join up and more trucks or tractors are likely to pass. Beyond this point it's a long and dusty walk, the lake and environs are beautiful, and extra time spent here, even an overnight, is not burdensome. Keep an eye on your gear, though, if camping – some people we met had things lifted.

# Ağrı Dağ (Mt Ararat)

Ağrı Dağ, or Ararat as it is known in the west, is at 5137 metres (5165 in some sources) the highest mountain in Turkey. It is traditionally considered to be the spot where Noah's ark came to rest after the Great Flood, and numerous expeditions have been mounted in recent years to try and find a chunk of it. In 1987 an American researcher claimed to have found traces of the keel of the ark on a lower, neighbouring peak, but it remains to be seen whether the bubble of Ararat's mystique has been burst or not.

'Ararat' is what the ancient Assyrians called the Urartu kingdom which was centred here as early as the 13th century BC; the word appears to be an elision of 'Uraratu', meaning 'mountain of mountains'. The Armenians, who succeeded the Urartus, merely called it Marsis or Massis, which translates as 'worthy of reverence'. Perhaps the first name, of Semitic origin, was Tanniz, while the current official name of Ağrı has actually been in use for almost 1000 years.

'Ağrı' is claimed by some to be an old Yakut word for 'great god' (the Yakuts were a pagan shamanistic tribe, one of

many Turkic tribes that migrated from Central Asia at the beginning of this millennium). Others dismiss this and assert that the name is really Ağra, a corruption form of Ahora (Ahıra) village on the north slope of the mountain, and that its is neither Turkish nor Armenian but Arabic. So the etymology of the toponym is shrouded in mists, as is frequently the peak itself. However we find the modern Turkish translation of *ağrı* – 'pain, ache' (as in 'pain in the neck') – to be more apt, for reasons which will become clearer below.

The peak in question looms in splendid isolation some 35 km south of the Soviet-Turkish frontier formed by the River Aras (the Araxes of the ancients). From the low-lying flood plain of the Aras, inhabited predominantly by ethnic Turks, there is a steep but steady rise to the summit. To the south another broad plateau, populated mostly by Kurds, extends all the way to some lower mountains and the town of Doğubayazit (sometimes spelled Doğubeyazit).

The blunt-topped mountain, permanently glacier-capped, is in fact a dormant volcano which last erupted in 1840. As is the case with the other dormant or extinct volcanoes of Anatolia (Erciyes, Hasan Dağı, Süphan) the lower slopes consist of basalt while the crater zone is characterized by andesite. All sides of the mountain are treeless, as much from the severe climate as the intermittent volcanic activity, but by no means lifeless. There is sufficient year-round water (most of it from the glaciers, some of it potable) to support green turf where the local Kurds establish their summer *obalar* (tent clusters).

The north and east flanks of Ağrı are the most attractive and offer the most interesting approaches, but unfortunately as of this writing they are off-limits to both Turks and foreigners. We have nonetheless included some information on these areas in the hope that someday soon they will be reopened.

They have been closed since 1985, not (as one might think) because of Kurdish-related troubles – Ağrı province is relatively quiet in that respect – but because the Soviets complain that mountaineers spy on their territory from the north slopes. (The question of how hikers could cause more security breaches than the NATO radar station purportedly on the same side remains unanswered).

Access to the top is therefore restricted to the one southern route, certainly the easiest but also the dullest itinerary. Furthermore, would-be climbers are hamstrung by a welter of prohibitions and regulations which effectively kill all the joy of mountaineering.

Foremost among these restrictions is the requirement to have a guide. This has led to the establishment of a racket, jointly run by outside trekking companies and the local Kurdish guides and muleteers, which will be uncomfortably familiar to anyone who has experienced the almost-identical rigmarole on Tanzania's Kilimanjaro. Climbing Ağrı is an unnecessarily complicated and expensive undertaking, and while we are not saying flat-out not to do it, we do suggest that under the current conditions there are lots of other mountains in Turkey, as good or better, to hike on. For those who want to do this trek, the options of going in a group or hiring your own guide are compared below.

### Securing a Trekking Permit
All foreigners going up Ararat must have a permit, and this is perhaps the one thing that a tour company can do better than you can acting alone. You must start the application process in your home country at least 60, and preferably 90, days in advance.

Contact the closest Turkish embassy and ask for the one-page, two-line mountaineer's application; make sure they don't send you the five-page, 20-question 'ark hunter's' questionnaire! Upon receipt of the completed form the embassy forwards this to the Ministry of Foreign Affairs in Turkey, which in turn refers it to the Ministry of Tourism & Culture.

After this the trail is somewhat murky until a notification of action taken is sent back to your embassy. This is what takes the 60 to 90 days, and you will probably have to persist in contacting them, not vice versa, as they will have probably forgotten all about you in the interim.

If you have to leave home without confirmation of permit issuance, you'll need to contact the Ministry of Tourism & Culture, *Tanıtma ve Pazarlama Müdür-lüğu* (Promotion & Sales Division), in Ankara. If they come up empty then try the Security Division of the Ministry of the Interior *Emniyet Müdülüğu*.

Once the permit is cleared, the *jandarma* station in Doğubayazıt is notified, usually by telephone. You the applicant will never actually see a piece of paper; the permit, known as *Ararat Çıkısa Katılacak Yabancı*, consists merely of a six-digit number and a date of issuance. It should be reiterated that applying for, and actually getting, the permission to climb Ağrı are two different things – you must shepherd the whole process along as outlined above, don't think that you can just apply and forget about it (the various ministries are talented enough at doing the forgetting for you!).

If you decide while in Turkey that you want to climb Ağrı, it is certainly possible to apply to Ankara directly, despite what some sources say. İstanbul-based tour companies do it all the time, successfully, on behalf of their clients. Contact the Ministry of Tourism & Culture, Promotion & Marketing Division, directly and expect to wait a minimum of 45 days for an answer. You confirm approval of in-Turkey applications by the same procedures described above for overseas petitions.

### Guides & Regulations
To escort foreigners up Ağrı, a prospective guide must be an official *mihmandar*

(literally, 'escorter of distinguished visitors') certified by the Turkish Mountaineering Federation. The couple of dozen certified guides who hang around Doğubayazit are either city Turks affiliated with the TMF or local Kurds. In theory a particular guide is assigned to you when your permit is issued but this does not always work out in practice. It might happen that you show up in Doğubayazit with a perfectly good permit but then have to wait a few days for a guide to be available.

Each guide is allowed to accompany up to 10 persons, ie if there are 11 in your party you'll have to hire two guides. Your escort's main duty, other than showing you the way, is to preclude spying, or actual entry, into restricted areas. To this end they require their clients to stay in a group – ie everyone within visual contact of each other – and of course on the trails.

The guides themselves must be equipped with walkie-talkies to maintain contact with the *jandarma* post in Doğubayazit. Most guides will accompany you all the way to the summit, though by the letter of the law they are only required to be with you until Camp II (4200 metres).

## The Kurds of Ağrı

Another sensitive point with the guides, especially since many of them are Kurdish, is that you not enter the *obalar* (tents) of the Kurds living at Eli and İbrahimkara unless specifically invited in by the menfolk. To do otherwise, even if you are female, violates their *namus* (honour), particularly of the Kurdish women.

Similarly, don't expect to point a camera at most Kurds without objections, again with respect to their *namus*, though money has a calming effect and is usually demanded. Many children in fact don't mind posing as they've learned that *baksheesh* generally is forthcoming. This is quite frankly to be discouraged; the kids, and indeed even the young adults, along the way up have become importunate and greedy over the last five years.

If you must give something, offer coloured pencils or balloons instead of 'bonbons' or money, and hand out to everybody – or nobody – if you don't want to provoke a brawl. Lastly, and sadly, don't leave small items lying around loose at Camp I; petty thefts here have become common, an inevitable consequence of the continual exposure of the Kurds to the disparity in wealth between themselves and visitors.

More positive cultural interaction is possible at Camp I. The Kurds will obligingly sell you rather idiosyncratic wool socks and gloves (see Equipment

At a market in western Anatolia

below) if you've forgotten a pair, as well as jewellery, rugs, saddle bags, etc. Expect to pay $US5 maximum for gloves, perhaps half that for socks.

## Going with a Company

At the moment no North American or British trekking companies operate their own trips on Ararat, although there is one German company (*DAV*). Any overseas organisation catering to English-speaking clients has until now subcontracted to Turkish operators with their own trucks and/or field reps in Doğubayazit.

Currently the most active of these are *Trek Kosmos* and *Trek Travel*, both based in İstanbul. We accompanied one of Trek Travel's groups up the mountain and after observing their methods we cannot highly recommend them as a tour operator.

Guides were mostly young university students from İstanbul, and while well-meaning, were inexperienced and did not display sufficient concern for the safety and comfort of their clients. Food service was haphazard and usually of inadequate caloric value to ward off the cold at high altitudes or support the level of physical activity involved in getting to the peak. At a price tag of approximately $US700 (from İstanbul and back), we consider their services poor value for the money and reckon that you can do much better yourself.

## Outfitting Yourself

The first order of business is to retain a reliable guide in Doğubayazit. In budgeting for one, there is another legal stipulation in addition to the one-per-ten customers rule: while the Kurdish guides' standard rate is $US40/day, the minimum charge is for five days, or $US200.

Hire of a truck or other vehicle capable of reaching the trailhead is another invariable – about $US24 (round-trip). Unless you're a masochist – and the guide will probably refuse to come along if you are – you'll want to hire mules to transport all gear, both yours and your escort's. Animals are about $US10 per head per day; the price includes an appropriate number of animal drovers who double as cooks and camp-setters. And don't forget the hire of the walkie-talkie: one per party, at about $US10 a day.

Putting it all together, for two people we have $US200 (guide fee) + $US100 (2 animals, 1 drover for 5 days x $US10) + $US50 (walkie-talkie for 5 days) + $US50 (groceries), for a total of $US400, ie $US200 per person.

For four people, the hypothetical breakdown would be $US200 (guide fee) + US$150 (3 animals, 2 drovers for 5 days x $US10) + US$50 (walkie-talkie for 5 days) + $US75 (groceries), for a total of $US475, ie about $US120 per person.

Either of these figures represents a substantial savings over booking with a trek company, plus you might get to eat what you want and when you want it – and not feel so much that you're participating in a circus.

## Rating/Duration

The climbing of Ağrı is strenuous though not technically difficult; most anyone who is reasonably fit will make it to the top, provided they do not have an acute attack of altitude sickness.

The requirement to hire a guide for five days is not totally unreasonable, since most parties spend two consecutive nights at Camp I either to acclimatise or wait for space to open at Camp II, where the third night is spent, and then overnight at Camp I again on the way down. If you are lucky, quick and not prone to altitude sickness you might get away with one night at Camp I, another at Camp II, and the third back in Doğubayazit if you're willing to put in a very long final day.

There does not seem to be a *hamam* in Doğubayazit, and only the luxury hotels booked by various tour groups have hot water, so a visit to Diyadin hot springs, some 45 km west of town, may be in order after the trek.

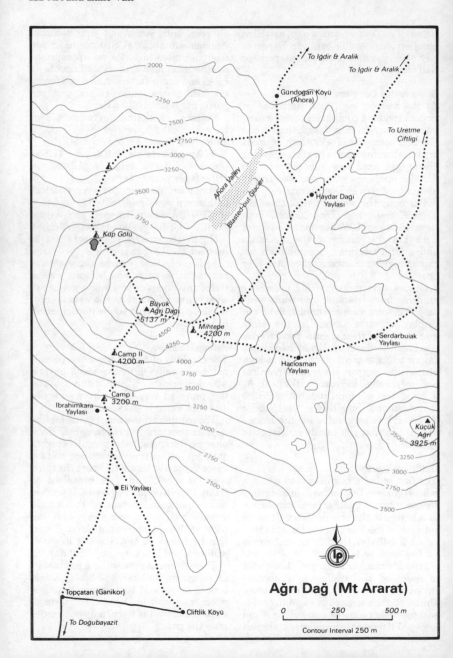

Ağrı Dağ (Mt Ararat)

0      250      500 m

Contour Interval 250 m

## Season

The best time for stable weather and good visibility from the top is July and August, with late June and early September being marginal alternatives. Even in mid-summer you can only count on being able to move around until about 2 pm, after which rain – hard rain – can occur at any time until about sunset.

## Equipment

The cold and wind in the early morning is considerable, so bring along your warmest clothing (gloves, hat, wool shirt, parka, etc). Trekking companies will only supply tents and perhaps a foam sleeping pad! Some sort of self-arrest device for the higher slopes is mandatory. A long ice axe would be ideal; ski poles are a second choice.

If the snow above İnönü is hard, crampons are very handy but quite optional if your boots have good tread. For the opposite condition gaiters are great – check in Doğubayazit beforehand.

Even if you don't get a full-blown case of altitude sickness, most climbers are pretty uncomfortable coming down from the final summit approach; aspirins and sweets to suck on are both immediately helpful measures, as is hot soup as soon as you can prepare it. (We strongly suspect that what many people experience on Ağrı is severe dehydration, not altitude sickness – but read the Health & Safety section in Facts for the Trekker for a better understanding of altitude sickness).

## Supplies

Doğubayazit, in its dual role of expedition base and last truckers' stop before shortage-plagued Iran, has just about everything you could want.

## Map

None now, or likely in the future, given that Ağrı is so close to the sensitive Soviet and Iranian borders.

## Getting to the Trailhead

Your party will leave Doğubayazit going east-north-east for seven km on the asphalt toward Iran. You then turn off left on a side road to cover 11 more km to Eli *yayla*. Your vehicle, however, will probably halt about two km below Eli owing to a freak summer storm in 1987 which washed out the road at this point.

## Stage 1: Eli to Camps I & II

From the site of the washout you will have to walk about one hour uphill to the pre-1987 trailhead at an elevation of 2500 metres. Assuming that you have pack animals, it will be 3½ to four hours on foot from there, past the Kurd *obalalar* at İbrahimkara, to so-called Camp I at 3200 metres. (The return trip, Camp I to Eli, takes two hours, with another 45 minutes necessary to clear the washout.)

There is space at Camp 1 for about 20 tents and the place is usually pretty full. Water comes from a snowmelt rivulet limiting the camp on the south-west, and one look at the debris in the streambed should convince you to collect water as high up as possible, perhaps even to boil it!

The onward trail from Camp I to Camp II is fairly clear, leaving the former on its east side, bearing north-east across two gullies and then heading north, first parallel to the easternmost gully and then up a small draw. The path is rather spongy, made more so by continual mule traffic, and it will take you 2½ to 3½ hours to reach Camp II – a cold, exposed ridge at 4200 metres. There is space here only for 10 to 12 two or three man tents, so often expeditions have to wait for an opening, which results in a lot of dickering and impromptu scheduling down at Camp I.

Water comes from an exposed pothole allowing you to get at a trickle running mostly under the rocks in a small gully west of the main camping ridge. The return to Camp I takes two hours at a leisurely pace.

**Stage 2: Camp II to the Summit**
On the day of the final push to the top, most of the trekking companies awaken their clients two to three hours before sunrise and give them a minuscule breakfast; both measures are idiotic. Wake up just before full daylight, eat your favourite energy breakfast, and you should be alright.

It takes 2¼ hours of toiling up through the andesite boulders, with minimal or no trail, to reach İnönü, a knoll with a bent metal marker at the edge of the permanent snow-and-ice cap. The worst is over here and it's an easy, pleasant hour more over the white stuff to the summit. That was our elapsed time, though, without special equipment; most people will take closer to four hours, assisted by some or all of the gear listed under Equipment.

Since 1987 the top has been crowned by a miniature wooden ark(!) (which doubles as the repository for the sign-in register) plus numerous altitude markers just to the south. The view east is dominated by 3925-metre Küçük (Little) Ağrı (you are standing on Büyük (Big) Ağrı), snowless and uninteresting except for its perfectly conical shape. Beyond, in the USSR, you can usually make out Lake Sevan.

To the south and north respectively the Doğubayazit and Aras basins sprawl at your feet, but a glimpse of Erivan in Soviet Armenia beyond the Aras is a treat reserved for extra clear days and cannot be relied on.

The descent to Camp II takes almost as long – more than 2½ hours in our case – because the 'trail' is steep and avalanche-prone below İnönü. Spread out and don't walk immediately above the person in front of you!

**Eastern & Northern Approaches**
If the following routes are ever again opened to mountaineers, all supplies and vehicle transport would be arranged in Iğdir or Aralık, the main towns of the Aras valley.

A long and gradual approach, but one which shows the mountain from its best angle, is that which begins from the *yayla* of Serdarbulak, at the north base of Küçük Ağrı. A full day's hike, via Hacıosman *yayla*, is required to reach the second camp of Mıhtepe at 4150 metres. Six to eight hours suffice for the round trip to 5137 from there.

Reportedly the most spectacular itinerary on the mountain is that up the Ahora (Ahura, Ahıra) valley, which begins in the village of Gündoğan. This valley, seven km long, is overhung for part of its length by a huge crevassed glacier which still bears the marks of an explosion of steam and hot gases which flashed down this way in the 1840 eruption. Buried somewhere under the lava here are the remains of the town of Ahora, an important medieval Armenian cultural centre whose original name was probably Argouri.

Further west, and probably reached by a separate path, is the lake of Küp Gölü, just below which are said to be the remains of a small fortress and an Armenian church. Küp Gölü is also reported to be the lair of a bandit known locally as Kurd Ahmet. If and when the government succeeds in capturing him then perhaps this side of Ararat will be opened once again, Soviet opinion permitting. As it is we were quite sorry not to be able to visit these areas and hope that some of our readers will be luckier than us in this respect.

At the summit of Ağrı

# Black Sea Region

**THE RİZE KAÇKAR (THE LITTLE CAUCASUS)**
The Rize Kaçkar mountains cover an area of approximately 1400 square km in the north-eastern corner of Turkey. Despite the formal 'Rize' prefix they are actually centred around the point where the borders of Rize, Artvin and Erzurum provinces meet, very near the highest summit of Kaçkar Tepe (3932 metres). To the north-west, forested misty slopes decline quickly to the Black Sea, while the Rize-Erzurum road marks the south-western limit of the region. On the south-east and north-east, the area is bounded by the roiling waters of the Çoruh River and the tawny, jagged peaks of the dryer side of the range.

Going from south-west to north-east, the Kaçkar range is conventionally divided into four massifs, namely Verçenik, Kaçkar proper (Kavron), Bulut and Altıparmak. Their underlying strata are predominantly granite, cyanite and granodiorite – unusual ingredients for Turkey.

From the tell-tale trough shape and rounded edges of the north-facing valleys, one can surmise that glaciers were at work here during the Ice Ages, much more so than on the angular south slopes or anywhere else in Turkey except for the Cilo/Sat. Today there are more than 100 lakes on both sides of the watershed, and every valley bottom contains a rushing stream. The warmer seasons see an explosion of wildflowers and butterflies: wolf, bear, deer, ibex and birds of prey still frequent the more remote districts of the mountains.

The fact that the Kaçkar's two aliases – the little Caucasus, and the Pontic Alps – refer to more famous and romantic mountains hints at the legendary quality of this range. Their designation as alpine, often fearsomely so, would certainly be confirmed by Xenophon and his hapless 10,000, who were trapped in the snow here while retreating from the Persian campaigns.

Throughout recorded history the Kaçkar has had some political or ethnic connection with the larger Caucasus just to the east. From the 10th century until the 15th century AD it constituted part of the territories of semi or fully independent Georgian or Armenian kingdoms, and as recently as 1877 to 1920 was partly in the grasp of imperial Russia. This capsule history disregards the sundry raids, incursions and brief tenures of the Byzantines, Seljuks, Persians and Mongols, as well as long periods of Ottoman rule. Although there has been a quiet half-century under the sovereignty of the Turkish republic, one cannot forget that this region has always been an outpost or doormat for powerful states en route to greater conquests.

It is therefore not surprising that the receding tides of empire have left a colourful assortment of ethnic minorities and monuments stranded in the folds of the Kaçkar. On the Erzurum side, pockets of Georgian-speaking Muslims continue to exist and, reportedly, communities of rural Armenian Christians (as distinct from the İstanbul population) still live near Yaylalar (Hevek) and Kurşunlu.

A generous sprinkling of ruined and intact churches and hilltop strongholds, both Georgian and Armenian, bear further witness to past turbulent centuries. The very name Kaçkar is the Turkish spelling of the Armenian word for cross, specifically the ornate bas-relief votive crosses and finely worked tombstones to be found on and around Armenian churches. It's an appropriate name considering the cultural heritage of the region and the layout of this intricately sculpted chain, with its various perpendicular ridges and spurs.

The Black Sea flank of the Kaçkar is

home to the Hemşin, a Turkish-speaking tribe concentrated above the coastal towns of Pazar and Ardeşen. The natives here, whether Hemşin or not, form a virtual caste of confectioners, and a sweet-shop anywhere in Turkey is likely to have at least one baker or pudding-pourer from this district.

The northern foothills are also heavily populated by Laz, an extroverted people of Caucausian origin who speak a language only distantly related to any other. They are famous seafarers, having founded several shipping lines, and employing ships' crews from even the most isolated mountain hamlets. The often elaborate headgear and ornate vests worn by the Laz women are quite striking, and it is not hard to imagine their ancestors, dressed in similar splendour, greeting Jason and his Argonauts at landfall in nearby Colchis, part of the traditional Laz homeland.

Indeed our impression was that life on the seaward slopes was easier than on the Çoruh side; smiles and hospitality seemed more forthcoming. Perhaps it has something to do with the contours of the land being softer and greener. Certainly the trails were clearer and more gentle in Laz territory, and one could see that struggling with burdens up a harsher, less fertile landscape on a daily basis would be enough to harden those living on the 'sunny side' of the peakline.

Toponymy (the lore of place names), always a problematic subject in Turkey, acquires an almost ludicrous dimension in the Kaçkar. Many locales have names of Georgian, Armenian or Laz origin, along with a new official Turkish alternative, which may or may not be understood by the inhabitants.

The ubiquitous '-vit' ending is an Armenian suffix denoting a *yayla*, while '-şen' is another particle meaning population in both Armenian and the local Black Sea dialect. Thus Hamameşen ('Town of the Baths'), the old name for the district around Ayder with its hot springs,

was readily contracted to Hemşin, and this new epithet was applied not only to various villages in the area but also to the Turkic subgroup living nearby.

Vowels and consonants alike still change with exasperating impunity in the mouths of various speakers whose first language may not be Turkish. Thus what may be Beravan or Burevan on a map is Borivan (though officially Sarıbulut) for your informant, and Avucur is locally called Avusor, to cite two examples. The numerous variant forms on the existing maps (eg Piskankara versus Pişenkaya) are probably more the consequence of cartographers listening to dialectic pronunciation than of careless typesetting.

The names of streams in particular tend to change every few km, and the phenomenon of non-unique names (eg Karagöl) is pushed to new extremes in the Kaçkar, even by Turkish standards. Add to this a tendency of locals to foreshorten the terrain and displace the names of peaks, passes, etc by a valley or three – it is hard to say whether this is out of uncertainty or local pride. We were for instance solemnly and repeatedly assured, against the evidence of our maps, that Altıparmak was Karataş, that the Büyükapi pass was the Demir Kapı, and that summit 3332 of Marsis was called Didvake – which it may or may not have been, though suspiciously another Didvake was marked next to Karataş on our maps. *Aman aman*, as they say in Turkey . . .

Despite any orientation problems, we found the Kaçkar mostly congenial for long-haul trekking. As in the Aladağlar, the Turkish and foreign trekking company offerings were initially perused for ideas and found to contain their usual quota of questionable judgements and outright absurdities. The route presented here either visits or skims close to three of the four main groups of the Kaçkar and provides a representative overview of its attractions. Nonetheless we realised, even while still en route, that it would take a couple more expeditions of approximately the same duration to exhaust the area's potential, rarely if ever visiting the same valley twice.

## Rating/Duration

This is a rigorous, though not murderous, nine-day to 10-day trek requiring previous similar experience. You can extend the time course – say to 12 days – by using extra or alternative campsites and so turn the expedition into a moderately strenuous one.

## Season

The snowpack has receded enough by mid-June to permit the *yayla* dwellers, as well as trekkers, access to the alpine zones, but there remains another complication.

Until the end of August, severe mists boil up on the Black Sea (north-west) slope of the Kaçkar, creeping up to the 2800-metre, sometimes the 3000-metre, level by noon. The fog is great for the local tea plantations but it effectively halts all movement. Trekking under these conditions is somewhat akin to trekking in the Himalayas at the onset, or tail end, of the monsoon. You can do it, as long as you pay attention to the weather, ie get over the high passes and down to the *yaylalar* (where clear trails commence) before the whiteout strikes.

This problem is almost entirely absent on the dryer south-east flank of the range, and the mists also abate on the ocean side during September and early October, which are said to be two of the best months to visit, if you don't mind the absence of any human life in the *yaylalar*.

Water is not a seasonal factor in the Kaçkar. In addition to the streams in the beds of the various valleys, there are countless springs, mostly fed by deep-welling ground water and not superficial snowmelt.

## Supplies

Get these principally in Kars, Erzurum or Artvin; Yusufeli is OK for last-minute afterthoughts, Barhal's cupboard is pretty bare. Rize and Pazar are fine for stocking up if approaching the Kaçkar from the north.

## Map

We have a beauty, at a scale of 1:50,000 and dimensions of approximately 60 x 90 cm, called simply 'Kaçkarlar' – without the cartographer's credit. Since it was passed on to us through the *samizdat* channels described in the chapter on maps, we have no idea who drew it up. In the absence of a copyright statement, Marc has arranged for the production of an improved version. Contact *Pacific Travellers Supply* (tel (805) 963-4438), 529 State St, Santa Barbara, CA 93101. This revamped product shuld be ready in 1989.

Most Turks who hike regularly in the Kaçkar know about the original map, and we even saw a very detailed quad (1:10,000) in the hands of a party from Ankara camped at Dilber meadows. Incidentally coverage on the 1:50,000 sheet includes only the Marsis, Altıparmak, Bulut and Kavron (high Kaçkar) massifs, between Barhal and Ayder; the Tirevit-Çat sector is cut off, as is the Verçenik group, and we know of no commonly available map for those areas. Good luck.

## Guides

You can contact one of us (Enver Lucas) at the address given in the chapter on helpful people, or through *Wilderness Travel* (tel (415) 548-0420), 801 Allston Way, Berkeley, CA 94710, USA; or through *InnerAsia* (tel (415) 922-0448), 2627 Lombard St, San Francisco, CA 94123. As of 1988 Enver conducts a 10-day hiking tour similar to the one written up here.

We can also provisionally recommend Metin Akıncı, whom we met in Ayder. He tends to frequent the same restaurants that young and active tourists do. He is actually from Şenyuva, near Çamlıhemşin, as is Savaş Güney, another guide with whom he cooperates.

### Getting to the Trailhead

You can get to Barhal, the start of our itinerary, fairly easily, albeit indirectly, from either Erzurum, Kars or Artvin. One bus a day leaves Erzurum, sometime between 7.30 and 9 am, for Artvin and makes a detour to Yusufeli, a town at the confluence of the Çoruh and the Barhal rivers. Likewise a single bus leaves Kars each morning at 7.30 am for Artvin, pausing at the junction on the main Erzurum-Artvin highway 9 km below Yusufeli at about 2 pm.

From Artvin there is a more frequent, direct service to Yusufeli, but the important thing is to get to Yusufeli by 3 pm to catch the daily minibus up to Barhal. If necessary take a taxi from the junction; the gas station/tea house there has a phone to summon one.

You can have one last elaborate restaurant meal in Yusufeli, at one of a couple establishments next to the bus stop; food will be pretty simple from here on, whether out of your pack or offered by those you meet along the away. Once clear of Yusufeli, the minibus follows the trout-laden waters of the Barhal Suyu 32 km upstream, wending its way through a legendary landscape. This was the edge of medieval Gruzhya (Georgia), and small ruined castles or fortresses on several bluffs overlooking the river attest to this.

Barhal (officially renamed Altıparmak) is a tiny but friendly village 1200 metres above sea level, with its houses scattered in long, straggling *mahalleler* and all but lost to view in a thick tangle of alder, walnut, mulberry and cherry trees. There are two inns, the best and most obvious one by the river, near the mosque and across the road from the two stores. Simple meals are available at the teahouse on the lower floor, and weather permitting you can take them – or even sleep – on an attractive wooden gazebo almost overhanging the water.

Family group met near Barhal

### Stage 1: Barhal to Karagöl

Before setting off for the high peaks, it's well worth taking a slight detour to visit the Georgian church just above Barhal. Leave the village on the jeep track heading north, not the one going west toward Yaylalar. After 10 minutes you should pass a wood bridge, then four tiny sheds perched on the south (left) bank of the Barhal Suyu. Opposite, on the right, a narrow muddy trail leads up through lush foliage for five minutes until linking up with a bigger trail coming from one of Barhal's numerous neighbourhoods. Turn left, and within a few moments you'll arrive at the primary school, right next to the old Georgian church.

This was built in the 10th century AD and is reputed to have been repaired by the famous Georgian queen Tamara in the early 13th century AD. The church is also purported to contain an inscription referring to Marsis, the nearby peak of that name, and at least one scholar, pointing out that this is a form of the traditional Armenian (and possibly Georgian) name for Ararat, has inferred that the local mountain was the true resting place of Noah's Ark. However he has neglected to account for the fact that 'Ma(r)sis' is probably a generic term for 'big mountain' in the Caucasus, just as the word 'Olympos' filled a similar role around the Aegean. We were unable to gain entrance to see this inscription since the church serves (until the new one is completed) as the village mosque, though it was probably used by Georgian Christians in the area until well into this century.

After returning to the main track, continue up the valley past the last buildings of Barhal, where you use a shallow ford to cross to the far bank of the river. Ninety minutes above Barhal, though, the track is disrupted to such an extent that you must hop back to the right (north) side of the water. Switchback up for 30 minutes more, then leave this thoroughfare in favour of a footpath to the left which parallels the river. From just before this trailhead you'll have your first glimpse of the Altıparmak group on the horizon and, much closer, the upper *mahalle* of Kumru hamlet.

After your first half-hour on the trail you cross the river yet again and toil up to Naznara hamlet, following the utility poles. Naznara, at 2100 metres, should be reached just over 2½ hours out of Barhal. Continue south-west another 20 minutes to the hamlet of Amaneskit, at 2250 metres, where the power lines end. These two settlements are really more *yaylalar* than hamlets, since the population, like that of the other settlements in this valley, move down to Barhal at the first sign of winter.

Above Amaneskit an irrigation sluice follows a most unusual course – right down the centre of a small ridge! Follow this unmistakable landmark up to a clump of trees, and leave the aqueduct

where an obvious trail takes off to the left (west). This in turn climbs severely to another aqueduct; turn right to follow it upstream until, some 5½ hours beyond Barhal, you arrive at a cirque where a waterfall pours off the far wall.

Facing the cascade, turn left and angle up a scree pile stabilised by clumps of rhododendron to intersect a path leading up to Karagöl (Borivan Gölü, 2600 metres), just beyond the edge of the 'lip' overhead. The total walking time from Barhal is six hours.

A small grassy patch on the north lake shore has enough space for several tents. Just below and to the north, among the rocks, is a small *oba* of four families. Altıparmak Tepe (3301 metres, but 3480 metres in some sources) looms just above, and beyond the *oba* sprawls the head of the valley of the Barhal Suyu. All told it's a fine base for a couple of nights with a dayhike sandwiched in between; the lake water is potable.

10th century Georgian church above Barhal

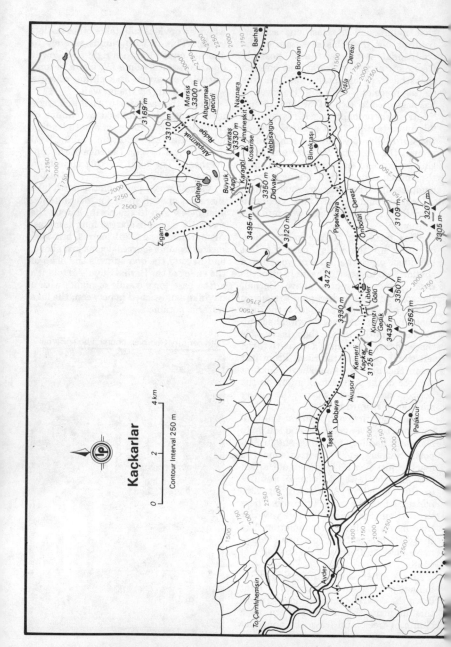

**Dayhike from Karagöl**

The obvious excursion, up into the cirque enclosed by Didvake (3350 metres) and Altıparmak, is a satisfying one. Follow the inlet of Karagöl, first on a path of sorts leading past a shallow tarn, then cross-country to a pair of small lakes known as the Alaca Göler. These lie more or less astride the way up to Büyükapı Pass, another 45 minutes distant.

Beyond the Büyükapı ('great gate') a route continues, down past two small nameless lakes at the foot of Karataş (3495 metres) to Zigam *yayla* and the head of the Zigam gorge. Karataş is the highest point in the Altıparmak group but it is a technical climb; its neighbour Didvake is also difficult to climb.

Alternatively, in the same amount of time you can hike up to the gap (impassable) directly overlooking Gölteği *yayla* and its two small lakes; by craning your neck a bit you can see Samli Gölü as well. From this vantage point you can easily pick your way up and to the right (north-west) toward the saddle joining Altıparmak with the main south-west to north-east line of peaks. Whether or not you climb all of Altıparmak (a walk-up), this saddle is an excellent reconnaissance point for those considering walks in the Marsis area.

**Marsis Group & Beyond**

Marsis is virtually a separate massif at the north-east end of the Altıparmak group. It doesn't make much sense to try and reach them from Karagöl; the recommended base camps for ascents are either Kosarise *yayla*, a collection of corrals below Karagöl at about 2300 metres elevation, or flat spots at the head of the Barhal Deresi, as close as practicable to the base of Marsis. Even from these lower campsites it's reportedly eight and six hours round trip, respectively, up to summit 3300 via a steep and snow-clogged couloir. The saddle just north-west of the peak also gives onto a spectacular basin containing a half-dozen lakes at an altitude of 2750 metres.

Just opposite the couloir, amongst the last of the Altıparmak pinnacles, is the Altıparmak Geçidi, which allows passage to two lakes on the other side and onward progress to either Gölteği *yayla* or a handful of other settlements just north-east of Zigam.

We were also told of a second Karagöl just to the north of summit 3332 of the Marsis group; this is said to be cradled in a deep chasm and while not possible to visit, is quite striking in appearance from above. You can get to the overlook most conveniently by camping just above the *mahalleler* across the Barhal valley from Naznara.

**Stage 2: Karagöl to Libler Gölü**

Locals counsel most trekkers to backtrack slightly from Karagöl to the aqueducts and pick up a trail circling the ridge east to Borivan (aka Beravan, Sarıbulut) *yayla*, and from there to veer east into Kısla Deresi, the valley leading up to the Kırmızı Gedik ('red gap'). This is the most conservative routing and may hold its attractions, but the requirement of going east to go west is so time-consuming as to compel you to camp at Pişenkaya *yayla* rather than at the more desirable Libler Gölü.

The preferred route presented here is initially more challenging but in the end saves you at least three hours.

From the tarn feeding into Karagöl a

Marsis massif seen from Altıparmak saddle

faint, steep but recognised trail zig-zags up for one hour through rhododendron patches and boulder piles to an obvious saddle just west of Nebisatgur hill (3050 metres). At the head of the trough-shaped valley on the other side is a pond, but if you can last the further half-hour necessary for the cross-country descent there's a year-round spring just above the start of some narrows. Skirt these to their left (east); about an hour below the saddle faint trails commence on the right-hand (west) side of this valley which leads almost due south down to the Kısla Deresi.

An hour below the spring, the roofs of Binektaşı hamlet come into view to your left, on the opposite side of the side valley.

Turn the corner, so to speak, into the Kısla valley at the point where an aqueduct crosses the trail, which links up with the main longitudinal path hereabouts in the upper *mahalle* of Kurdet hamlet. From this community the proper way leads down a slope, at the margin of a conifer grove, to a crude bridge over yet another tributary gully.

Once on the other side the path improves as it slips through the forest, passes just above Norsel *yayla* and gets to Pişenkaya 3 hours 15 minutes after leaving Karagöl. From a curve in the trail just before entering this *yayla* one has a particularly good view of the entire southwest end of the Altıparmak ridge.

Pişenkaya is set in tiers on the north side of the canyon, just above treeline; there are pure springs nearby but level camping space is at a premium. Continue upstream, passing the first bridge seen but crossing the second; a faint trail on the south bank of what is now known as the Önbolat Deresi crawls up to a cow pasture an hour above Pişenkaya.

Here you can verify that you're still on course and push on another 90 minutes to a set of narrows below Libler Gölü. A torrent gushing through the tight spot fans out over a broad meadowland in which any sort of path is lost. To get to the lake you must either go up over the rhododendron-covered bluff on the left, keeping as close to the narrows as practicable, or you can cross to the right (north) bank of the Önbolat valley and follow the cascades up to the actual outlet of the lake. There's no proper trail in either case. The lake, at 2700 metres, is attractive, though the shore is apt to be marshy; still you can find dry spots for four or five tents.

### Stage 3: Libler Gölü to Ayder

The Altıparmak group is arbitrarily considered to end above Libler Gölü, with the Kırmızı Gedik (around 3100 metres) being a logical division between the northeast end of the Kaçkar and the centrally situated Bulut massif. The pass is actually a double one, divided by a rock snout; the right-hand or northernmost option is the easiest to get over.

From the lake climb past the waterfall (cramped going but possible), attain a grassy plateau, and then bear straight left (west) toward the gap, which you should reach some 75 minutes after leaving the lakeshore.

Coming down from the notch, the footing is treacherous and there is no obvious trail; follow the only watercourse due west for 45 minutes until levelling off in a giant *ova*. Here a few cairns mark the continuation of an increasingly clear path descending to the *yayla* of Avusor (Avucor), 2½ hours beyond Libler Gölü.

Avusor is a large Laz community at 2400 metres whose inhabitants spend winter in Çamlıhemşin. Along with a meal you may be treated to a bravura performance on a *tulum*, the local bagpipe fashioned from a goatskin. Most of the men know how to play, and the contraption will be passed around those assembled until all have had a chance to get their licks in. Eventually everyone present may troop outside to dance the Black Sea *horon* on the turf to the accompaniment of the pipes.

Continue downhill and to the west, following the Küçük Deresi on its north bank; take left forks as they occur. When the weather is clear, the strikingly formed Kemerlikaya peak (3562 metres) dominates the skyline behind, and as you proceed you can feast your eyes on the green hills before you.

Forty-five minutes below Avusor, you wind through the small but prosperous-looking yayla of Dobaya, with buildings so elaborate it's hard to believe that this is merely a summer residence. Just over an hour out of Avusor, ignore the right fork going up to Peryatak yayla in favour of the left-hand bearing for Ayder. Shortly after the path serpentines down through Taşlık ('the stony place'), a scattered, aptly-named yayla, but stays on the same side of the river, avoiding two bridges to the far bank.

Treeline is about 1 hour 45 minutes past Avusor. The route now penetrates stands of hazelnut and fir, among which is a yayla unmarked on our maps, until the footpath ends (temporarily) at a logging road after the 2½ hour mark. This road leads to Ayder within 45 minutes, but it is more satisfying to turn off it some 400 metres along and keep to the path which continues down through a handful of farms on the north bank of the stream.

The trail finally ends much further down the same road, between two closely-spaced bridges near a small hut, but not before it has saved you at least 15 minutes of road-walking. The total hiking time from Libler Gölü to Ayder is around 6½ hours.

Ayder (1250 metres) is a sizable village, famous for its hot springs, and the tourist development folks have big plans for it; there are already eight hotels, with more planned and a grandiose new spa under construction. However we were quite pleased with an old wooden inn, the Cağlayan Oteli, and the old baths – a domed structure nestled in the trees across the river – were very fine indeed. Prices at the two restaurants in town

are already creeping up to unfriendly levels but at least the local trout is still on the menu. If you need to end your trek here there is a daily bus down to Camlıhemşin, but for those moving on up the mountain Ayder makes an excellent halfway stop, not least because the two or three stores are excellent for restocking your larder and eliminate the necessity of hauling 10 days' worth of food with you.

## Stage 4: Ayder to Kara Deniz Gölü or Yaylalar

Most days in summer a vehicle of some sort – perhaps a jeep, or a truck carrying both freight and passengers in the back – plies the dirt road heading upriver toward the two yaylalar of Aşağı (Lower) and Yukarı (Upper) Kavron. The latter of these is a popular base for technical ascents of the north face of Kaçkar Tepesi, but we advise trekkers to disembark after some 30 minutes at the junction for Palakcur and Çaymakcur yaylalar, just above the meadow of Kalerin Düzü.

As you begin to walk up the left-forking jeep track, there's an almost immediate right-angle turnoff for Palakcur which you don't take. Continue straight, following the stream and ignoring all logging roads to the side. Three houses on the left, about 45 minutes along, mark the start of an actual trail up to Aşağı Çaymakcur, visible on the left-hand (eastern) slope and reached an hour beyond the truck stop. If you miss the trail, it's easy enough to continue on the road along the west bank of the water until you're opposite the yayla, then cross to the correct side on a convenient foot bridge. Once clear of Aşağı Çaymakcur the path proceeds without ambiguity up the valley.

You should arrive in Yukarı Çaymakcur, a Hemşin yayla of about 35 houses at 2250 metres, 2½ hours after the divide in the Kavron and Çaymakcur roads. At the time of our visit (early August) the lower community was almost completely deserted. The families in the upper hamlet explained to us that they spent the first part of the summer in Aşağı Çaymakcur, and when their flocks had exhausted the forage there and the high meadows had come out from under the snowpack, then they moved up to Yukarı Çaymakcur. By the end of August they would be back in the lower *yayla*, probably engaged in making cheese, before retiring to their winter homes in Şenyuva (a village near Çamlıhemşin).

Before leaving Yukarı Çaymakcur in the direction of Kara Deniz Gölü we feel bound to mention the existence of an alternate route which is apparently very popular with some of the trekking companies operating in the area. From the upper *yayla* you can follow the Çennavit Deresi up to its lake, and then slip over the Körahmet pass (3100 metres) into the head of a valley containing several *yaylalar*. The lowest and largest of these is Körahmet, where the organised excursion companies camp for the night. This is probably a five- or six-hour tramp from the Çaymakcur valley and, except for the chance to subsequently descend another hour to Yaylalar (Hevek, 2100 metres) and visit an old bridge and a ruined Armenian church, is of dubious value.

The Körahmet pass is rated as more difficult than the one described below, the *dere* beyond is lakeless and probably nondescript, and in sum this route can only be recommended to those who suddenly decide to end their wanderings above Çaymakcur and need to get as quickly as possible to the roadhead at Yaylalar. Every morning there is a minibus from there, via Barhal, down to Yusufeli and the 'bright lights' beyond.

Resuming the suggested itinerary, you wind through the more populated half of Yukarı Çaymakcur on the east bank of the stream, then cross to the opposite side on a final footbridge. Within 20 minutes any clear path ends and the stream splits into a left, central and right upper reach. Climb up the turfy ridge to the right of the

rightmost torrent until meeting with a rather hesitant trail which soon crosses the water to another turf-and-stone ridge separating you from the middle fork.

The trick from here on is to stay on this elevation, always veering right (southwest) at every opportunity and shunning temptations to drift left or downhill. Bits of trail come and go but your main aids are cairns which appear about 90 metres above Yukarı Çaymakcur and lead you over a progressively less steep grassy slope to the east shore of Kara Deniz Gölü. They are lifesavers in the usual summer afternoon mist, when even the most detailed map is useless. Just over two hours of walking should suffice to get from Çaymakcur to the lake, one of the more beautiful in the central Kaçkar, with limited camping near its two outlets.

**Dayhike from Karagöl** You will almost certainly have had a short hiking day up to Kara Deniz Gölü, with time left over for a recommended dayhike. From the lake (2800 metres) a good trail zig-zags up to the prominent pass just to the south-west. This saddle overlooks a bowl-like valley containing the lakes of Büyük Deniz and Meterel, whose shores you can reach in 45 minutes and with a net altitude gain of 100 metres.

From there one could easily drop down in another 90 minutes to the *yayla* of Yukarı Kavron; there is a well-grooved-in path down the single-barrelled canyon.

However this would be a bit much for a day return to Kara Deniz lake, and is more properly considered as part of an alternative full-pack itinerary which would take you from Yukarı Kavron to the head of the Kavron valley and the traditional base camp for mountaineers aspiring to tackle the north face of Kaçkar Tepe.

**Alternative Route West from Karagöl** This is a technical, glacier-climbing route for experienced trekkers. About the only real option is to continue over the ridge separating the Kavron Deresi from that of Polovit, and resume the last day of the trek as outlined in Stage 5, but the trekker would be considerably poorer for having missed out on Kaçkar peak's southern approaches.

If you've come this far with your full gear, make it worth your while by heading north on a trail which skirts Memişefendi hill to arrive at Samistal *yayla* within two hours. From there you have unsurpassed views of the central Kaçkar high country, and you can subsequently descend by the onward path to Ayder via Hazıntak *yayla*. This has the advantage of being a circle route – extra paraphernalia can be stored in Ayder.

### Stage 5: Kara Deniz Gölü to Dilber Düzü

On the grassy elevation just east of the lake's outlet, reacquaint yourself with the cairns and find a good, clear path, with a general south-easterly trend, which goes up to the Çaymakcur pass. First you climb up past a monolith overlooking a small, semi-permanent tarn, then gradually switchback up boulder piles and fields of compacted rock to the divide at 3202 metres. This takes 90 minutes from the lake and compared to the climb up from Barhal, or to the Kırmızı Gedik, is a waltz.

However, on the other side, the terrain exacts its measure of revenge by compelling you to execute an almost complete circle to reposition yourself at the south-east foot of Kaçkar summit. From the pass you've an hour descent, first over the familiar compacted rock and then across flower-studded slopes to the high meadow of Düpedüz (2600 metres), rich in springs. This is the first suitable campsite since Kara Deniz lake, so if you've decided to augment a hiking day out of Ayder leave yourself enough daylight to get here.

The path, faint since the pass, improves and keeping to the north-west bank of the stream drops down within 90 minutes more to Döbe *yayla*, and from there in half

as much time on the east (left) bank of the stream, to Olgunlar. (This in turn is a mere hour or so above Yaylalar, discussed above).

Once through the village of Olgunlar, cross the Büyük Çay ('big stream') at the bridge next to a picnic pavilion (!) – handy since there seems to be no daytime teahouse in the village – and adopt the wide track on the south-east bank. It's 80 minutes up to the *yayla* of Naz(t)af; thereafter the path deteriorates markedly but is still followable, and remains on the same side of the canyon for the balance of the time course up to Dilber Düzü. This meadow, tucked just around the flank of Cağıl Tepe, is just over three hours above Olgunlar, and eight hiking hours beyond Kara Deniz lake.

There's good camping by the stream coming down from the cirque to the south-west (which also marks the continuation of the way on the morrow). Directly to the north and the west are fearsome palisades – the westerly ones being known as Şeytan Kayaları ('the devil's rocks') – and these are the toes, as it were, of Kaçkar peak itself. The headwaters of the Büyük Çay are triple; in addition to the creek by your camp, two other forks issue from couloirs flanking the summit. Although maps may indicate that the more northerly one leads up to a 3305-metre pass between Mezovit and Kaçkar, they are both inaccessible to ordinary hikers. For now just enjoy the view from the meadow and hunt for wild onions growing near water both above and below Dilber Düzü.

### Stage 6: Dilber Düzü to Nameless Lake, with Summit Dayhike

From Dilber meadow continue upstream, heading south-south-west in the direction of a red-dirt saddle. Just before reaching this, about an hour along, turn right for the ascent first to Deniz Gölü (not to be confused with *Kara* Deniz Gölü) and then to Kaçkar peak. There are no real trails here but the ascent is easy, heading due west for a maximum of 45 minutes until reaching the large lake at 3300 metres. It's a spectacular spot but there's really only one tiny campsite by the outlet.

Leave full packs in the vicinity and circle the north shore of the lake to the mouth of a broad valley whose head is under permanent snow in an ordinary year. Once over this, you descend briefly, traversing more snowfields at the foot of a glacier, then climb up and around rock– and snowfields to a point on the ridge ahead where rivulets pour off a sheer rock-face 90 minutes above the lake. A scree-laden trail becomes evident here, and toils up to a saddle in the ridge overhead.

While still under the glacier, resist the temptation to head up for the obvious pass '3705'. There's a sheer drop on the other (Kavron) side, and a traverse from this gap to the saddle just noted will take you north-east over a nasty, all-but-impassable ridge consisting almost entirely of crumbling rock.

Most hikers will cover the distance between the rock-face cascades and the summit in an hour, bringing the total from Deniz Gölü to 2½ hours. Of course there is a magnificent 360-degree panorama from the altitude marker (3932 metres). Your departure point, Deniz Gölü, is in plain sight to the south, as is the smaller nameless lake just beyond it where you will probably spend the night.

Closer at hand is the giant glacier on the north flank of peak 3864, plus one of two tiny, anonymous lakes lodged atop the Şeytan Kayaları. Turning around, you have an unobstructed view north as far as the previously visited lakes of Büyük Deniz and Meterel. The Mezovit massif lies immediately to the north-north-east, with bits and pieces of the entire Kaçkar summit-ridge showing beyond.

To the north-west the Kavron valley, with its dirty brown lake of Öküz Yatağı, is rather less enchanting, but Verçenik (variously Verşembek, Varşamba) peak to the west-south-west satisfyingly rounds off the list of highlights. Before your trip down, the climbers' register, double-

packed in a metal canister, makes for interesting reading.

The return to Deniz Gölü takes 90 minutes, and another 45 minutes is required to negotiate the slippery but fortunately low saddle on the south-west shore to the no-name lake on the far side. Although it's at roughly the same elevation as its neighbour, the shore of this medium-sized lake is grassier, offering several campsites near the outlet. With this so close at hand it seems a waste to return all the way to Dilber Düzü; as it is, you will have to budget the best part of daylight hours to accomplish all of the above comfortably.

In all fairness we should note that there is another, more direct way up to Kaçkar summit which may be of interest to those who intend to spend two nights at Dilber Düzü. Exactly opposite the camping area, in the Şeytan Kayaları palisades, is a fearsome gap known as the Dar Boğaz. You can go up this gallery – small parties only, with plenty of space between climbers, as there is danger from landslides – and come out atop the cliffs in the vicinity of the two little lakes visible from the standard route. From there make your way to the dripping cliff face and complete the ascent of Kaçkar.

It would be a shame to miss out on Deniz Gölü, so vary the return by looping by it. This circle route will be about an hour shorter than outings which pass Deniz Gölü twice, but of course you will not find your gear waiting for you at the latter lake and you must therefore stay another night at Dilber Düzü.

## Stage 7: Nameless Lake to Tirevit

From the outlet of the anonymous lake it's a half-hour climb up to the top of the pass marked 3415 on the map. Once down the back of this, you must choose between going directly over yet another scree-laden spur before you or dodging left around the more moderately pitched base of this ridge. Distance and timewise the result is virtually identical: you arrive at the grassy meadows below the Kavron pass, some two hours after leaving camp.

As you pick your way through flat granite slabs, you should find a cairned trail which is coming up from the Davalı valley and its *yayla*. Another hour of hiking suffices to attain the pass itself (3270 metres).

The view from the top is initially limited to the head of the Polovit Deresi and is not too informative. Coming down, the path, contrary to what you might expect, stays high on the right (east) flank of the valley for 45 minutes, almost regaining the altitude of the pass, until emerging onto a saddle at 3100 metres. To the right (north-east) the Kavron valley with Derebaşı Gölü sprawls at your feet, and Çukur Gölü is visible directly to the west on the far side of the Polovit valley.

A conspicuous trail threads its way out of the Kavron basin to join up with yours on the saddle, which explains why the

descent from the pass was so skewed in this direction.

Rather than follow it down to Kavron, however, descend instead left toward the *yayla* of Apıvanak. Initially there is no clear trail but you have easy cross-country progress down a gentle turfy slope to the point where a well-defined path materialises. Apıvanak, a maximum of 75 minutes below the saddle, or a total of two hours beyond the Kavron pass, is a friendly place (2500 metres) sandwiched between two historic bridges which straddle the river.

Leaving Apıvanak, you have another choice to make: whether to proceed directly to Tirevit or to take the long way around via Polovit. The latter option involves continuing an hour down the valley, past the lower of the old bridges, to the substantial Polovit *yayla* at 2300 metres. From there you would have a steep though short climb over the ridge separating Polovit from Tirevit before dropping down to the latter *yayla* – a route

Bridge at Apıvanak, Polovit Deresi & Davanali pass

nearly an hour longer than the direct course which we, having had enough of sharp climbs and *yaylalar* during the past eight days, followed.

The inhabitants of Apıvanak will be glad to show you the start of the path which mounts the top the ridge to the west within 80 minutes. In a region that is no slouch when it comes to fine vistas, there is a particularly good one from this height, where you can simultaneously take in your destination, the majestically curving Tirevit Deresi; the concentrated *yayla*, virtually a village, of Polovit on the road not taken; and of course the various Kaçkar summits to the south-east.

Clamber down from the ridge for 45 minutes more until crossing the stream at Tirevit, a substantial *yayla* tucked into the bend of its valley. This brings the total of the leg from Apıvanak to just over two hours, and the elapsed walking time for the day to just over seven hours. There's ample, if none too private, camping space

in the meadows opposite Tirevit on the north-east bank of the stream, and most parties pitch their tents there. However, if daylight permits, you might want to walk the little extra to the site detailed in the next section.

## Stage 8: Tirevit to Çat

The main path down the valley stays on the south-west bank of the river for the 75-minute walk down to the hamlet of Elevit, where the road to Çat begins. However, if you are looking for an alternative to camping across from Tirevit, it's preferable to initially return to the north-east bank of the stream and then stride down past the *yayla* of Karıç to an exposed knoll just below treeline.

This spot overlooking Elevit also has a commanding view of the confluence of two rivers and perspectives up the main and side valleys and down toward Çat, where a bed of mist usually rides above the forest. You can stake your tent near the

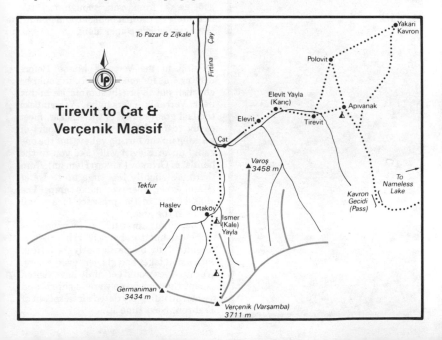

foundations of an old ruined Armenian church; water is furnished by a trough-spring just above. We reckoned it one of the most impressive camps in the Kaçkar, especially if the moon is out.

The apparent onward trail becomes impassable after a few hundred metres and the next day you must retrace your steps a bit to Kariç and from there descend to Elevit. Several days a week there's a minibus down to Çat; while you're waiting for it inspect the old Armenian graveyard with its headstone inscriptions. If necessary spend the night in the single inn; the bus, when there is one, tends to depart around midday. In any case try and arrange some sort of ride to avoid the seven-km road walk down to Çat.

Allacagöller

Çat itself, or at least the *mahalle* which most outsiders see, is something of an anticlimax. A fine old bridge just upstream augurs well, and the path leading right (north) from this supposedly leads up to an older residential quarter. However facilities are limited to two inns about 500 metres apart on the single street, both serving simple meals on request, with the higher one doubling as the store. If you are inclined to move on quickly, at least one or two daily minibuses down to Pazar on the coast will oblige you. These tend to come from further up the mountain – either from Elevit as noted above, or from Ortaköy – and roll through Çat at around 9 am and 1.30 pm.

On the way to Pazar it is worth trying to get the driver to make a brief stop at the little Armenian fortress known as Zir (Zil) Kale, perched on a crag overlooking the Fırtına Çay, just upstream from the first of several old bridges. But don't let the bus get away from you though, as it's definitely not worth being stranded until the next vehicle comes along!

**Sidetrip to the Verçenik Massif** Before leaving Çat for good, though, it would be churlish not to briefly summarise hiking near Verçenik (Varşamba, Verşembek) the last great massif of the Kaçkar, most easily reached from Çat. Four hours of walking up the Fırtına valley (*not* the one going up to Elevit) will take you to the hamlet of Ortaköy (Yukarı Hemşin); from there it's slightly less time up to Işmer (Kale) *yayla*, where you make camp. (The alias is due to the presence of a small castle in the area.)

The final approach to Verçenik is technical but the head of the valley is rumoured to be particularly beautiful, with small lakes and glaciers everywhere. We ourselves would certainly have visited except that our boots were in shreds and we had an inflexibly dated air ticket out of Trabzon. Next time . . .

# Index

## MAPS

... continued from page 4

supplying us with more maps impossible to obtain under other circumstances. Josephine also treated Marc to a lesson on the subtle differences between various nomad tents, a subject to which she has devoted much of her life.

Before actually setting out into the hills there were often marathon huddles with local guides or non-professional villagers. Tekin Kücüknalbant put us over Ericyes on paper, and Arif Tokatlyan, Cemil Özyurt, Mehmet Yalçın, Ahmet Pıçakçı, and Rifat Karahan of Barhal spent an entire evening plotting our course through the Kaçkar. Doğan Şafak of Niğde was a treasure trove of information on the Aladağlar as well as a map source, and in addition we spent a pleasant day discussing what the diplomatic communiques call 'matters of common interest'. On Ağrı Dağı, Mecit Doğru, former head of the Turkish Mountain Federation, furnished us with an etymological history of that peak.

For genuine Turkish hospitality we are indebted to Emil Galıp Sandalcı in İstanbul; the families of Menderes Güzel and Mehmet Elvan in the *yaylalar* of the Toros; Ali Osman Yılmaz, Mustafa Gölge and Ali Kasagöz at Avesor; and the villagers of Değirmenözü, Barazama, Yıldız and Maden. We are particularly grateful to the Evcan family of Turgut on the Hisarönü peninsula, who hosted us for two days and showed us around their giant 'backyard'.

Rarely did we have any other hikers along with us, though we are grateful for the company of Jane Wills and Necla Baytaş of the British Embassy in Ankara, and Necla's aunt Hürriyet Çilingiroğlu, in the Ihlara valley, Matt the Welshman in the Kaçkar, and Barney Summers of Croyden on Süphan Dağı. Mostly our thoughts turn to the dozens of Turkish villagers and *yayla* inhabitants, full names not known or remembered, who were always ready with *çay*, a meal, or directions. We thank you all and say *eksik olmayiniz* – may you never lack for anything.

## Temperature

To convert °C to °F multipy by 1.8 and add 32

To convert °F to °C subtract 32 and multiply by ·55

## Length, Distance & Area

|  | *multipy by* |
|---|---|
| inches to centimetres | 2.54 |
| centimetres to inches | 0.39 |
| feet to metres | 0.30 |
| metres to feet | 3.28 |
| yards to metres | 0.91 |
| metres to yards | 1.09 |
| miles to kilometres | 1.61 |
| kilometres to miles | 0.62 |
| acres to hectares | 0.40 |
| hectares to acres | 2.47 |

## Weight

|  | *multipy by* |
|---|---|
| ounces to grams | 28.35 |
| grams to ounces | 0.035 |
| pounds to kilograms | 0.45 |
| kilograms to pounds | 2.21 |
| British tons to kilograms | 1016 |
| US tons to kilograms | 907 |

A British ton is 2240 lbs, a US ton is 2000 lbs

## Volume

|  | *multipy by* |
|---|---|
| Imperial gallons to litres | 4.55 |
| litres to imperial gallons | 0.22 |
| US gallons to litres | 3.79 |
| litres to US gallons | 0.26 |

5 imperial gallons equals 6 US gallons
a litre is slightly more than a US quart, slightly less
than a British one

## Lonely Planet

Lonely Planet published its first book in 1973. Tony and Maureen Wheeler had made a lengthy overland trip from England to Australia and, in response to numerous 'how do you do it?' questions, Tony wrote and they published *Across Asia on the Cheap*. It became an instant local best-seller and inspired thoughts of a second travel guide. A year and a half in South-East Asia resulted in their second book, *South-East Asia on a Shoestring*, which they put together in a backstreet Chinese hotel in Singapore in 1975. The 'yellow book', as it quickly became known, soon became *the* guide to the region and has gone through five editions, always with its familiar yellow cover.

Soon other writers started to come to them with ideas for similar books – books that went off the beaten track and took an adventurous approach to travel, books that 'assumed you knew how to get your luggage off the carousel,' as one reviewer described them. Lonely Planet grew from a kitchen table operation to a spare room and then to its own office. It also started to develop an international reputation as the Lonely Planet logo began to appear in more and more countries. In 1982 *India – a travel survival kit* won the Thomas Cook award for the best guidebook of the year.

These days there are over 60 Lonely Planet titles. Nearly 30 people work at our office in Melbourne, Australia and another half dozen at our US office in Oakland, California.

At first Lonely Planet specialised exclusively in the Asia region but these days we are also developing major ranges of guidebooks to the Pacific region, to South America and to Africa. The list of walking guides is growing and Lonely Planet is producing a unique series of phrasebooks to 'unusual' languages. The emphasis continues to be on travel for travellers and Tony and Maureen still manage to fit in a number of trips each year and play a very active part in the writing and updating of Lonely Planet's guides.

Keeping guidebooks up to date is a constant battle which requires an ear to the ground and lots of walking, but technology also plays its part. All Lonely Planet guidebooks are now stored and updated on computer, and some authors even take lap-top computers into the field. Lonely Planet is also using computers to draw maps and eventually many of the maps will be stored on disk.

The people at Lonely Planet strongly feel that travellers can make a positive contribution to the countries they visit both by better appreciation of cultures and by the money they spend. In addition the company tries to make a direct contribution to the countries and regions it covers. Since 1986 a percentage of the income from each book has gone to aid groups and associations. This has included donations to famine relief in Africa, to aid projects in India, to agricultural projects in Nicaragua and other Central American countries and to Greenpeace's efforts to halt French nuclear testing in the Pacific. In 1988 over $40,000 was donated by Lonely Planet to these projects.

---

## Lonely Planet Distributors

**Australia & Papua New Guinea** Lonely Planet Publications, PO Box 88, South Yarra, Victoria 3141.
**Canada** Raincoast Books, 112 East 3rd Avenue, Vancouver, British Columbia V5T 1C8.
**Denmark, Finland & Norway** Scanvik Books aps, Store Kongensgade 59 A, DK-1264 Copenhagen K.
**Hong Kong** The Book Society, GPO Box 7804.
**India & Nepal** UBS Distributors, 5 Ansari Rd, New Delhi – 110002
**Israel** Geographical Tours Ltd, 8 Tverya St, Tel Aviv 63144.
**Japan** Intercontinental Marketing Corp, IPO Box 5056, Tokyo 100-31.
**Netherlands** Nilsson & Lamm bv, Postbus 195, Pampuslaan 212, 1380 AD Weesp.
**New Zealand** Transworld Publishers, PO Box 83-094, Edmonton PO, Auckland.
**Singapore & Malaysia** MPH Distributors, 601 Sims Drive, #03-21, Singapore 1438.
**Spain** Altair, Balmes 69, 08007 Barcelona.
**Sweden** Esselte Kartcentrum AB, Vasagatan 16, S-111 20 Stockholm.
**Thailand** Chalermnit, 108 Sukhumvit 53, Bangkok 10110.
**UK** Roger Lascelles, 47 York Rd, Brentford, Middlesex, TW8 0QP
**USA** Lonely Planet Publications, PO Box 2001A, Berkeley, CA 94702.
**West Germany** Buchvertrieb Gerda Schettler, Postfach 64, D3415 Hattorf a H.
**All Other Countries** refer to Australia address.

# Trekking Guides

### Bushwalking in Australia
Australia offers opportunities for walking in many different climates and terrains – from the tropical north, to the rocky gorges of the centre, to the mountains of the south-east. Two experienced and respected walkers give details of the best walks in every state, plus notes on many more.

### Tramping in New Zealand
Call it tramping, hiking, walking, bushwalking, or trekking – travelling on your feet is the best way to come to grips with New Zealand's natural beauty. This guide gives detailed descriptions for 20 walks of various length and difficulty.

### Trekking in the Indian Himalaya
The Indian Himalaya offers some of the world's most exciting treks. This book has advice on planning and equipping a trek, plus detailed route descriptions.

### Trekking in the Nepal Himalaya
Complete trekking information for Nepal, including day-by-day route descriptions and detailed maps – this book has a wealth of advice for both independent and group trekkers.

# Lonely Planet Guidebooks

Lonely Planet guidebooks cover virtually every accessible part of Asia as well as Australia, the Pacific, Central and South America, Africa, the Middle East and parts of North America. There are four main series: 'travel survival kits', covering a single country for a range of budgets; 'shoestring' guides with compact information for low-budget travel in a major region; trekking guides; and 'phrasebooks'.

# Mail Order

Lonely Planet guidebooks are distributed worldwide and are sold by good bookshops everywhere. They are also available by mail order from Lonely Planet, so if you have difficulty finding a title please write to us. US and Canadian residents should write to Embarcadero West, 112 Linden St, Oakland CA 94607, USA and residents of other countries to PO Box 88, South Yarra, Victoria 3141, Australia.

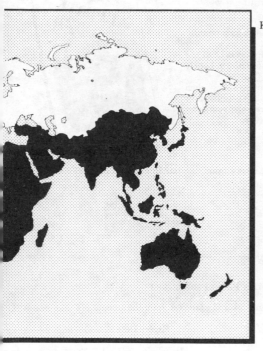

## Indian Subcontinent
India
Hindi/Urdu phrasebook
Kashmir, Ladakh & Zanskar
Trekking in the Indian Himalaya
Pakistan
Kathmandu & the Kingdom of Nepal
Trekking in the Nepal Himalaya
Nepal phrasebook
Sri Lanka
Sri Lanka phrasebook
Bangladesh

## Africa
Africa on a shoestring
East Africa
Swahili phrasebook
West Africa

## Middle East
Egypt & the Sudan
Jordan & Syria
Yemen

## North America
Canada
Alaska

## Mexico
Mexico
Baja California

## South America
South America on a shoestring
Ecuador & the Galapagos Islands
Colombia
Chile & Easter Island
Bolivia
Peru

# Lonely Planet Update

We collect an enormous amount of information here at Lonely Planet. Apart from our research there's a steady stream of travellers' letters full of the latest news. For over 5 years much of this information went into a quarterly newsletter (and helped to update the guidebooks). The new paperback *Update* includes this up-to-date news and aims to supplement the information available in our guidebooks. There will be four editions a year (Feb, May, Aug and Nov) available either by subscription or through bookshops. Subscribe now and you'll save nearly 25% off the retail price.

Each edition has extracts from the most interesting letters we have received, covering such diverse topics as:
• how to take a boat trip on the Yalu River
• living in a typical Thai village
• getting a Nepalese trekking permit

## Subscription Details
All subscriptions cover four editions and include postage. Prices quoted are subject to change.
**USA & Canada** – One year's subscription is US$12; a single copy is US$3.95. Please send your order to Lonely Planet's California office.
**Other Countries** – One year's subscription is Australian $15; a single copy is A$4.95. Please pay in Australian $, or the US$ or £ Sterling equivalent. Please send your order form to Lonely Planet's Australian office.

## Order Form

Please send me

☐ One year's subscription – starting next edition.     ☐ One copy of the next edition.

Name (please print) ....................................................................................................

Address (please print) ..................................................................................................

.....................................................................................................................................

.....................................................................................................................................

**Tick One**

☐ Payment enclosed (payable to Lonely Planet Publications)

Charge my     ☐ Visa     ☐ Bankcard     ☐ MasterCard     for the amount of $ .....................

Card No ...................................................................... Expiry Date ...................................

Cardholder's Name (print) ...........................................................................................

Signature ................................................................... Date................................................

**US & Canadian residents**
Lonely Planet, Embarcadero West, 112 Linden St,
Oakland, CA 94607, USA
**Other countries**
Lonely Planet, PO Box 88, South Yarra, Victoria 3141, Australia